HOUSE OF SOULS

A PSYCHOLOGIST'S
JOURNEY
TO GOD

HOUSE OF SOULS

A PSYCHOLOGIST'S JOURNEY TO GOD

JUDY MARSHALL, PH.D.

PSYCHMASTER *PRODUCTIONS/PRESS*

www.psychmaster.com

PSYCHMASTER *PRODUCTIONS/PRESS*

First Printing   February 2012

Copyright © 2012 Judy Marshall

Library of Congress Control Number: 2011939497

ISBN-13: 978-1-933816-16-6

ISBN-10: 1-933816-16-3

All rights reserved. No part of this book may be reproduced, mimeographed, scanned, or distributed in any printed or electronic form without permission from the publisher or the author. Brief quotations used in literary reviews or articles are excepted. All brand names and product names used are trademarks, registered trademarks, or trade names of their respective copyright holders. Names have been changed to protect confidentiality.

Psychmaster
PO Box 17025
Chapel Hill, NC 27516
www.psychmaster.com

Graphic/Cover & Book Design: Judy Marshall
Cover Art: Joseph F. Ferraro

Printed in the United States of America

*For those who are
still searching...*

Contents

Prologue   xi

1	THE ALMIGHTY SELF-ESTEEM	1
2	WHATEVER HAPPENED TO GOD?	19
3	SPIRITUAL BEINGNESS	31
4	STILL THERE AFTER ALL THESE YEARS	47
5	THE MIND ON TOP OF EXPERIENCE	61
6	RANDOM PIECES OF SOUL?	77
7	FAITH MAY NOT BE SO BLIND	95
8	FEAR AND GOD-FEARING	115
9	HOLE OR WHOLE?	131
10	HOW BARBIE GOT FIXED	145
11	REFUGE IN THE UP ESCALATOR	161
12	LIGHT THY FIRE	177
13	RIDING THE GOD RAILS	195
14	SOUL SCHMOOZING	213
15	HOUSE OF SOULS	233
16	REVVING THE SPIRITUAL ENGINE	251
17	SOFT HEART	271

Epilogue: RUSH OF BLESSINGS   287

God, as Truth, has been for me a treasure beyond price. May He be so to every one of us.

                    - Mohandas Gandhi

Prologue

This book is my way of understanding emotional experience. It is about faith and a relationship with God.

As a psychologist with a strong belief in God, an essential question for me has been the interaction between faith and psyche. Are there differences mentally and emotionally between someone who truly believes in God versus someone who does not? Does faith result in distinct ways of coping with difficulties, approaching relationships, and defining self-esteem? Are there alterations in perception and feeling, behavior or attitude that occur with the practice of genuine spirituality? Once we enter into a relationship with God, what happens psychologically? Does that change things? How does faith affect our inner and outer life?

For me personally, I know the answers to these questions because I haven't always had faith. Coming from an agnostic background, turning to God came later and actually took me by surprise. What followed was unexpected as a wave of regenerative transformation seemed to expand out into every aspect of my life and has only grown stronger in the intervening years. Having walked on both sides of the road, I can attest that it is always more comforting to walk with God.

For many, turning to faith would seem a new and revolutionary approach to psychology. I've worked in the field for many years and only lately is there any talk of spirituality but almost never of God. It's not just the scientific professions. Our modern culture has become so secular. Any serious consideration of a true Higher Power seems to have evaporated from mainstream consciousness. We have had decades of academic research, myriad theories of human behavior, and an endless parade of self-help formulas that promise everything from an improved personality to the ability to find perfect love and an expensive car. Developing a connection with God is something that most people would not even think about.

Of course, this hasn't always been so. Long before the practice of psychology, on the most intimate level, individuals found solace and self-understanding through their religious experience. Throughout most of human history, it has been spiritual devotion, not therapy or self-help, that has been the vehicle for emotional healing and provided guidance as to how to lead a life of value and fulfillment. There was a time when being subservient to God and a sense of personal integrity, the latter arising out of "doing the right thing," were much more important than having self-esteem.

Human life is immensely challenging. It always has been. Less so now than in prehistoric times when you had to brave a treacherous wilderness and the creatures within on a daily basis. Still, for many today, dealing with the ups and downs of living and the emotional monsters within can feel very precarious. All of us have our share of disappointments and losses. All of us have at least relatively good and bad days. Some are clearly more sensitive and reactive than others, but we all have our highs and lows.

As a psychologist *(and human being)*, I know the heady but brutal power of emotion. We all *feel*, which can be blissful or painful or both and a lot in-between. Feelings can surge, buoying us up to a brilliant height, but just as easily explode outward or implode inward, catapulting us down to a desperate and dangerous level. Even for those who never see the depths *(or the heights)*, we all run an emotional gamut as part of the human condition. Life is a beach, and then you die. All of us face the inevitability of loss and our own death.

How do we understand our personal experience? As we ride the cycles of our lives, we try to make sense of it all. There seem to be patterns weaving in and out, at times appearing to strike a straight line. Or circles within circles, expanding and merging with others, then doubling back to start anew. Where does it end? Or is it without end? It is natural to wonder: Is there something larger than and beyond ourselves?

It has long been recognized by philosophers and psychologists alike that how we view the world affects how we experience the world. See the glass as half empty, and it will be. See the glass as half full, and it can be that, too. If our expectations are high as to the available opportunities and our ability to flourish, we tend to feel overall optimistic. If we expect success or a reasonable facsimile, we tend to move forward. We'll take the risk and make the effort, at least opening up the possibility that something good could occur in our lives. If we expect the worst, we tend to get it and end up feeling eternally beaten down. We ask *(with good reason)*, why bother anyway?

In fact, it is modifying this half full/half empty dynamic which is what so much of psychotherapy is all about. The theory goes, if we can change the self-sabotaging assumptions we hold, often on an unconscious level, and replace the *negative* beliefs with more *positive* ones, the individual will feel and act accordingly, and there will be a lifting of depression and improved self-esteem.

This gets back to the question as to what, if any, is the impact of faith? The nature and strength of faith can vary greatly. But, in general, true faith in a Higher Power introduces *positive* assumptions, many of which are incompatible with what is taught in the mainstream culture. In faith, life is no longer random but has inherent meaning and purpose. In faith, death may no longer be feared but is simply part of the humanly unknowable truth and reality beyond the physical world. Faith also involves clear and absolute moral principles that, if followed, only add to a sense of personal wholeness and provide direction in living. In faith, the individual is no longer alienated but belongs to a greater spiritual unity or family, with the potential for a loving, caretaking relationship with God.

Not only in my own life, but in various aspects of my work as a psychologist, I have repeatedly observed that those of genuine faith hold a tremendous emotional gift. This is not based on scientific research but rather clinical impressions after spending thousands of hours with those who were going through a difficult period in their lives. What do I mean by genuine faith? People of genuine or true or committed faith go beyond philosophical assumptions and attempt to *live* their beliefs in their day-to-day existence. Whether through organized religion or simply a deep, personal inner conviction, they seem to experience distinctive perceptions, feelings, and values. Despite wide variation in background, they appear to react *similarly* to each other but *differently* from those for whom faith is unimportant.

What are the differences? For people of *living* faith, often the psychological reaction is less severe than would be expected. They may not get as depressed to major losses or negative events. More often they do become depressed, but it is as though there is another *positive* dimension within their experience and this competes with the painful feelings. This other dimension seems to involve a perspective of wisdom or greater vision as though the person is able to connect with a larger picture, to get above the despair of the moment, and to hold onto an awareness that this too will pass. There is also a sense of connection to some other force or Higher Power, perhaps distant at times but still a haven or refuge from the emotional storm.

A perspective of *living* faith can open up unexpected avenues of relationship and connection with others. Going beyond ego, the relationship with God tends to develop a sense of one's self in a truer identity on a purposeful journey that is lifelong. This does not mean that people of faith do not face challenges or crises or struggle with psychological issues like everyone else. They do, and they can become discouraged, despondent, and even suicidal or behaviorally out of control. Yet their faith seems to offer a healing and guiding pathway unattainable in any other way.

This book is about my own transformation and my reflections about what committed faith and a relationship with God can bring to a person's life. It is based on my own spiritual journey and interactions with others, including friends and clients over a long career. Although traditional, it is not founded in any one religion or denomination but flows from those core spiritual principles that underlie all religions to some degree and to which people have turned since time immemorial for wisdom and guidance. *Living* faith reflects universal and eternal truth but flourishes in the individual human heart.

While this book is about psychological transformation, it is important to emphasize that the intent is not to set forth a therapeutic program to be followed or to define an exclusive in-group of the enlightened, super-healthy, or self-actualized. It is also critical to keep priorities straight. True faith in God can never be a means to a predominantly self-oriented end. In overview, this book is about how the journey of genuine faith can lead to an increased sense of subjective well-being and meaning. It is not about seeking and using faith as a strategy or trick to obtain self-fulfillment or personal gain.

Rather, the intent is to share what I have learned and to honor each individual's journey as a very unique endeavor. No matter how deep the spiritual conviction, as human beings, we live our lives through the prism of our psychological experience. This raises unique opportunities and challenges for each of us. Developing faith and spiritual connection offer unparalleled strategies for transcending difficulties and finding the path of our greatest good. No one is too damaged, but many are lost.

It is my belief: We are all whole before God.

1   THE ALMIGHTY SELF-ESTEEM

When I was a little girl in the 1950s, it seemed that everyone belonged to a religion. Every Sunday we traipsed off to church, my sisters and I decked out in white gloves, dress hats, and Mary Jane pumps, although it was never clear why. Talk of God or bedtime prayers, even saying grace, rarely occurred in my house. A few times I approached one of my parents with queries about spiritual matters, but they never appeared to know what to say. Nor seemed to think such things held any importance.

My father was a university professor, an intellectual, and our weekly churchgoing was most likely his attempt to adapt to the placid conformity of *Leave It To Beaver* suburbia. Ours was a stimulating household but did seem different. Instead of gathering together to watch Johnny Carson, as occurred in the homes of my friends, during our family time my father would read aloud from *Beowulf* and *David Copperfield* with great theatrical flare. When I was thirteen, one Sunday he decided we were agnostics, and we never went to church again. At first I was thrilled by my "Get Out of Church Free" card, but quickly this turned to feeling very sad. Despite the limits to my religious instruction, I had a simple, childlike love of God. From my young perspective, it felt like we had abandoned an old friend.

Predictably, as a young adolescent, at some point after we stopped going to church, I ceased thinking about God entirely. I had a lot of growing pains to attend to, and being agnostic became glamorized in my mind as chic and existential in a European or Bohemian sort of way. Initially, it did seem strangely nonconformist not to go to church, even for my unconventional family. Now, as I look back, it appears my father's pronouncement may have been a year or so ahead of its time. In the mid 1960s, *Time* magazine *(April 8, 1966)* ran a famous cover asking "Is God Dead?" which caused expectable outrage.

The next few years were politically stormy and socially revolutionary for the country. Amidst the cultural disquiet, people seemed too riled up about other things to think or worry about God. On college campuses, the most important ethical ideal became "make love, not war" in protest against the Vietnam conflict. By the 1970s, it seemed that traditional religion had become associated with an antiquated mindset and was definitely uncool. Few people I knew went to church or temple, except on holidays or special occasions. This no doubt reflected my peer group *(in the bell-bottom strewn university setting I existed in at the time)*. Yet it did seem something fundamental was transforming in the society at large.

To a young person, the late '60s and early '70s were a visionary, iconoclastic period. There was a clear attempt to break through constraints of all types, from experimentation with mind-blowing drugs to sexual liberation, new gender roles, and alternative lifestyles, all eventually trickling into mainstream fads. Unmarried couples were shacking up with the pros and cons of birth control methods discussed publicly by young women *(like myself)* who ten years earlier barely knew what sex was going into their teens. In the exhilarating arrogance of youth, there was the sense that we were on the crest of something monumental, risqué, and world-shattering Utopian. Esoteric philosophies *(meaning they were exotic to modern Americans but institutional in other societies)* became popular in a recreational, pick-and-choose type of way.

For a student of psychology in the 1970s, there was a lot of optimism about human possibilities and how we could apply the knowledge of the field. Out of the 1960s had come a belief in innate and untapped human potential, with the hope that liberation from repressive societal restraints would unleash vast creativity and harmony, both personally and in the world at large. On the popular front, increasingly there seemed to be the idea that an inherent, pure, and authentic "self" existed within each of us *(almost like a young child untainted by society's teachings)*. The assumption was, if the individual could just get in touch with this true and innocent core and allow it to blossom unfettered, a happy life was sure to follow. Taking this one step further, ultimately we could have an idyllic and productive society if all of its members were allowed to thrive.

"Do your own thing" became the clarion call although too often it seemed everyone was doing the same thing *(again, the bell-bottoms were everywhere)*. Still, there had developed a clear focus on the importance of individuality, self-actualization, and the supremacy of personal truth. This wasn't just a temporary craze despite the 1970s stereotype as the "Me" Decade with long sideburns and bad clothes. People were beginning to think differently about themselves and how to live their lives.

In retrospect, it did seem an underlying shift was occurring, from the *external* authority of an all-powerful God and absolute moral principles to the *internal* authority of the *self* as knowing what was best *(at least for the individual)*. With everyone trying to do his or her own thing, it was becoming a relativistic world. But there remained a sense of moral clarity in terms of absolute good and evil, which no longer exists today. When I see television programs from the 1970s, for the most part, there was still a classic, moral undercurrent in terms of heroes and villains, a lesson or fable sewn into the plot line, the playing out of traditional ideas of "right and wrong."

In some ways, notwithstanding the patina of hip, the '60s and '70s were a naïve, almost juvenile period. Socially and sexually, the culture appeared to have come unhinged like a rebellious teenager who was enjoying the power of hormones and shock value for the first time. There also seemed to be a bit of the adolescent attitude of "biting the hand that feeds you." Despite the scathing rejection of parental social and moral values, paradoxically the pumped up optimism regarding human knowledge and power seemed to be an extension of the straight-laced 1950s establishment *(against which everyone was supposedly rebelling)*.

The military-industrial complex crowd. The NASA scientists with their horn-rimmed glasses and crew cuts. Since the end of World War II, there had been the undaunted promise of unlimited technological prowess and expertise, which was only affirmed by the rapid progression of technical advances that seemed to proliferate with every passing year. Breakthroughs in medicine, industry, communication, and lifestyle. The expectation in the potential for human control was unprecedented. The idea was that once man *(and it was man then)* was able to understand something, whether disease, the physical environment, or the human mind, we could eventually fix and manipulate it, ideally towards our own beneficial ends.

As children of the 1950s, we had imagined the year 2000 was going to be the deadline and jumping-off point for a man-made, high-tech Nirvana. As a young psychologist in the 1970s, it still seemed we were evolving in an astonishing direction. After all, we had just walked on the moon. Less than ten years before that and my fourth grade class had been herded into the elementary school cafeteria to watch Alan Shepard, the first American in space, take a 15-minute suborbital flight on a tiny black-and-white screen. We closed our eyes, clutched each other's hands, and prayed for America. Now, in the wake of the

Vietnam era, the university professors may have sported ponytails and tie-dyed ponchos, but it was still about human vision and control. Surely, the progression of social science and unleashed personal potential would lead to one giant leap for human consciousness. *(Had Divine knowledge and authority simply become irrelevant?)*

But then enter the 1980s. Priorities changed. Almost overnight, the "Me" Decade appeared to go into overdrive and erupted into an era of unadulterated self-indulgence. The idealism of the two previous decades gave way to a more practical but somewhat cynical pursuit of materialistic and hedonistic pleasures. *Self-actualization* of inner potential soon became reformulated as *self-gratification* of personal needs and desires, even at the expense of infringing upon others. Consistent with a decade in which excess was glorified, there developed a popular sentiment *(and moral justification)* that narcissism, like greed, was adaptive, even necessary, to achieve one's goals and live the most fulfilling life possible. That inner authentic "self," assumed a decade earlier to be the wellspring of greater creativity and more humanly responsible attitudes, had caved into a bottomless pit of untamed wants and needs.

By the late 1980s, self-esteem had become the prime psychological commodity. Everybody wanted it. Like money, the assumption was the more you had, the better. It was *high* self-esteem that was presumed to be the vehicle for getting what you craved and for having enough hubris to go after life so unabashedly. If you had it, you should flaunt it. If you didn't, you should get it. People without an adequate sense of self-worth *(interpreted to mean a lust for success)* were admonished for being passive and unassertive or avoidant of taking risk. *Low* self-esteem became identified as the quintessential human tragedy, sentencing an individual to a life of emotional hardship and defeat, both in career and relationships.

Among practicing psychologists, there was a lot of excitement. Here was a concept that could easily be understood by clients and the population at large. We all have self-esteem or lack thereof. Deficits in self-esteem began to be used to explain almost every problem in human functioning from codependency to criminality. As the self-esteem movement took hold, the importance of early childhood relationships, always emphasized in therapy, became popularized as the root cause of shortages in self-regard. The theory went, if you didn't get enough unconditional love and stable parenting from your primary caretakers, there were bound to be mega-problems later on.

It seemed that untainted, authentic "self" within was begging to be hugged. On daytime talk shows, in therapy offices and self-help books, everyone was analyzing the trauma or neglect in childhood, the deficits in their mother-child bond. The mother hadn't responded when the child cried *(the rejecting mother)*. No, she responded too much *(smothering)*. Actually, the child never knew what to expect *(inconsistent, mixed messages)*. It soon became evident that everyone was damaged. That every important relationship or life choice was simply the playing out of unmet early childhood needs.

It also followed that self-esteem in the young child was crucial for strong emotional development. Books for conscientious parents, childhood enhancement programs, and school systems throughout the country began to advocate heaping on love and acceptance like gravy on a Thanksgiving dinner. In some places, self-esteem classes were even part of the curriculum. It also wasn't just about creating *good* feelings but protecting the child from *bad* feelings that had become so important. Playground teasing, competition, punishment for wrong behavior, and even normal disappointments were now considered emotionally dangerous and should be avoided. While such experiences are traumatic at the extreme, it seemed the intent was to entirely psychologically sanitize and anesthetize childhood. The premise was, in a totally positive environment, the youngster's growing sense of self-worth could then thrive unimpeded.

These childrearing trends had been developing for awhile but by the end of the 1980s appeared to coalesce as scientific fact, at least in the popular mind. Since the 1990s and over the past twenty years, the importance of self-esteem has seemed to become institutionalized in the media and mainstream culture. Good self-esteem has seeped into societal consciousness as something of fundamental importance, a must-have, including for those who are not psychologically minded but only trying to find out how to be successful and provide the best for their families. Yet self-esteem has not been consistently supported by academic research as the be-all and end-all in psychological adjustment. Nor have the theories about how to treat it.

Certainly, there are a number of positive things that have come from the self-esteem movement, such as greater acceptance of others, more understanding of personality and relationships, and less stigma about having psychological problems. On the other hand, the obsession with self-esteem has appeared to correlate with disturbing societal trends that have burgeoned over the past twenty years. Specifically, we see the glorification of *self* and relentless pursuit of *self*-interest encouraged in an increasingly materialistic, harsh, and morally bereft or relativistic world.

The quest for self-esteem seems to have morphed into a pursuit of *self-*aggrandizement and pernicious narcissism. Beyond the expectation of a life of pampering and *self-indulgence, self-love* and *self-fulfillment* have crept into the societal mindset as inalienable human rights. We are taught we deserve to have it all by just being who we are. We are told "Love yourself" first and foremost and to charge ahead at all costs in as competitive and aggressive manner as necessary. The new ethic is to "get mine," whatever that means for the individual.

True self-esteem means you like or respect yourself but based on a realistic appraisal. Not who you want to be or feel you need to be *(according to parents or society)*. Who you are. Genuine self-esteem starts with self-acceptance and suggests some degree of surface insight. What are my strengths and weaknesses? What am I good at? Where are my vulnerabilities? True self-esteem also implies that the person feels lovable and competent enough to achieve goals or, at least, to make the effort.

Is this enough? It no longer seems to be for a lot of people. Sure, at some level, we all want a genuine sense of self-worth, just as we all want love and security and health and a feeling of personal effectiveness. It could also be argued that self-esteem has mutated into an entirely different animal, and what is now called self-esteem *(or what everyone seems to be seeking)* has nothing to do with a genuine feeling of self-worth at all. The pursuit of self-esteem as a balanced and reasoned sense of personal value and individual potential seems to have bloated into grandiosity and voracious self-entitlement.

Psychologists are apt to point out that it's not narcissism per se, but whether it's *healthy* versus *unhealthy* that's important. It is *healthy* to seek a sense of accomplishment, positive self-regard, and yes, self-love, all of which may be critical for life satisfaction. But too much or out of control narcissism, which many would argue we have today, is toxic and spawns insatiable neediness, manipulative attention-seeking, and shallow self-absorption. There is also an angry and mean-spirited undercurrent to *unhealthy* narcissism. For example, in recent decades, our society has become so self-focused, egotistical, and cocksure that many people seem to think they can only feel good about themselves by feeling superior to others. There is also the potential for bitter envy and vindictive aggression if desires are not fulfilled or the grandeur of one's self-image is not appreciated in the outside world.

How did this happen? For one thing, at some point during the past twenty years, the hunt for self-esteem seems to have shifted from nurturing and building up self-confidence through unconditional love and positive opportunities... to the perception of *victimization* suffered in childhood or from the outside world. Once self-esteem began seeping into mainstream consciousness as a primary need, providing self-esteem *(or the perfect circumstances to develop it)* appeared to become a parental and societal responsibility, almost on a par with insuring adequate nutrition. To *not* do so became equated with abuse, not only of children, but of all those who are weaker and cannot fend for themselves. Deficits in self-esteem were no longer damage that everyone seemed to incur to some degree in the course of growing up *(although some was severe)*. Low self-esteem now implied you had been victimized or abused.

Anything or anyone that impeded self-worth was considered an outrage and righteously engendered a lot of anger. The message seemed to trickle into popular consciousness that most people had become traumatized by just being alive. I've heard friends and clients describe themselves as having been emotionally abused because their parents argued in front of them. Not hitting or cursing or nastiness, just arguing about the things that families tend to argue about. Or they didn't get the birthday present they wanted. Or Dad was always too tired after working 18-hour days to pay attention. Or the teacher looked at them funny. Or they didn't have a Dad. All these situations surely can affect a person and cause pain or self-doubt, but this is part of living, not abuse.

Real child abuse is always tragic as is the victimization of fellow human beings. Yet at some point it seemed that *understanding* what went wrong in one's childhood evolved into *blaming* one's childhood with absolution from any personal responsibility for anything. It was no longer simply about productively changing and coping with the emotional issues and maladaptive patterns arising from the past. Now everyone and anyone could rationalize anything and everything *(from the most atrocious to the truly trivial)* due to the personal harm inflicted by others. Abuse or victimization *(past or present)* became the great excuse and exonerator and the new defining principle for almost every negative feeling or act in society at large.

It seems our culture of blame strikes a double whammy. Not only do we assume we are *not* responsible for any bad stuff that we do, but it is mandated that we *deserve,* without condition, to have all the good stuff we can get. Sounds like easy living, but what happens when we don't get what we want? The mindset of victimization seems to have advanced even further in a dynamic of hurt, entitlement, and rage. If we don't get what we want, we feel like a failure and anxious... but, of course, it's automatically somebody else's fault. We then assume it's also unfair, and we've been victimized further. *(Again, whatever it is we want, we assume we have the right to as human beings.)* So we're allowed to act accordingly. For too many, this gives free rein to, not only being covetous and self-pitying, but begrudging, bitter, scornful, and mean *(and still hurting inside).*

Even from the beginning of my practice, I saw how devastating the narcissistic societal messages could be on a person's well-being, including for those who were just trying to live normally productive and interactive lives. The intensive focus on *self* ironically left most people feeling empty and wanting and inevitably wanting more. The hyper-indulgence of ego or sensual and material appetites never fulfilled but led to a debauched or gluttonous boredom and stagnation down-the-line.

Being regular or ordinary in any aspect of one's life *(or self)* seemed to imply a lack of value that felt intolerable to many. Yet the drive to be special, with unlimited potential and choice, also backfired. The impossible standards of perfection or happiness that people seemed to be creating for themselves could rarely be met, let alone sustained. When perfection couldn't be reached or didn't fill up, this was taken as proof of unworthiness or "loser" status, the pain of which was then directed onto others through resentment or collapsed the individual into self-loathing, even despair.

Even as far back as the 1980s, listening in therapy sessions to how the pursuit of self-esteem played out at times made me feel uneasy. Clients who had identified themselves as having low self-esteem would recount all their perceived failings, how they wished they could be different, and whom they admired and wanted to emulate. Often I was astounded but found it tragic, hearing the ways people wanted to change. Before me would be this sensitive, caring, conscientious, true blue, and delightful person, but the goal seemed to be to become self-obsessed, uncaring, aggressive, exploitative, and unfeeling. At least, that was the fantasy. Usually, it wasn't conscious. These weren't unkind or selfish people. They felt inferior and suffered greatly but clearly imagined this was the way of being self-protective and assertive in such a competitive and pressured world.

There also was the sardonic joke, "In my next life, I want to come back as a psychopath. It would be so much easier." I actually heard this sentiment from quite a number of clients. I've even had a few people seek my services with the frank intent of learning to manipulate others or to feel superior. I remember one woman *(as though ordering the most expensive meal on the menu)* saying she wanted the type of self-esteem that would allow her to walk into a room with such assurance that she could condescendingly look down on everyone else. She saw nothing wrong with this but just felt lacking in the qualities that she thought were necessary to be happy *(which was why she thought contacting a therapist was appropriate)*.

While it felt something was so wrong, what was more disconcerting was that I could also relate to what my clients were expressing. As someone with a sensitive nature, I had struggled with issues of self-worth and wanting to fit in since my teenage years. Life just appeared smoother for a lot of other people who seemed better able to go with the social flow, took things in stride, and cared less about the feelings or reactions of others. This was long before I had any spiritual interest or understanding. Like so many of my clients, I was only trying to find a way and doing what I had been taught in order to exist and thrive in an environment that often felt empty or incompatible.

In fact, it seemed the ultimate irony that those very qualities that I resisted in myself *(because they made me feel so weak and vulnerable)* were the ones I found so appealing in my clients. Yet they had sought me out in the first place because it was those exact qualities they had wanted to change. I began to question the supremacy of the self-esteem paradigm as the thought nagged at me: Is it self-esteem we all want or is it unbridled narcissism? Or is it just unbridled narcissism that we feel we need to get by? Were people really unhappy with themselves? Or were they unhappy with their lives and the ways of the society in which they found themselves?

There's a lot of hurt and discouragement for people who live from the heart in the modern world. For some, it's their basic nature to be gentle and sensitive. To be themselves means to be emotional,

THE ALMIGHTY SELF-ESTEEM

humble, empathic, and caretaking. To hold onto these inner values and authentic feelings is an ongoing battle, and too often they end up feeling repeatedly exploited, disappointed, denigrated, or ignored. The level of manipulation and competitiveness that it takes to succeed is something many have difficulty tolerating or don't even have the capacity for in their behavioral repertoire. All this would suggest a moral issue, but ours is a world without much moral consideration. Such people can end up blaming themselves.

Morality isn't necessarily linked to self-esteem. We all know people with high self-esteem who are moral midgets and very self-satisfied with their own egregious behavior. In theory, it would seem that some moral standard is implied if a person is really going to examine his or her own thoughts and actions. Today little emphasis is given to character. With God archaic *(or at least exiled)*, is there a higher standard anyway? Moral values have become relative and are rarely factored into the formula for self-esteem. Gone are the days of holding up for inspiration the strong but humble and self-sacrificing movie hero *(larger than life on a black-and-white screen)*. Modern people tend to be judging themselves as to whether they have the goodies that society has deemed are worthwhile or will get them something in the external world. We measure ourselves *(and others)* in terms of material possessions, nice looks or special talents, fame, status, our power quotient, and the aura of being cool.

Such criteria have always been part of the social equation, but this is surface stuff. It has nothing to do with one's real worth or emotional core. Nowadays, the superficial externals seem to have become so prominent that little else matters. Whether you're a good person or a nice guy is irrelevant at best and may be looked upon negatively *(it suggests weakness)*. In the current mindset, the winner is self-interest and the person who embodies it. We idealize aggressive ambition, a kind of crafty intelligence and social cunning, and the posture of being so together that "nothing really bothers me," least of all other people.

Even those who are sensitive and want to be caring often are self-absorbed. Again, there's such a stigma associated with expressing anything too tender or being emotionally exposed. Many retreat behind a wall of pretense through constant activity. Underneath, they're fixated on their own emotional pain. We're also advised not to take the eye off of *self* if we want to make anything out of our lives. People who would be mortified at being labeled self-centered can be so preoccupied with their own issues that they actually are in the day-to-day. We're all so programmed to be involved in our own little narcissistic bubbles, even without realizing it.

What's worse is that wrong or unethical *(even some illegal)* behavior doesn't seem to matter anymore. It's not relevant unless it affects our individual needs and our own little world. Too often transgressors seem admired, rather than shamed, for their brazenness and guile. Basically no one cares. *(It's not my problem...)* We've become numb, at most turning a bored eye to the litanies of inebriated and victimizing politicians, celebrities, and corporate scammers who, once caught, seem to think remorse means blaming something or someone else. *(Whatever...)* On the societal level, we appear to be moving from moral relativism to moral apathy. On the personal level, there seems to be a lot of confusion and misunderstanding.

This last was underscored for me several years ago when I was giving a workshop on sensitivity and brought up the importance of having strong personal moral values to guide and center emotional experience. To me, the logic seemed fairly obvious. Strong moral values provide a compass and anchor. You have a clear definition of how to behave, what brings meaning and is worthwhile. You also have a straightforward direction as to how to proceed in any situation although figuring out the details can be complex. Such clarity offers ballast against external influences *(such as the reactions of others)* or one's own emotional tailspin. Finally, adhering to strong moral standards can lead to a sense of personal integrity and honor, which ultimately is positive for real self-esteem.

The participants of the workshop were confused. What did I mean by strong personal moral values? No one appeared to know what I was talking about. This made me confused. These were educated, psychologically-minded people in their 20s and early 30s, but they seemed genuinely puzzled about what I meant by personal moral values or how these could have any impact on emotional experience.

As we clarified further, what became evident was that, for many people today, personal morality has come to have a totally different meaning. It is equated with the endorsement of certain intellectual ideas having to do with social justice or tolerance, compassion for the disadvantaged, or creating environmental balance. These values are presented more like personality traits *(or proof of holding the socially correct attitudes)*. They have more to do with what a person *subscribes to*, rather than what is *struggled with*. Personal values have become more like a resume of idealized theoretical principles, rather than a compass and anchor in day-to-day behavior and interaction. These ethical standards may be admirable and can affect some of the person's choices but usually remain in the background most of the time.

This was disturbing. Of course, there have always been those who have worn their morality like a badge. But it seemed that something important and psychologically worthwhile had fallen through the cracks. Just one generation earlier and there was the cartoon of the devil and angel on one's shoulder in consciousness, which played over and over again in TV shows, storybooks, actual cartoons, even commercials. We were taught there were "right and wrong" choices in our thoughts and actions, which were based on agreed upon higher standards beyond self-interest or personal needs. There was a lot of instruction about *conscience,* a word rarely heard anymore. We were told to let our conscience mentally punish us when we behaved badly and to turn to our conscience for guidance when needed. The conscience became a dynamic part of the psyche from a fairly early age. Back then, you had to *earn* feeling good about yourself.

Today this kind of thinking is looked upon as rigid, potentially unhealthy, and ironically intolerant. In our relativistic world, there is no absolute "right" or "wrong" *(other than it's absolutely wrong to judge absolutely).* In traditional morality, there are both tried and true standards and guides for behavior, and then we can judge ourselves and act accordingly. Now, in a relativistic or apathetic morality, we are taught that it depends on the individual's vantage point based on personal history and cultural teachings. There is always a reason or other perspective or context to consider. This feeds right into the idea that no one is responsible. Taken to the extreme, this means anything goes. Everything can be explained away.

Traditional moral values may even be looked upon as destructive. We are advised that too much conscience in our feel good world is oppressive and stifling and holds the potential to breed negative self-judgments, such as guilt. This could be counterproductive to self-esteem, which is mandated should never be contingent on behavior anyway. A sense of self-worth based on "who I am, not what I do" is assumed to be an elemental right and optimal condition. Anything that detracts from this is considered dysfunctional *(i.e., "You're being way too harsh on yourself.").*

This would seem to be the crux of the matter. In the contemporary view, moral issues of "right and wrong" are secondary *(if considered at all or even understood)*. Consistent with a culture in which the authority of God has been replaced by the authority of science and human experts, people today are taught to first see things in terms of *health* versus *dysfunction (or disease)*. It is often said that science is amoral. It doesn't render judgments but is about observation and how things work. For the modern secular person, consideration of God is simply off the radar. *(Or is it that Self has replaced God?)* It is not spiritual or moral behavior but being psychologically *healthy* that has become the preeminent goal.

But what do we mean by psychological health? By whose criteria? What if the societal norm has become unhealthy or self-destructive? What happens when the moral standard has been reduced to the level of a grabby, screaming child within and anything goes? When the ideal of earned self-worth has been repackaged as a license for audacious conceit and rapacious self-enhancement? When, instead of personal honor through courage, honesty, and disciplined accomplishment, it is intimidating power or envious admiration from others that is the sought-after reward?

It does seem off kilter. In an age when the pursuit of *self* has become elevated to the primary purpose for living, real self-esteem seems so hard to come by, and people appear so lost and unmoored.

2   Whatever Happened to God?

A surprising sidebar to the secular narcissism of mainstream culture has been the explosion of interest in spirituality. One doesn't have to surf too far up the cable channels to hear attestations to the power of spiritual practice... from scripture quoting preachers to low-lit astrologers to white robed worshippers meditating on the beach at sunset. In local bookstores, shelves of "metaphysical" titles bear witness as to how this theory or that technique can transcend real-life problems and enhance personal well-being. In print, on the screen, and on the web, testimonials abound as to how *positive energy* and *positive attitude*, God, the god within, and "the Universe formerly known as God" can work wonders in our individual lives.

The classic association to spirituality is a belief in God or the supernatural. In contrast, modern spirituality is often marked by confusion, and it's unclear exactly what it involves. Enter a New Age bookstore or website and be bombarded with ancient texts, trendy witticisms, and all sorts of recuperative and meditative practices. From the major Eastern religions to homeopathy, channeling, extraterrestrials, and Women's Studies, the offerings are plentiful. Add on the workshops and gurus, plus all sorts of alternative healing techniques and specialized products. Spirituality has become big business. Some might argue this modern movement is nothing more than successful advertising. Even so, it does raise the question: Is there a void or need that is being tapped into and not otherwise served in contemporary life?

For many today, there is a cafeteria or smorgasbord approach to spirituality. They select elements from various belief systems and do the same with different types of practices, developing a customized program uniquely for them. For instance, people who identify themselves as spiritual may express this by attending yoga class or a Zen retreat. Others have private rituals, such as lighting candles or taking a walk at sunset. Some meditate through gardening or doing crafts, even in the midst of driving home during rush hour. It seems that many people are finding spiritual meaning through activities that are not usually associated with worship or meditation but have come to have intense personal significance for the individual.

Between the marketing and range of spiritual topics, there seems to be a lot of uncertainty. I have met people who meditated regularly, were conversant about the latest healing workshops, and maintained a vegetarian diet for spiritual reasons but acknowledged they were unsure what spirituality really involves. Even those who have a regular practice and affirm the transformative benefits, on another level, may be unclear and still searching. I have also been told that a person was turned off to spirituality by a bad experience with a healer or trancelike technique or other people who profess to be spiritual.

There's a lot of chaos in spiritual interests these days. Typical was one gathering I attended where the conversation turned to religion and personal belief. An earnest hush came over the room as everyone tentatively started to weigh in. This one was a Taoist, another a Buddhist but also had a sense of a collective human consciousness. Two endorsed some form of Native American beliefs. Another had been to a New Age sweat lodge but followed a particular East Indian guru. Someone else was reading books on metaphysical healing and was also into journaling.

This is not to disparage. When people speak of these matters, it is very heartfelt. But it seemed so superficial as nothing about the substance of the beliefs or basic philosophical issues was being discussed. After everyone announced their preferences, the faces were so expectant, like children who had enthusiastically brought their new notebooks on the first day of school, then the teacher hadn't shown. Everyone seemed truly interested, even hungry, but for what? Real information? Permission to feel spiritual hunger in the first place? I have been in several scenarios like this one. It always seems so jumbled and as though something is missing, perhaps emblematic of the clutter and mixed messages in modern life.

Today's spiritual quest comes in many forms with various objectives. What is striking is that so much of contemporary spirituality does not include any traditional concept of God. The institutional religions *(East and West)* and many of the healing practices and esoteric belief systems that are popular today do have a belief in a Supreme Being or Higher Power as a basic assumption. A lot of modern spirituality does not. It has more to do with healing, personal empowerment, or what feels good, and clearly when some people talk about spirituality, there is no consideration of God at all.

So what is the attraction? For some, modern spirituality is associated with a sense of haven or retreat. It becomes a personal refuge from the hyperactivity and turmoil in the external world. As opposed to the frenetic and grueling pace of daily existence, spiritual practice may be looked upon as an opportunity to replenish mental and even physical resources, to get back in touch with one's *self*, and to feel centered, however briefly. We have grown accustomed to nonstop stimulation through all sorts of media, family and work demands, and instant accessibility via cell phone, email, and texting. Life has become an endless To Do list marching by. Rarely are we able to hit the *Pause* button and take a breather.

In this milieu, a person's private spiritual practice becomes a kind of peaceful pit stop amidst the daily race. There may be a well-defined belief system, including devotion to God, attached to these activities, but often there is not. For some, there is no interest in higher values beyond the sense of replenishment or filling up of *self* or *life force* that such practices provide. For others, there may be an interest or desire for a fuller spiritual life but just not enough time for more extensive reflection or exploration.

Modern spirituality may also be sought because of its association with deeper meaning, higher values, and compassion. It becomes a sanctuary, not only from the frenzy, but the harshness of our dog-eat-dog world. Organized religions and many of the nontraditional spiritual disciplines today do address greater philosophical questions, provide ethical direction in living, and offer connection with others who have acknowledged similar needs. There tends to be a comforting and protective feeling connoted by a community that has come together towards spiritual ends or helping others. In its popular image, spirituality has an aura of gentleness, kindness, and inner peace. It represents the softer side of life, a place where tenderness not only can be expressed but is nurtured and appreciated.

It is interesting that, with the exception of blind, cultish fanaticism, there has arisen the general consensus that spirituality is "good for you." Modern spirituality is often conceived as synonymous with optimal, extraordinary functioning or healing and practices that are life-enhancing. On the pop culture front, spirituality may be touted as a magical version of self-help, a kind of intuitive or visionary branch of psychology. Sometimes the emphasis is so predominantly on *self* and psyche that any connection to traditional spiritual concerns, let alone God, seems secondary or lost altogether. There has also been the distortion through massive commercialization. At the extreme, with its promise of providing relaxation and bliss, the contemporary spiritual quest may be more about self-gratification, even being pampered on a purely sensual level, rather than any spiritual or even personal truth.

Yet, for many, modern spirituality is a serious endeavor. There is a sincere intent to advance the individual and common good through healing and wholeness although ironically the focus is primarily on what happens on the earthly plane. For example, on the *physical* or bodily level, "spirituality" may be associated with wellness, alternative medicine, organic nutrition, homeopathy, and the idea of a mind-body *(sometimes mind-body-"spirit")* connection. The goal is to take a more harmonious, natural, and holistic approach to health and disease, using techniques that are either not fully accepted or even known in Western medicine or through scientific research.

On the *emotional* level, even mainstream psychology has begun to acknowledge a "spiritual" part within the human psyche. Typically, this is associated with an area of life where the person finds depth, unique meaning, or a feeling of peace. There may be reference to a *higher self* or *soul*, but usually this is more colloquial, describing certain traits or needs or dreams within the individual's personality. It has no relation to the traditional idea of *soul* as connected to and created by God. There may even be some discussion of a "spiritual" quest by going within, but there are differences with the traditional concept. In this psychologically oriented, earthly "spiritual" model, the person goes within to get in touch with the *self* in order to *enhance* it. In the traditional spiritual quest, the person goes within to find God and greater Truth and meaning and get *beyond* the psychological *self*.

Some therapists and pastoral counselors do deal with traditional spiritual issues or the teachings of a particular religion although this usually occurs only when the client is specifically seeking this type of counsel. Among the helping professions, it is generally considered inappropriate to discuss ethical or religious ideas without the client's permission to go in that direction. Other psychotherapists may encourage "spiritual" practice solely for the purposes of relaxation, regrouping, and self-actualization without reference to a Higher Power at all.

On the research front, there have been a few studies that have supported a positive effect of spirituality on mental health although such findings tend to be explained using familiar *(and scientifically acceptable)* psychological and biological concepts. People who are religious are thought to have greater social support. There are noted to be physiologically relaxing effects associated with meditation and prayer. In other words, the benefits of spiritual practice are seen as similar to receiving biofeedback or listening to a soothing tape in a therapist's office. In recent years, there has been groundbreaking work in the neurology underlying "spiritual" experience *(e.g., defined as mystical feelings of egolessness or compassion)*, including correlation with actual brain activity. Still, given the scientific bias of academic endeavor, while there have been some studies of intercessory prayer, there is rarely consideration of a true spiritual dimension or Higher Power affecting human consciousness.

Plainly, modern spirituality is a mixed bag. At the other end of the spectrum from an entirely earthly focus, there may be emphasized *metaphysical* knowledge or practices, which seek to heal or empower through the understanding of *supernatural* forces and laws. Many of these ideas, such as the power of attraction or astrology or the channeling of healing spirits, are obviously outside accepted science and assume the existence of a spiritual *(or at least nonphysical)* dimension or reality *beyond* the natural world. Since *metaphysical* means "beyond the physical," theoretically *metaphysical* knowledge would include traditional spirituality, and sometimes there is a focus on a Higher Power or the intent of communing with the Divine.

But often the pursuit of *metaphysical* knowledge is geared solely towards helping people in their *physical* and *psychological* lives. It has nothing to do with God at all but is just as focused on healing and personal empowerment as a more conventional self-help program. The difference in the *metaphysical* approach is that it is assumed the best way to do so is through understanding and manipulation of the paranormal world, which is thought to affect human beings. On the other hand, some traditional religious systems warn against dabbling in *metaphysical* practices, which are considered magic. In the traditional view, an individual defers to the authority and mystery of God. Any attempt to tamper in the *metaphysical* realm is presumed to be like walking into an arena that human beings can't begin to understand and could be dangerous, possibly opening up the person to false knowledge or evil forces.

For many today, the idea of *metaphysical* influences, whether evil or benevolent, is just too far-fetched, even among those who describe themselves as spiritual. The pervasiveness of science and technology has placed such a predominant emphasis on the natural world and *physical* explanations. Any interpretation or interest that goes beyond the physical is considered irrational, superstitious, or out of touch with reality. Such judgments can be so strong that those who do seek to go beyond the limits of scientific explanations may try to hide this from those who don't.

Sometimes it feels like there's a kind of Believers' Underground. You wait for the sign, a word or look or emphasis that lets you know you can speak your mind. It can be socially dangerous to say that you truly believe in God, who gets really bad press in the modern era. A genuine, committed faith in God tends to be denigrated as the way of the uneducated, psychotic, or those who can't think for themselves. A sincere belief in God, at least in the sense of a Supreme Being or all-powerful Creator, is viewed as reasonable for the primitive person or in the world of our forefathers. For those who have been exposed to scientific reality, the assumption is that holding onto such belief can only be seen as a psychological crutch.

Ask people today if they believe in God, and the answers are all over the map. Except for those who are traditionally religious, God may be equated with forces of energy, a Higher Self, global consciousness, the anthropological similarity of all human beings, a sense of creative dynamism or *life force,* even that God is solely a linguistic device to capture certain feelings deep within. The concept of God as energy, particularly in line with the findings of quantum physics, is popular and scientifically palatable.

Sometimes within such definitions, there is the idea of a real Higher Power, inclusive of and always greater than the individual. Yet a lot of the time there is the impression that God has been redefined as an adjunct to physical or psychological existence *(i.e., potentially under human control).* The emphasis is on *explaining* God in understandable, human *(and physical)* terms, rather than acknowledging that there *is* a Higher Power *beyond* human explanation. The sense of deference or yielding to the Higher Power may also be missing. Instead, we scramble in pursuit of the God particle and the God gene in order to once and for all scientifically explain it all... as well as to explain our human need to explain it all.

Many times I have been in a conversation about spirituality, either socially or in a workshop setting, and at some point it dawns on the other person that my concept of God is that of an actual Higher Power and Supreme Being. *(Yes, God does exist. Really.)* The reaction is often of hesitant incredulity. *(Oh no, she's NOT taking this stuff literally!?)* The throat gets cleared. There's an uncomfortable pause, and I'm asked something to the effect of "You don't mean you *really* believe in a Supreme Being? A supernatural God?"

It's as though I just admitted to killing my mother. Sometimes the other person politely drifts off and then avoids me for the rest of the function *(although I may occasionally catch hostile glances from across the room)*. Sometimes there is immediate anger and defensiveness with civil but sarcastic overtones. I have been ridiculed, even verbally attacked, as stupid with a "thou doth protest too much" intensity that suggests a hidden vulnerability. There seems to be such staunch, emotional antipathy within the secular mainstream to the possibility of a real Higher Power or spiritual reality.

What most typically happens is a heated debate of sorts although nothing is ever accomplished. I have been accosted numerous times for buying the "God is an old man with a long white beard" routine. I'm quite sure I've never said that I believe "God is an old man with a long white beard." I have said that I believe in God as the Supreme Being. *(Apparently many think it's all the same nonsense.)* Sometimes the intensity of the anger makes me feel as though I betrayed the person's confidence because such a brittle, sensitive chord seems to have been struck. The message I get is, as an educated person not identified with any formal religion, I'm not supposed to have such irrational, old-fashioned views.

To be fair, I used to be equally surprised at these meltdowns, which can occur after twenty minutes or more of heartfelt discussion about spiritual matters and God. *(I always wonder... what did this person think we were speaking about?)* In fact, I've sometimes felt a bit taken as people seem to love to talk about these things, even when it makes them furious. Since I am a psychologist recognized as interested in spiritual matters, I tend to immediately get asked questions and others seek to share their opinions regarding spiritual belief or lack of it. People seem so compelled to talk about this in the first place. The question of God is a very serious one, an emotional and at times agitating trigger, with deep meaning for most, even if the individual spends a lot of time discounting it.

At the same time, I understand what these people are feeling. I used to be one of them. I know how threatening the idea of a true Higher Power can be. I've made all the scornful and condescending remarks, rolled my eyes, and hissed with disdainful laughter whenever God's name was mentioned. Once I even proudly gloated about having a pastor ejected from my hospital room when I was undergoing surgery the following day, and he was just offering kind support. That was how desperate I was to maintain a barrier between myself and any suggestion of spiritual reality.

In retrospect, I can see how defensive it was and how threatened I must have felt *(at least subconsciously)*. Even though I was young, it wasn't that I was trying to be cool or put on a brash, sophisticated face to the outside world. To acknowledge the real possibility of God is the opening of a psychological Pandora's Box. It could mean we might have to throw out a lot, if not everything, of what we think we know. But it's not just about losing intellectual control. The possibility of a Supreme Being with actual influence over our lives is even more forbidding on a raw emotional level. It takes us back to the position of a helpless child, entirely dependent on the will and decisions of others. In this case, the other is an all-powerful God, an unknown quantity and force.

The potential consequences are huge and raise terrifying questions. What would an all-powerful God mean for our existence? Is God fair? Are we judged? Are there absolute standards with consequences for how we live our lives? And what about beyond? Do we have any say at all? It's an unnerving proposition, especially for people who find emotional security in being independent thinkers, objective and logical, smart and in control. This isn't only a matter of pride. When these are the cards one holds, it is frightening to acknowledge the possibility of a true Higher Authority and Power beyond the *self*.

At the same time, there are also those who seem to be at a point in their experience that they want to open the door to serious discussion of God. In these same social and professional situations where I encounter such strident disregard as a person of faith, I also meet people who are intrigued, even thrilled, that they have found someone who will talk about spiritual matters in the true sense of the term. Once it is ascertained that this is the direction we're headed, the tone becomes hushed, the posture secretive. Slowly I get edged towards a corner or kitchen or outside porch where we can speak privately. I feel an undercurrent of anxious confusion. There is always such mystery and awe in thoughtful conversation about God. Usually these people do not have a strong religious background but immense hunger for any tidbit of direction with regard to deep-seated spiritual inclinations, questions, and experience. Sometimes I feel uncomfortable. It's almost as though they are projecting onto me a lot more wisdom than is warranted just because I am allowing them to speak about what they truly feel.

What typically are shared are unusual occurrences and feelings that haunt the person and cannot be explained rationally. These are presented in earnest, even timid, inquiries somewhat in the manner of children seeking confirmation and validation of their experience.

They want to know that they're *not* going crazy… that what they saw or intuited or felt *did* or *could* occur… that what they *know* happened *could* be true. Also sought is information about feelings or ideas that are unacknowledged or denigrated by secular attitudes, such as a sense of fate or an inner communication with or being led by God.

I also know what they're feeling. Before I had faith, whenever I would even slightly open that door to a genuine spiritual possibility, there always seemed to be two inconsistent versions of reality that simply could not be reconciled. Faith assumes there is innate *spiritual* knowledge within each of us. Our scientific ethos directs us to assume we can explain all of life's experience in *physical* terms.

What happens if you can't?

3 Spiritual Beingness

Was this a portal to an unseen world?

When I was a child, sitting in church always made me feel very small. Ensconced in the solemn, cavernous darkness, I would look up to where the arches, stained glass, and flickering candelabra created an ornate, lofty web of light and shadows that I utilized to pass the time. Gazing above my pew, I would be carried off into gauzy, pleasant nothingness. Sometimes I imagined I could fly away, somewhat in the manner of Peter Pan.

The religious service always felt so long and suffocating. Usually a well-behaved child, after ten minutes I would begin to squirm. The sitting was the worst. During prayer on the uncomfortable, creaky kneelers, at least my sisters and I could play finger games, making signals to the kids across the aisle and scrambling to see who could find any droppings underneath the next pew... an old prayer book, mimeographed program from last year's Christmas service, a matchbook, even a clunky earring.

Interspersed with the tedium, there was one part of the communion service that I loved. When the minister came to the recounting of the Last Supper, his voice would drop in tone and cadence as though a ghost story was being spun around a Girl Scout campfire. There would hang a breathless space of hushed anticipation that seemed to shoot through my heart and that of everyone in attendance. It was a tale of betrayal and secret knowledge. I knew what happened, but I'd hunker down, crouching tightly between the kneeler and the next pew, and close my eyes so I could take it in fully.

I also became fixated on the phrase "the Peace of God which passeth all understanding" *(The Book of Common Prayer;* also *King James Bible, Philippians 4:7)*. I loved that phrase. Several times I inquired of adults as to what this meant or felt like but to no avail. One day I got it. My heart and being briefly filled with an enthralling, soft, and serene stillness I had never experienced in all my nine years. It was delicious. Definitely deserving of the name. I ran to tell my mother, but she was unimpressed.

Given that I was a psychologist-to-be *(although I didn't choose that course for many years)*, this "Peace of God" became catalogued in my mind as a bona fide human emotion of which I needed to be aware. I think it became my favorite. I would feel it from time to time, rare and fleeting compared to other emotions, so I knew it was something special. It was always a sensation of benevolent and radiating warmth, thrilling but soft, like a whisper, tickling and smothering the heart area. It seemed to occur at least once during the holidays when all the people I loved would be visiting and gathered around the fire or dinner table. The world seemed to sparkle in festivity, but underneath there was this quiet bond of softness and love. These felt like perfect moments in time. Even as a child, I knew they were ephemeral.

I tended to feel "the Peace" most during summers at the shore when my father and I would take walks on the empty beach in the early evenings. Sometimes I would ask him about mermaids or shipwrecks, even eternity. Mostly we spoke very little as dusk flickered across and closed in on the ocean's darkening, mysterious surface. There was a plaintive, ominous quality mixed in with the warmth, but it was still oddly comforting. I knew it was "the Peace of God" all the same.

The longest I ever felt "the Peace" was when I learned that Denise had died. The younger sister of one of the boys in the neighborhood, she had been the brunt of a lot of teasing. I hadn't really played with her much, other than joining in with the teasing from afar. No one had. She always had this strange and stilted quality and never seemed to understand that we were teasing, which made us tease her even more. She also seemed so chronically sad.

I was devastated. I had never known a peer who had died. I kept thinking of the way we had treated her and that no one could change that now. My mother said she had a heart condition, which was why she seemed so off and stiff, but it seemed so unfair. Why didn't she tell us she was sick? If only I had known. I would have treated her so differently, especially if she was going to die. My mother explained that her parents wanted her to live a normal life for as long as possible.

For days, I struggled with a sadness and searing guilt that I had never experienced previously. Retreating to my room, I just sat and stared, fighting tears that kept welling up from my young heart. It all felt so wrong. I did feel a kind of presence which I attributed to God although I felt too angry to care. I didn't think to be angry at God but at myself for the way I had treated Denise and the way that life is and that people have to die. And that children can die. I may have asked, "Why?" It was all so final. My mother tried to talk to me about what I was feeling, but I wanted to be left alone.

At some point, the emotional pain receded, and my heart became infused with a soothing and steadying calm. It seemed softer than I had ever felt it and more subtle, but the distinctive warmth was strong. Here was "the Peace of God, which passeth all understanding." Suddenly it came over me that it wasn't just "the Peace" but also the "passeth all understanding." My young mind took this as a directive. I wasn't supposed to understand, so I stopped trying. Immediately I felt reassured although I didn't know how or why or what this feeling meant. I still wanted to be alone, so I stayed in my room a bit longer, and "the Peace" didn't leave like it usually did, not for a long while. It was like I had curled up in the arms of God.

How do we know God? Spiritual knowledge is never intellectual, neither fact nor theory. From a mental perspective, knowledge implies the accumulation of information, the substance of libraries, laboratories, or encyclopedias. Knowledge may also involve a sense of achievement through training or experience, an expertise or advanced skill. In a social sense, we get to know someone after spending time together. To really *know* someone suggests a degree of intimacy, familiarity, or sharing.

The idea of spiritual knowledge is more akin to this last meaning. We know God through sharing with God. It is direct and personal. Religious texts may set forth Divine Truth, the Word of God, or the doctrines and history of a particular religion, all interpretable by scholars. This body of religious knowledge may be very important for the enhanced understanding of specific philosophical and moral questions or even personal guidance regarding a certain issue. But true spiritual knowledge is a state that comes from an individual's *connection* to God and sharing through a committed relationship. It also acknowledges the Absolute Truth of God and that, as human beings, we can never know this Truth fully.

Spiritual knowledge is paradoxical. On the one hand, the human perspective is always limited. We cannot know God fully and directly. On the other, we can have an awareness of God in everything and all that there is. This awareness tends to be accompanied by an actual sense of belonging to and intrinsic connection with God. We *feel* emotionally bonded. This is not just in the head but in the heart. We also feel connected with others and the world around us through God.

SPIRITUAL BEINGNESS

How this awareness is experienced by each individual or how each person arrives at this place internally will vary. Traditional spirituality does assume there is innate spiritual knowledge within each of us. This means, no matter what our religious background or the teaching of the family or culture in which we grew up, as human beings, we all have an inherent spiritual awareness. This is true, even when this is suppressed by what we have been taught, including if we have been taught not to see it.

Such awareness begins to open up once we understand the reality of God and this ultimate mystery. Again, this is a paradox. The more we accept the Truth of God but that we can never know this fully, the more aware of God we become. From a human perspective, we give up some measure of mental control. We begin to defer to God. The result *(or what we get)* is a sense of another loving, harmonious, and knowledgeable presence, embracing and guiding us. Sometimes there is an associated feeling of *spirit* or light. The person feels this light, within and without, and at times will recognize it in other people.

For many, the idea of spiritual awareness or connection is confusing. Usually, we associate spirituality with *belief*. We describe people as spiritual because they believe in a Higher Power or otherworldly forces. Go to any website or poll about religion or spirituality, and it's all about beliefs. Does God exist? What does Christianity or Islam or Judaism believe? What constitutes a devout versus a sinful person? Is the Bible really the Word of God? Is there an afterlife? Is abortion considered murder? Is there evidence for reincarnation? What about fate versus free will?

Belief involves ideas and assumptions. There is a clear intellectual quality. Even if we believe something with all our heart, it is still a decision we make in our head. We also assume that many beliefs are acquired through learning, again suggesting a mental phenomenon. We are taught by parents, teachers, and other authority figures about God, what is real versus fantasy, what is important in life, and what is "right and wrong." Sometimes we just accept what we have told, but usually this is tinctured by what we have learned through experience. Most of us develop a very personal philosophy about the way things are in the "here and now" and beyond.

What is generally overlooked is that spirituality is as much *experience* as it is belief. This goes beyond thoughts or theories or personal philosophy. Spirituality as *experience* involves changes in emotion, perception, and bodily feelings. Again, it is not just what we believe in our head but affects us in our heart and our gut, even throughout our body. Like other types of experience, this can be all encompassing.

In other words, we don't just evaluate spiritual ideas and then decide whether we want to accept them as true or not. We also participate. This is the power of spirituality for so many people. Spirituality as *experience* makes us feel a certain way. This could range from worshippers becoming so possessed that they seem to go into convulsions and speak in tongues to feeling uplifted and more connected with others after a meditation session. It can be a sense of a specific, personal communication with God or a vague but intense feeling of clarity and awe while watching a sunset.

In contemporary times, we tend to explain what goes on inside our minds in *psychological* as opposed to religious terms. This is true of much of modern spirituality as we discussed previously. We don't worry about having unholy or sinful thoughts, but we do worry when we have dysfunctional attitudes or unhealthy emotional issues. In the current era, we are concerned with health and abilities, not moral or spiritual responsibility. We want to *feel* good, rather than *be* good.

So what does go on inside our minds? We have thoughts and feelings *(positive and negative)*. We cope with fantasies and impulses *(creative or destructive)*. We have perceptions and real bodily sensations and a vast memory bank at our disposal. We have a sense of our *self* or ego as the driver along the road of life, but we also assume that a lot of what drives us is unconscious or biological and thus beyond our control. How it is all put together will affect how we behave, how well we do, and how satisfied we feel or not. In psychology, we assume this is mostly determined by our genes and personal history.

Yet this is theory. *Subjectively,* what is it really like inside our minds? All those thoughts, passions, dreams, and memories create a sense of personal *consciousness.* A never-ending internal landscape, to which only we are privy. At least, so it seems. Personal consciousness is unique to each of us, gives life meaning, and makes us who we are. It is our consciousness that is the source of our individuality. We are both actor and audience. As the person actually living it, each of us has an ongoing, interactive, multilayered movie inside our minds that only we can see.

No one can get inside your mind in any significant way unless you share what you are thinking or feeling. Sure, there are psychics who can tell what number you are thinking. Nonverbal facial cues or electrodes hooked up your nervous system may expose whether you're lying or offended or in a good mood. You can try to record through stream of consciousness techniques what is going on inside, but this is superficial. Even then, it's only what you choose to disclose and fairly minimal information compared to all that is going on, kind of like postcards sent from inside your mind.

How do we explain consciousness? What is this personal and subjective unseen world? Or seen only by us? In the scientific view, human consciousness is assumed to be explainable through *physical* phenomena. It is the aftereffect of brain processes. Our inner experiences *(all those emotions, dreams, memories, urges, etc.)* are felt to be the result of biological mechanisms, such as neurons firing or chemical reactions. Plus, the fact that human consciousness arose in the first place is thought to be an accident of evolution. It was adaptive for the survival of the species, solidifying our superior place in the animal kingdom. Obviously, this perspective is entirely biological. It is devoid of any spiritual considerations.

Even in professional psychology and much of pop psychology and self-help, it is usually assumed that the workings of the mind are dependent on biology. This is particularly true with the increasing use of medications to treat emotional problems, such as depression and anxiety. All our long-term issues, dysfunctional behavior patterns, deficits in self-esteem, addictive tendencies, and day-to-day moods are ultimately seen as arising from our biological make-up although the physiological processes are complicated and not entirely known. The same goes for our personality traits, preferences in a romantic partner, and sense of *self* over life's course. Everything about us, for that matter, and what we think and feel.

This biological view is accepted by the culture at large, at least on the surface. In a society where science is such an authority, this makes sense. No other explanation really competes in our secular world. Still, when it comes to consciousness, do we really know what's going on? Even when scientists are able to identify and measure how biology and psychology go together, this isn't necessarily the whole story. We can measure the *brain* but not the *mind*. There may be other factors involved that are influencing us but have not yet come to light or can even be observed or quantified scientifically. That doesn't mean they don't exist. Science attempts to explain natural phenomena *objectively*. The mind is a *subjective* experience. There may be other forces or a power beyond ourselves, perhaps beyond explanation or even discovery by human beings on the natural, physical plane. This would be consistent with spiritual teachings.

Of course, from the standpoint of a living, thinking, feeling human being, the biology that is presumed to underlie our consciousness seems pretty remote. And who cares? We may return to ashes and dust at the end of it, but right now, while we're in the midst of it, we want to get the most out of what human existence has to offer. As we travel our lives, it is the richness of consciousness that makes it all worthwhile and also haunts us.

What is the nature of consciousness from a spiritual perspective? Is this the portal to an unseen world? A window to a greater reality? To God? Is consciousness at least partially founded in *spirit*? Or does it connect us in *spirit* with others and beyond ourselves? Spirituality as experience does create the impression that we are accessing another realm *beyond* physical reality. Most of us do have a sense that normal psychological processing isn't the entire story.

We hear people talk about something happening on a "whole other level." This typically means it cannot be explained in the usual way. The state of dreaming also seems to involve another dimension or domain altogether. We have all been educated regarding the unconscious and may see this as operating in our own lives. Most of us are aware of trancelike, hypnotic, or altered states, whether or not we have experienced these.

Clearly, we don't have to look to spiritual explanations to confirm multiple levels or states of consciousness. But no one really knows what happens in our internal depths, other than we all travel there during appreciable portions of our lives. All of us experience what appear like cycles of consciousness. A deepening, fading, resurfacing, and then deepening again over the course of the day and into the dreamworld of sleep. The deeper we go, the more we seem to enter a realm of infinite boundlessness. As we do so, there is a feeling of egolessness and separation from our usual sense of *self*.

Is our consciousness ours alone? A major question is whether, in consciousness, we could be connected with others. The idea of a *transpersonal* consciousness or realm is that there may be a collective or group or pool of consciousness among human beings. In other words, at the deepest levels, do we *share* consciousness with others? Is there a point that we go so deep into our internal world that we leave it and enter a spiritual dimension or collective domain beyond ourselves? Are there ways that we communicate with others, and they with us, through consciousness alone?

The idea of an actual transpersonal consciousness is controversial in mainstream psychology. Conversely, most spiritual systems of thought would seem to assume a transpersonal consciousness of some sort, even if the idea is not directly discussed. Religions and spiritual philosophies may describe God differently, even vastly so. Yet there is a spiritual DNA, core principles that have occurred in most belief systems in some form throughout the world and recorded time. The most essential principle is the existence of God and a spiritual unity beyond the *self*. This is the fundamental belief in God as Supreme Being, Higher Power, or greater order, creating and embracing all living things.

How does a transpersonal consciousness fit in? This would be in the idea of a spiritual *unity*, that we are all connected at some level beyond ourselves, with and through God. The idea of a greater unity of *spirit* is easily associated with Eastern religions that tend to conceptualize the Divine as a harmonious Universe or Oneness, sometimes even the idea of a Higher or unified Consciousness. In the traditional Western religions, the idea of spiritual unity is less direct but still applies. God is depicted as the Supreme Being but also the Father or Creator, with the power and love of God seen as embracing and giving life to all living things, thus unifying us all. There is also the idea of a family of God with a unity among spiritual brothers and sisters.

How God is defined may vary, but the implication is that there exists a unity or other transpersonal reality that transcends the material world of our senses and psychological awareness. One way of looking at this is that there is *physical* reality, which may be conceived as an actual plane, a dimension, or level of consciousness. This involves our senses, usual perceptions, and familiar psychological experience. There is also the plane of *spiritual* reality, which represents a truer level of being and is beyond human comprehension. This *spiritual* reality is assumed to be the source of Truth and therefore the *higher* and primary reality. The *physical* world and our *psychological* experience are considered *lower* and secondary, even though this is the reality of our everyday lives. Some belief systems even suppose the physical and psychological are an illusion. Others assume there are various dimensions, some of which harbor forces that are negative or evil, such as Satan.

From a personal vantage point, what all this means is that we seem to exist on multiple levels at once. In the traditional spiritual view, our consciousness is influenced from various sources. Part of what we experience, including our psychology, may be explainable as the end result of *biological* forces and brain mechanisms, but that's not all there is. Since we are created by God, we are also affected by the *spiritual* level of experience. As human beings, we live in at least two possible worlds although we may not be consciously aware of this as we go about our lives.

During the 1960s, the hip and fashionable sentiment was that we were "spiritual beings within physical bodies." At the time I never thought much about what this meant, other than deciding to live in an ashram. It seemed a lifestyle choice associated with the rejection of materialistic values and most exemplified by alternative hippie living, which did include some unconventional religious practices. The "spiritual being" part didn't seem religious but more about being a "spirit" in the sense of feeling free and floating through life, again to "do your own thing," to release that inner essence, to fly, and to thrive. In the college mainstream, the "spiritual being" phrase seemed to touch a chord that life *(meaning the expanse of life before us, as young people)* was supposed to have greater meaning than just the pursuit of materialistic status *(like the lives of our parents)*.

There was also burgeoning interest in exotic metaphysical ideas and practices, such as astrology, psychic phenomena, and Tarot cards. All became prime entertainment at parties but also increasingly were seen as vehicles for personal growth. This suggested a whole other transcendental dimension to personal psychology. As discussed previously, such trends have become integrated into modern approaches to spirituality, which may or may not involve God or more traditional ideas.

Yet the idea that we are *spiritual beings* within *physical* bodies is very traditional. It is another of those core principles that underlie most religions. How we are *spiritual beings* and what this means for the individual will vary from one belief system to another, as do conceptualizations of God. Still, the underlying concept makes sense and it's all connected. If there is a Higher Power who creates and embraces all of us on the spiritual level, logically there is a part of our being that exists on that level. Sometimes this is referred to as the *soul* or Higher Self. And, if the spiritual unity is assumed to be the level of Truth and meaning, then this spiritual part within each of us would presumably be the most important and authentic part of who we are.

So, as *spiritual beings*, we can all know God and find within that spiritual part of ourselves. This is why many religious systems assume there is innate spiritual knowledge within each of us. Because we are *spiritual beings*, we instinctively recognize and can access a connection to God, a sense of Absolute Truth, and inherent spiritual values. It doesn't matter what we have been taught, including that God does not exist. The assumption is that, on some level, we know differently. Our *spiritual beingness* has the potential to trump everything else. Our true identity is that of a child of God. As such, we instinctively feel we are part of a greater spiritual family, and our nature is to seek to connect with and serve God and our spiritual brothers and sisters.

But – there is a huge dilemma in this line of thought. If we are *spiritual beings*, why don't we know this? Why are we so out of touch? How can we be so unaware of the most important part of ourselves? Why is the awareness of God or spiritual reality so limited or nonexistent for so many people? If spiritual reality is the true level of being, why do human beings behave in such ugly and evil ways?

The answer is that we lose touch with who we truly are, that *higher* part within, because of other *lower* level needs, energies, or forces. Some belief systems assume there are negative or evil forces that may influence, even possess us. Another explanation is that our *lower* physical and psychological experience is so compelling that we are taken away from our spiritual core. As human beings, we have dual citizenship in two different universes. We are innately *spiritual beings* but within *physical* bodies with all the *lower* level demands and problems that are part of living on a physical plane.

To illustrate, just think about how immensely challenging and consuming *physical* reality actually is. For our very survival, we have to attend to our biological needs. It's not a matter of choice. We also do so within an environment of finite resources and external threats. Even beyond survival, there's the physical reality of sickness, aging, pain, and limitation as well as sensual pleasure and sexual drives. If that weren't enough, there's the *psychological* realm, presumed to be an extension of the *physical*, with a whole other set of needs, impulses, motivations, emotions, temptations, and reinforcements.

Even on the most superficial level, we all know how unsettling it can be to concentrate under the influence of emotion. This can even be to the point of disruption and loss of focus and personal control. Additionally, there are all the social and economic complexities that arise as a member of a family and human society. Bottom line is that there's a lot of commotion in the earthly realm. So the idea is that the nonstop noise and stimulation of our existence on the *physical* plane get in the way of paying attention to or having time for anything else. Our *spiritual beingness* moves to the background and may disappear off the radar entirely.

To complicate matters further is the matter of human *conditioning*. This is what our culture teaches us is important and real. Much of *conditioning* is valuable in that it helps us to understand the physical and social world around us. It helps us to function and accomplish things in life. Our *conditioning* also narrowly focuses us on a certain version of reality, actually locks us in. It creates a lens or camera angle through which we see the world before us and is so automatic that we do so unconsciously. By the time we are adults, without realizing it, we are generally experiencing our lives through only one lens from only one camera angle. It becomes very difficult to see things any other way.

This camera angle of our *conditioning* tends to focus us on certain things but hides others. Anything that suggests an alternative version of reality, especially anything in our experience that contradicts the accepted version that we hold, is likely to be ignored, rationalized, or discounted. We may not even be aware that we are doing so. The modern trend to look towards science as the final authority is the perfect illustration. The scientific mindset urges a rational approach and deals fairly exclusively in *physical* phenomena and explanations. It denigrates nonphysical points of view as superstitious nonsense. It is easy to see how inner *spiritual* awareness could become obscured.

This was how "the Peace of God" fell by the wayside for me. As I grew into adulthood, I stopped trusting the entirety of my experience and began to see things only the culturally accepted way. Or I did and I didn't. Definitely, I tried. Once I was in graduate school, with the help of all the psychological theory I was learning, I could easily redefine "the Peace" without any connection to God at all. Was it… a "preverbal, emotional state" *(i.e., similar to what a child experiences before learning words)*? The fantasy and limited understanding of an overly imaginative child? Sometimes I just conveniently didn't allow myself to think about it. The point is that I was able to *reframe* those very real feelings, perceptions, and sensations that I had remembered *(as connected to God)* within a new version of reality, in which I was now heavily invested *(and had nothing to do with God at all)*.

Despite my educated calisthenics, there still remained a nagging awareness of something more. Much as I tried to deny it, I continued to sense an underlying realm of nebulous rhythms in life, of which I had been aware since childhood and seemed perceptible in the depths of my consciousness. From the time I was very young, it always felt like something else was going on *above* or *beneath* or *beyond* the surface of things. It just seemed that there was more to reality than what I was being taught was real. I never thought of this as spiritual, but there did seem to be another fabric in life that linked things in ways that were never spoken about or acknowledged. There appeared to be another flow or pattern in addition to the discernible world, certainly a lot of synchronicity in events, at times a sense of deep connection with others, a kind of tapestry of fate and meaning. The circles within circles that couldn't be explained. The older and more educated I became, the more I feared this was insanity. So I never shared it and tried to shut it down.

There is a great disconnect between the possibility of spiritual reality and the *conditioning* of our hyper-secular culture. People who are brought up in traditional religions may be more open to spiritual ideas because of what they have been taught. But even very religious people can end up compartmentalizing their experience or restricting spiritual awareness because the scientific messages of the mainstream culture are so pervasive. On an unconscious basis, *conditioning* is very powerful. Yet, whatever one's background or however rational our world may be, the assumption is that innate spiritual wisdom exists within. This is our gift, inheritance, and privilege as given by God.

As I would later discover, it is when we open to our *spiritual beingness* that our human lives can begin to expand across a promising and totally new horizon.

4 Still There After All These Years

In the early 1990s, I embarked on a period of spiritual awakening. It is somewhat ironic because it was a client who started me on this path. Out of her own enthusiasm, she kept suggesting that I read a certain spiritual book that she had found transformational. I didn't pay much attention at the time. I just wasn't interested in these types of matters. I also questioned why she kept bringing up the book in sessions. Was this an unconscious ploy to avoid dealing with real psychological issues? Was she trying to tell me our therapy wasn't working and she needed something more? For some reason, I did get the book, but it took me about a year and another six months to read it. I was not that impressed. It was about miracles and just seemed too implausible, coming from the agnostic and scientific background I had at the time.

From time to time, issues of spirituality did come up in my practice but not that often. During the first years of doing therapy *(before I had faith)*, I was always amazed at how deeply entrenched the religious ideas from childhood seemed to be. So many of my clients were intellectually sophisticated, agnostic, even atheistic and devil-may-care on the surface. From the innermost levels, particularly during periods of great distress, echoes from their religious past *(e.g., of the nuns or Hebrew school)* came through loud and clear. When it really mattered, the disbelieving public persona was thrown out in a heartbeat. Suddenly there would be concern about offending God or sinning, and my client would seek spiritual solace or guidance, even sheepishly admit to praying, during times of emotional turmoil.

This always threw me. I was the therapist and supposed to know this person well. Sometimes the most intimate details of heinous abuse or frightening depression had been easily shared because of the trust in our therapeutic relationship over the course of many sessions. There never had been any talk of God nor seemed to be any interest. Then suddenly when the crisis struck, God would be everywhere for a session or two until the person began to feel better, at which point predictably God would be packed off to the emotional hinterlands once again.

Ever since my teenage years, when my father had shut down our churchgoing, I called myself an agnostic. Theoretically, this meant I didn't know whether God did or did not exist. Certainly, God didn't exist for me. Frankly, I never thought about it, other than when someone was trying to convince me otherwise and I became nastily defensive or during late-night inebriated discussions at smoke-filled college parties *(when we would solve the problems of the universe and then go out for breakfast)*. The question of God seemed irrelevant, personally and professionally. From the time I was in graduate school and from that point onward, it was the writings of the great psychological thinkers, like Freud and Jung, that structured my world. This was how I understood myself and human beings in general. For the first ten years of my career, I would have discounted any suggestion that spirituality could positively change or even affect a person's life.

In the first part of my clinical practice, I took a classic approach to doing therapy. I would help the client identify long-term issues and maladaptive behavior patterns *(e.g., poor self-esteem, addictive tendencies, self-sabotaging relationships)*. We would then look towards early influences to explain how such problems arose and to attempt to work them through. Therapy is not always focused on the past. Often there are real world issues that have to be dealt with, such as when someone is working through a crisis or going through a personal transition. But, in general, the tendency in psychology is to look towards *(or look backwards, I should say)* to the experiences of childhood as forming who we are.

Sometimes the classic approach worked well but not always. As would be expected, it seemed to work best when the problem was clear-cut and in the present, such as dealing with miscommunication in a relationship or helping someone going through a divorce or even providing coping support in the aftermath of life-threatening trauma. As time went on, I began to feel that many of the longer-term challenges that people dealt with were vague and underlying. It went beyond self-esteem. Among my clients and many of the people I knew, there was an emptiness, a kind of amorphous dissatisfaction and lack of meaning. From the outside looking in, this made no sense as these were successful, intelligent, and attractive people and seemed to have all those things that we all want or at least presume are important.

Sometimes there was a feeling of a more authentic identity, a sense of truer *self* deep within, although often the person was at a loss as to how to express this. Sometimes there was conflict as to whether this sense of truer identity was a good or a bad thing. Definitely, it was not the role that most were playing in their day-to-day existence. Many seemed to present a type of *shadow self* that was based around the standards and expectations of society at large. Others seemed to define themselves in terms of whether or not they had the trappings of success. Sometimes relationships were used in this same way as an emblem of self-worth or accomplishment. The goal seemed to be to feel good about one's self by having what it takes although this worked marginally at best. They never seemed to feel really good about themselves or their lives.

From the beginning of my career in the 1980s, I had glimpses of this, not only in the people I worked with, but with many of the people I knew, and I also showed some of these tendencies, myself. As time went on, increasingly I felt such underlying existential issues were extremely important in psychological growth and healing but were not being adequately addressed by classic psychological concepts, including in my own life.

Like many of my clients, I had sought out therapy and read self-help books. I had come to understand my triggers and maladaptive patterns, developed coping strategies, and pursued avenues of potential strength. In some ways, things always seemed to be getting better or at least clearer. On another level, nothing seemed to ever change. No matter how much self-knowledge I obtained, I was still an unconventional person with a sensitive temperament. Coping with an emotional roller coaster and fluctuating self-esteem remained pivotal themes of my adult life.

But overall, in the early 1990s, I was doing well. This was a period of transition for me but nothing traumatic. I had moved across country, which was a positive, even exciting, change. At one point I came upon the book my client had recommended and leafed through the pages *(to be honest, with a scornful eye)*. It still seemed far-fetched.

Yet there was something about even considering a spiritual book that was like a door had been opened. I wanted to know what this "spirituality" was. At first, it was more out of intellectual curiosity, at least on the surface, but this soon progressed into a process of intense exploration. I began to read widely in various religious and metaphysical traditions. I attended services of different faiths. I also started talking to people who had a strong spiritual foundation in their lives. With my psychological background and being naturally curious, I basically was trying to find out what spirituality meant for them and how it affected them.

Although I kept it to myself, it was also during this time that, for some unknown reason, I decided to give prayer a chance. It was this last that jump-started a transformation that continues to this day. While I initially felt silly and told myself this was nothing more than a joke or experiment, one night I honestly opened up to God in a way that I hadn't since I was ten years old. Then I kept praying but didn't think about it and have kept praying. In retrospect, it was like a gentle earthquake, soft and subtle at the time, but something indefinable had been reordered in my awareness.

How do you just start praying to God? I have been asked this many times when I recount this story. You just do. It doesn't even have to be with words. Even though I was keeping my emotional distance by pretending this was an experiment, I remember how tentative and awkward I initially felt. Once I began, it didn't matter. In fact, I recall feeling oddly welcomed and encouraged on some subliminal level *(although I continued to keep my emotional distance)*. This was to remain an experiment. Still, the words and the feelings behind them tumbled forth so easily and in an entirely heartfelt manner.

It was awhile, maybe a month, that I kept my emotional distance, and then it just kind of faded away. There wasn't a clear decision or moment in time when I began to trust God. I just did. At some point, it was no longer an experiment but had become reality. God had become a real presence in my life. Looking back, I can see that, from my simple nighttime prayer, there seemed to have rippled out an awareness of God and my closeness to God in so many aspects of my daily experience although I didn't think about it that way at first.

What was striking was that I began to have a sense of *connection* to something beyond myself. I could actually *feel* it. It was as though I was next to or enveloped by a harmonious but nonspecific presence. I often had a feeling of pleasant warmth and stillness around the heart area, sometimes throughout my body, so reminiscent of "the Peace of God" that I had discovered as a child but less intense or transitory. For the most part, these perceptions seemed to stay with me and were more in the background of whatever I was doing from putting away dishes to reading or driving to work. They were most noticeable when I was home alone although at some point I stopped feeling alone because of this underlying sense of *connection*.

But it wasn't only when I was at home that I would have this awareness. When I was out and about, I also began to experience these same feelings of *connection* although more focused and with other people and the surrounding world. A rewarding interaction or an unexpected and genuine smile from a stranger might lead to a transient, soft but uplifting sense of exchange with that person. This would linger a few minutes, even after we went our separate ways.

I would feel a more generalized but transcendent and peaceful sense of *connection* while watching the sunset, a favorite time of day for me. Now it meant more. Even when stuck in traffic, sometimes I seemed mentally transported above the stress of the moment and would feel a kind of collective empathy with the other drivers, all of us immersed in the same freeway chaos at this same point in time. It was very odd.

Did I just see what I wanted to see? Perhaps. That would be the psychological explanation. Another might be that such perceptions were due to the fact that the more spiritually oriented I became, the more I was motivated to approach the world differently and so may have been eliciting a different response. This was especially true in dealing with others. Based on what I was learning through reading, speaking to spiritually committed people, and within myself, I was making a conscious effort to apply core spiritual principles and higher values in daily living.

I tried to approach other people with respect and care and the awareness that we are spiritual brothers and sisters, whether friends or associates, even strangers. I would take a little more time to focus on their concerns and what they might be feeling or offer a smile or upbeat comment, even if it wasn't always easy or sometimes didn't seem to have any impact. I also tried to back off from disruptions of stress and anger or discouragement that would occur throughout the day, by taking a moment to try to refocus on the positive or bigger picture, sometimes even saying a prayer, which calmed me. I directed myself to look for the lesson and opportunity in negative events.

While it felt silly or unrealistically Pollyannish at times, there were immediate rewards. I did feel more positive day-to-day. I learned that maintaining a larger and deeper focus and not allowing myself to be pulled into daily crisis or petty craziness was more productive and did seem to keep me centered. I got the lesson that sweating the small stuff accomplishes nothing. The new way of connecting with others, even in brief snippets throughout the daily routine, did seem to lead to a general lifting of spirits.

Sometimes it felt like I was being led to an interaction just when I needed it. A brief and socially superficial but sincere exchange could pull me back from the temptation to dive into the small stuff. I learned it wasn't so much what was said but how it was said that mattered. The sense of transcendent exchange with others, even if fleeting, along with the subtle impression of harmonious *connection* I felt in general, created a comforting undercurrent to my experience. Sometimes I even felt a quiet, omnipresent sense of guidance but to where or what or why was unknown.

Outside of work, it was also during this period that I began spending a lot of time alone. Partly this was due to increasing disinterest at the crisis-ridden din of so much of modern life. It seemed that almost everyone I knew *(myself included)* was caught up on a treadmill of personal problems and agendas, anxiety and frustration. No bigger picture here. No resolution. The working through of one negative situation just ushered in the next. We all had our crisis du jour. This isn't to say there weren't wonderful moments, and many of my relationships I valued greatly. Yet I often found myself having a hard time relating as I had in the past. It wasn't any one particular person or interaction, but just everyone seemed programmed *(again, myself included)* to be tense, a little angry, and hypervigilant to crisis and the soap operas of our lives.

The more distant I became from the crisis and negativity, the more I could see how others were embroiled in it without insight into how crazed and pessimistic their lives had become. My new motivation to be more positive and spiritual felt too fragile and wasn't understood. I didn't want to proselytize or appear so wide-eyed and saccharine in my attitude that people thought I was obnoxious or had gone off the deep end. But, when I tried to share some of the things I was going through and pondering, including the timeless philosophical questions, others seemed confused and bored, even threatened. This was too outside the narcissistic bubbles in which everyone seemed to be functioning.

Probably what I was experiencing was similar to an alcoholic who is able to maintain sobriety but begins to avoid spending time around drinking friends. As time went on, some of these friendships worked out and some drifted away, and I learned to accept that. I also began to explore different social avenues and activities more in sync with my new perspective.

The other reason I was spending so much time alone was because I had begun to paint. This was a monumental step for me. I have always loved color. On rainy days during my childhood, many hours were spent lining up the crayons from my Crayola 64 Superbox and testing out the various color combinations in looming abstract forms. I could never draw realistically, so I abandoned any serious pursuit of artistic expression for many years. I dabbled in crafts here and there. I also loved art, especially abstract art. One of the more productive activities of my teenage years was that I would sneak into the city *(against my parents' rules)* to spend Saturday afternoons wandering the galleries of the art museum, like a young child pleasantly lost in an intricate fairy tale. I came to know all the paintings and artists by heart.

The fact that I began to paint seriously so much later in life seemed a part of my spiritual awakening. I had been wanting to do so for quite some time but never pulled it together until one day I did. Spending hours immersed in colorful abstract shapes *(as I had as a child)* was like the opening of an immensely blissful and meaningful door. My art had become my consuming passion, almost a visceral need that continues to this day. It was like something within me had been unleashed and was being guided.

To me, this art blossoming seemed quite a mysterious thing. At the same time, it also felt so natural, almost "written." One of my colleagues laughed as he fondly reminisced, "I had a girlfriend who was an artist. Talk about obsession! I would wake up in the morning and she'd be at her easel, just like I left her the night before. Are you one of *those* people?"

I was and proud of it. I knew exactly what he meant. To be sure, there was a lot of playfulness and pleasure similar to being a kid in a sandbox, but beyond fascination, discovery, even obsession, there was something more. Indeed, I was spending large expanses of time in front of the canvas into the wee hours of the morning and barely moving. Even at the time this seemed akin to meditation, and the sense of transcendent *connection* to another presence that I had been feeling in general was so strong. As I mentally accommodated to this awareness, I began to feel that, through painting, I was going to a place within where I was embraced by and communicating with God although mostly on a nonverbal level.

Sometimes while painting, I seemed to drift off into productive reflection. Much of the time, I entered into a state of harmonious mindlessness, and the hours would tick by. There was a feeling of timelessness. Or was it an interruption of time? After a day or night of nonstop painting, I would feel strangely refreshed. The extended effort and concentration just expended should have led to exhaustion. At other times, my painting spree seemed to have resulted in a clear as a bell answer regarding an issue or solving a problem in another area of life although I had not been consciously thinking about it.

There was also the egolessness as I seemed to go into a suspension of personal consciousness, merging into and moving towards something greater beyond the boundaries of *self*. This was very subtle. I would be mentally engaged in the painting before me, often intensely. At the same time, I seemed above and beyond whatever I was doing while peripherally aware of the surrounding room. It wasn't an out-of-body experience. It didn't feel that I had left my body although it was no longer part of my awareness in the usual way. It did seem I had left my ego or *self* as though the focus of my awareness was elevated and elsewhere beyond normal experience.

When I look back, I have the profound conviction that so much of what I was experiencing through painting was about developing a relationship with God. Bizarre as that may sound, it would feel as though I was enveloped in a Divine embrace *beyond* psychological process and physical presence. These perceptions seemed so strange but beneficial, even healing, although this wasn't just a lulling off into some meditative sleep. There was a feeling of dynamic sharing, caretaking, and guidance as well as the creativity emerging in the images on the canvases before me. A joint endeavor? It was as though, through painting, which was giving me such joy and a sense of accomplishment, a loving bond was being nurtured and solidified.

There was also something else. The process of painting seemed to contain greater philosophical and psychological truths. It became a metaphor for living. Beyond the transcendent and loving feelings I was experiencing, I began to feel I was being given distinguishable life lessons. For one, since my art was abstract, the result was open-ended. I wasn't realistically trying to copy a scene *out there*, but I began to have the distinct impression that the designs I painted already existed *in there*. Not necessarily inside the canvas, but they were supposed to capture something that already had been determined or created but had not yet been manifest in the physical world.

The process was not so much to create but to discover or uncover. I just had to find it. Even the uncovering seemed symbolic for so much of what we do in life. It was my "creation," but I had to commit to letting it breathe, to find its own way. There was also a point when I intuitively knew the painting was finished, and I needed to let it go. One brush stroke beyond and the final painting would never be what it should be or as good as it could be. It then remained unfinished *(tired and past its prime)* despite endless reworkings.

I often resisted and pushed too far, leading to regret that I hadn't listened to that inner sense, and now it was too late. It almost seemed as though I had been given a gift or truth, and now it was gone. All this felt intertwined with some need to maintain control and to create something in a preordained image that I desired, rather than what was artistically true. I could also end up intentionally destroying work I later wished I hadn't. At the time I had captured and produced something that consciously or unconsciously was too disturbing or lacking, and I wanted to dissociate myself from it. Again, it was as though I was choosing to ignore some truth I had been given, which was ultimately sacrificed for my emotional comfort zone.

I also learned a lot about the power of perspective. Sometimes this had to do with my own self-assessment. Pride and contentment with a painting completed the night before easily turned to dismay and disgust the next morning *(sometimes returning to pride two days later)*. I would find and be thrilled with pieces that I had vehemently disliked and abandoned months earlier. It became clear that my evaluation was entirely dependent on my emotional state.

Even those favorite pieces I loved or was particularly proud of, I loved less on some days. It was all about my mood. I also saw the reactions of others, which were so variable, both in terms of their approval and what they thought my abstract forms represented, kind of like artistic Rorschach cards. I began to accept that I couldn't predict or control the reactions to my artwork, good or bad. In a way, this was freeing. It was about doing the best I could and trying to do so in accordance with that inner truth but then letting it go and giving it up to some greater dynamic.

Finally, I also learned the gifts of frustration. Even with the insights I was achieving, the process of creating could be so nerve-racking. I would feel that I was squandering a lot of effort and blame myself. Over time, I began to see that fallow expanses and wrong turns are rarely a waste in terms of creativity but an essential part of the process, as important as any other. Something is always happening below the surface. For me, painting was not only a mode of creative expression. It was a discipline, an exercise in tolerance with myself.

Over the next ten years, I would spend a lot of time in solitary creative pursuits. This seemed an integral part of my spiritual journey, which progressively moved me to a place of ever greater faith and opening of experience. I knew that others wondered why I was less available and often reclusive. Did they ask, what is she doing? Why is she so avoidant? Why doesn't she get on with her life? For the first time, I didn't care. I was living authentically. Creative endeavor had become my passion and joy, my meditation and calling, a place of worship and mystical communion. It wasn't that I didn't want to be in the world, but there were other things I needed to pursue, at least at that point in time. Again, I felt guided. I had also learned the most fundamental given – that God is the most important relationship, from which all others derive. I was content and never felt alone.

5   The Mind on Top of Experience

A sense of mystical communion with God? This is an odd, even bizarre, idea for the contemporary world.

My period of artistic solitary confinement didn't last forever although it did for quite awhile. It was a time of incredible richness, growth, and peace for me. And when it ended, it wasn't that I got tired or restless or had learned all there was to learn. Nor did it mean the mystical feelings receded. It was just different. Life intruded, and I was led in another direction.

What do we mean by *mystical* experience? Traditionally, spiritual experience has been associated with mysticism, which is not well understood in modern life. *Mysticism* is formally defined as the immediate consciousness of or direct communion with an ultimate reality or God. In other words, it is a sense of personal connection, even union, with God or a Universal Power beyond the *self*.

I don't remember if there was a sense of communion, but I was about twelve years old and very bored when I had my only classically transcendental mystical experience. It was one of those aimless and empty afternoons when the space between the school dismissal bell and dinnertime seemed like an eternity. I must have been really tapped out of things to do because I had decided to count the books in our dark and stuffy living room. Why? Why not? I was twelve. It seemed a challenge, and we had a lot of books.

Since my father was an English professor in love with the Victorian period, there were heavy, wooden antique bookcases everywhere, packed and stacked with volumes of deeply colored leather. Our house looked and smelled like a library. Although an avid reader, I have always found the physicality of books *(at least the older ones)* distasteful. It's that fermenting smell, the dusty moldiness. But many people love it.

Although I didn't know it, I was approaching the end of that long expanse of childhood, in which an hour is a lifetime, and you have to fill so many of them. As adults, we look back on the endless spaces of growing up with idealized nostalgia. We fantasize that someday we will be able to reclaim a perspective of boundless, unspoken for time. Of course, when you're a kid and trapped in the midst of it, the boundlessness sometimes becomes smothering. I must have been desperate and probably a little bit crotchety if I was counting books.

It didn't go well. Almost immediately the leathery tomes began blending into one another. I had to keep doubling back to recount, but the books kept merging, seeming to pick up increasing speed as the singsong rhythm of my counting began to take on a life all its own. It felt oddly exhilarating as if the books were becoming animated. Or was it me? Suddenly it was like looking out the window of a car speeding so fast along a country road that the fence posts seem to be whipping by instead of the other way around. Now it was the books, not fence posts, that were streaming by... in unison... dancing off the shelves... converging and melding into one whizzing blur as though swirling around me.

I wasn't moving physically, and I knew it was in my mind *(i.e., it wasn't a hallucination)* although my brain did seem to be racing with a calculated, crystal clear lucidity that I've never experienced before or since. I began to see logical connections between things, all things, starting with the books, which were connected to the house... which was connected to the family… to the trees… like a kaleidoscope of rushing ideas until the connective patterns of everything in the world seemed to emerge and be laid bare before me. It was all perfect and clean and then fused into an infinite whole. Of Truth? Of Oneness? Of how everything came together? I could see the Whole of everything and how it all worked. I felt God there with me, but it wasn't like "the Peace." That was in my heart. This was in my mind, a perfect coherence and clarity of all things.

I don't know how long it lasted. Maybe a minute. Maybe five. Perhaps, ten seconds, but it seemed longer. When I tumbled back down to reality, there lingered a certainty that I had been privy to how everything in the world came together. I had seen the ultimate and final Truth *(although I couldn't remember what it was)*. That didn't matter. Immediately I tried to walk through the connections again in my mind, but it was mental mush. Several times over the next year, I attempted to kick-start the process by counting books, but it never worked. I just got a roaring headache.

Within the modern mainstream, mysticism *(or at least what is known about it)* tends to be viewed as peculiar and mysterious, even a bit perturbing. While most people are aware that many religions have monastic and mystical traditions, they are unaware that the intent of such practice is to encourage communion with the Divine. Current associations to mystical phenomena seem to have more to do with superordinary powers or alternate realities but more in the mode of science fiction, not specifically spiritual. In contemporary language, *mystical* appears to be more associated with an altered state in consciousness, the Dance of the Fractals of One's Mind, or an aesthetic quality. It connotes an aura of tinkling lights and haunting music, a kind of murky or misty serenity *(perhaps, merging "mist" and "mystical?")*. It is the stuff of Hollywood at its quirkiest and most surreal... or esoteric magazines and internet sites about yoga and unusual meditation practices.

In the popular media, there also seem to be two common and more traditional stereotypes of mystical experience. The first has to do with an austere life of ascetic and solitary worship and the rejection of worldly values. This is the caricature of the inspired but eccentric religious mystic... the barefoot and disheveled wanderer in the desert in olden times... the shaven monk in inscrutable introspection over a flower... the cloistered nun who doesn't speak... the wise and wizened elder, uttering sagacious one-liners. There is also the idea that this odd existence is rewarded by special knowledge or the revelation of mysteries although not necessarily related to God.

Obviously, the true religious mystic would be an alien figure in the modern world. Most contemporary people could not even begin to comprehend why a person would choose this kind of lifestyle or what it's about. Spending large amounts of time in contemplation, let alone trying to connect with God, for most, is just too strange. A boring time-waster, at best, if not very weird. In fact, those who do choose an existence outside usual social values or devote large amounts of time to meditation or prayer are typically viewed with suspicion. We assume they are misfits or loners, who did not develop normal social and sexual needs. In the secular mind, abstinence and religious discipline may also be associated with a dark, even masochistic, side.

At the other end of the spectrum, there is also the stereotype of the spectacular mind-blowing experience. This is the caricature of supercool mysticism. A collision of worlds. Roller-coaster for the mind. Extreme spirituality. Glorified acid trip of the *soul*. Ride the Psychedelic Hippie Bus within. What actually occurs during these episodes may not be as consistently 4th of July fireworks as the explosive descriptions suggest. But individuals recount a truly mind-altered state, sometimes lasting momentarily, sometimes for an extended period of time.

This scenario is similar to my experience at twelve years old, only more so. What typically is described is the perception of merging into a cosmic unity in consciousness beyond the limits of a separate ego. There may be a sense of embrace or of dissolving into the dynamic Oneness of all things. Some people report being outside space-time dimensions or observing two incompatible realities at the same time. They may describe a visual symphony of energy forces, the conviction of seeing ultimate Truth, or being led to the primary elements that make up the universe. There may be a sensation of intense power or spiritual intimacy far beyond any pleasure the ego or body has known. Some describe coming face to face with or touching or *knowing* God.

When such experiences are genuine, they are extraordinary, perhaps to a life-changing degree. One would think this would particularly be so in terms of the spiritual meaning and implications. Still, the popular tendency is to discount or make fun of such experiences, at the same time glamorizing them as the supreme high or hallucination. Subjectively, this type of mystical state is often likened to what happens with the use of psychoactive drugs or substances, such as hallucinogenic mushrooms. These episodes may also be triggered by intense physical activity or rigorous endeavor.

Sometimes transcendental mystical episodes may be sought and encouraged within religious practice *(including through the use of mind-altering substances)*. Within a religious or spiritual context, such mind-shattering experiences are supposed to be transforming and purposeful. They are intended to expand the individual's perspective beyond the limits of normal human perception and draw the person closer to God. They are not recreational or the latest way to get high, which is often lost on the modern secular person.

The experience when I was twelve wasn't life-changing, but I probably was too young to understand how extraordinary it was or to question what had happened although I did for awhile when I was in graduate school. Even then I never doubted what had occurred but rather managed to explain it away within psychological theory, similar to what I had done with "the Peace of God." Specifically, I decided that it was simply one of those *peak experiences,* as described by the psychologist Abraham Maslow, who had attempted to interpret such transcendental or religious ecstatic phenomena in humanistic terms *(i.e., without spiritual explanations).* I never quite understood how one could accept such experiences without reference to some other consciousness or force or realm *(but as a gung-ho young graduate student, I had stopped questioning).*

Most of the time as a young adult, I rarely thought about what had occurred. It was part of that sense of something happening beneath the surface of things that I had felt since childhood and tried to deny but usually could not, despite my best intentions. So I would analyze and discount. Yet there had been such realness to this awareness as though reflective of another order or domain. It was also this realness that always stuck with me *(despite my attempts at denial)* and was reinforced when I heard other people speak of similar experiences.

Over the years I've been quite taken aback at the conviction and intensity of others in describing moments or brief spaces of time when, like myself, they seemed to have pushed past the curtain or membrane of consensual awareness and entered into an alternate, transcendent world with a clarity of perception that feels truer. Often these incidents occur without the mystical bells and whistles that are stereotypically described but as a flash of Absolute Certainty. In an instant, the individual knew God or the quintessence of the universe or ultimate and pure Truth or that God exists... before the curtain comes back down with a return to more normal human perception. This mental awareness isn't a turn of belief or insight or waking dream or even a sense of understanding, but rather there is the impression of having gone somewhere or having seen something real *beyond* the physical world or in another domain.

It is always the realness that is described and the conviction that something happened which is so striking and compelling. Nor is it easy to rationalize these experiences as wish-fulfilling, attention-seeking, or recreated in retrospect. Most of the people who share these types of experiences do so only in the context of extreme trust within a long-established therapy relationship or friendship or in an intimate spiritually oriented setting. Such experiences are profoundly meaningful and deeply private for the individual.

Beyond the secular distaste for anything having to do with God, what may also be intimidating today about true mysticism is that it is so private. It involves a purposeful exploration within the secret and unspoken recesses of our minds. What the stereotypes *(whether monkish or mind-shattering)* have in common is an intense inner focus, a kind of inward journey that is entirely subjective, with the destination being solitary communion with God. This is why the image of the traditional mystic is so hermitic but mysterious. We can never see or appreciate the richness of what is going on inside.

It is interesting that retreats have become so popular in recent years. While some are religious and the association is well known, the term has come to mean a time-out from usual activities to separate from the noise of contemporary living, typically in a focused group setting, where it is assumed a lot can be accomplished without the usual distractions. It is almost as though retreats provide a socially acceptable vehicle for more intense inner focus and exploring within. Whether through meditation, massage, or corporate brainstorming, the objectives are varied but suggest a recognition that spending an extended period of time in an insulated and tranquil setting can access potential and stretch existing limits. Unless the intent was simply a weekend of pampering, education credits, or straightforward business meetings, participants come away from retreats of all types feeling inspired and reinvigorated.

Do retreats speak to something people need? Many religions tend to think so, at least in the context of furthering spiritual knowledge and connection to God. Traditional religious or spiritual retreats tend to emphasize internal focus and reflection *(even if part of a group)* amidst quiet and serene surroundings, where the stillness allows the individual to listen to God. Most religions stress the importance of regular contemplation and private worship in addition to participating in more formal and celebratory group services. Some people are able to schedule reflective or devotional periods into their daily lives, but many simply cannot. Thus, the retreat maximizes the journey inward by removing external distractions and providing a planned respite from human responsibilities to attend to spiritual ones.

Some people choose a life of contemplation and discipline, devoted to developing spiritual awareness. Some choose to live their entire lives this way. Individuals who choose such a path tend to describe a sense of calling to do so. Others spend a period of time in extended contemplation or spiritual searching, isolated from worldly distractions, but eventually return to a more conventional existence in the mainstream world. Following their quest, they may have a renewed sense of purpose to somehow help others, serve God, or create a better human existence by trying to teach or change the world in accordance with universal spiritual principles.

On the other hand, periods of contemplation, meditation, or prayer are important for everyone as *spiritual beings*. We show devotion to God, our Creator, but we also listen and learn from God, who guides us in our human lives. Spiritual knowledge and connection are always enhanced through meditation, contemplation, and prayer. The quiet recess within is the hub of spiritual connection, where it seems that we can go so far into ourselves that we connect *beyond* ourselves. To use a cliché expression, it is here that we spend quality time with God.

It thus makes sense that one of the greatest teachers of spiritual awareness would be spending time alone. Certainly, the quality of the alone time is all-important. We can be alone for hours or days or even years and entirely distract ourselves through television, music, reading, or mindlessly doing chores, even through fantasy. Some degree of motivation and discipline would seem required to listen to or communicate with God at all. Yet it is sometimes when aloneness is forced upon an individual that there may be a gradual turning to God, such as during imprisonment, after the loss of a spouse, or when a person is isolated from the usual routine of life during a prolonged illness or convalescence.

Solitary time with one's thoughts is hard to come by in the 21st century. Is it an aversion to exploring too deeply? Or just that the environment is so alive with electronic baubles and flashy five-second pellets of media enticements that we can't turn away from the outside world? The 24-7 nature of modern life *(and now the internet)* allow constant stimulation if we so desire. It is likely most of us are addicted as witnessed by the anxious withdrawal that many report when the cable or wireless network goes down for even a few minutes.

In general, our culture has become so externally oriented and action-driven. Sure, we can turn off the television and cell phones and close the laptops, but just knowing that cyberspace is beckoning and waiting is a different vibe *(and temptation)* than when it's not. We also have the ability to contact others almost any time and anywhere, which is unprecedented in human history. It takes a lot of control to truly cut one's self off for a space of time. Introspection or extended quiet can also be emotionally threatening to some people. The usual noise and distraction may obscure underlying painful feelings, which then resurface if the outside frenzy is removed.

It wasn't always this way. There used to be a structure built into the routines of normal living that promoted inner reflection or spaces of extended thought. Historically, a reason for the Sabbath or religious day of rest was to allow an intermission from the necessary toils of the human world to focus on God. Before the age of the electric light, there was a limit to the types of activities in which people could engage. Prior to iPods and Walkmans or even car radios, there was relative silence when walking, which people did more of, or on long trips *(other than the sounds in the actual environment or of others speaking)*. This didn't mean that people thought about God or even deeper philosophical matters, but they did have to rely more on their internal experience for stimulation.

Even when the world became more technically advanced, I can recall Sundays as a child when no stores were open or how quiet it seemed after the playing of the "Star Spangled Banner" at midnight as all the television channels signed off. There was always something somber, almost sacred about it. It was the proverbial "You could hear a pin drop." Again, not that anyone seemed to be thinking about God or engaged in spiritual reflection, but there was a serious, inward pull. A forced period of downtime. You could fill it with all sorts

THE MIND ON TOP OF EXPERIENCE 71

of activities, yet there remained an underlying pensiveness, which is rarely experienced anymore.

It is ironic that, behind their digital curtain of external stimulation, many people today seem very much alone. They may be enmeshed in gaming or surfing the web or texting and social networking on all continents throughout the globe, but there's a sequestered or separate quality. It's as though they are traveling in a half-seen layer of fantasy and information gathering *(neither fully of the seen or unseen world)*. Yet this kind of aloneness is neither quiet nor still. Traveling deeply inward or spending large amounts of time in silence or contemplation is very difficult in the modern age.

This is the qualitative difference in mystical and spiritual reflection. The quiet is purposeful, even if the individual is not actively engaged in analytical thought. This doesn't mean that all deep thinking is akin to spiritual or meditative contemplation. Having lived around university communities for periods throughout my life, I can attest the absentminded professor isn't only a stereotype. I've actually seen oblivious faculty members so engrossed in their own mental workings that they narrowly missed bumping into trees as they walked through campus. Extended periods of deep thinking can be entirely rational and methodical, intently focused on solving a real world problem or addressing complex theoretical questions.

While focused, spiritual contemplation is neither formulaic nor task-oriented, other than being about surrendering one's will and one's thought to God. Generally, an individual doesn't contemplate in a rational or linear or even organized way, although if one reflects upon certain questions or choices with God, there may be some analysis or reasoning by the individual. Still, the larger intention is the opening to God... to *feel* the spirit... to understand and be guided by the unknowable… to encounter and merge into the greater transcendent reality to some degree.

But is it mystical perceptions and feelings we are experiencing or biologically-induced illusions? Are people really connecting with God and a *higher* reality? Predictably, there have been attempts to explain mystical experience scientifically, from the awe-inspiring, mind-blowing episodes to the less dramatic perceptions associated with spiritual practice. The fact that extreme transcendental experiences are so similar to drug-induced states would seem to lend support for a theory of underlying biological and neurological mechanisms. Another scientific observation points out that most human beings do not appear to use most of their brains most of the time. Research suggests there are vast areas of the brain that are underutilized. Thus, another possibility of what is happening in so-called mystical experiences may be stimulation of areas of the brain that are not commonly used in normal life.

In the biological view, the assumption is that it may *seem* that we're apprehending another mystical realm, but we're not really. It's only brain processes, such as neurons firing or chemical reactions, that are creating the unusual perceptions and causing us to think that we are. As we've discussed, just because there is a connection between biology *(i.e., the brain)* and psychology *(i.e., the mystical feelings and images)* does not necessarily rule out that there is also a connection with or we are being impacted by a Higher Power or other reality beyond the *self*. Logically, it's a chicken-and-egg question: Which is the first cause? Is something in the brain-body process causing the transcendent perceptions and then we label these as "spiritual?" Or is it a connection with the higher *spiritual* reality that is causing the biological responses, and we have entered or accessed another dimension or realm and truly are in communion with God?

THE MIND ON TOP OF EXPERIENCE

For people of faith, such explanations are irrelevant. Mystical experiences are meaningful within the context of their beliefs. They confirm awareness of and connection to a *higher* spiritual reality and God. For many, it is the mystical feelings that serve as personal evidence, if not proof, that God exists. The sense of mystical *connection* and embrace is tangible and dynamic. Skeptics often question people of faith because of the lack of any objective proof of their beliefs. For the spiritual person, faith is in the heart and intensely felt. Mystical feelings are powerful and all inclusive. They produce a sense of rock solid, in-the-bones knowingness, which cannot be reduced to intellectual facts or formulas.

For the person of faith, *mystical* or *spiritual* experience *(the terms tend to be used interchangeably)* covers a broad range. At one extreme are the transcendental states, occurring rarely if at all. At the other are the more subtle feelings and perceptions that may be present in the mundane flow of living. Spiritual experience is not necessarily restricted to periods of contemplation, meditation, or prayer although may be strongest during such activities. For many, there is a spiritual awareness that occurs as an underpinning, another dimension to life, softly perceptible but in the background most of the time.

What does *mystical* experience feel like? How does one recognize *spiritual* awareness? In fact, the more ordinary spiritual feelings and perceptions are similar to what is experienced during the mind-blowing states but to a lesser degree. First, there is that distinctive sense of *connection* or embrace or merging, which is tangible and real. The person actually *feels* it. This is what was so salient for me as I awakened to faith. It is this feeling of *connection* that is the hallmark of spiritual experience, whether ordinary or extraordinary, and always perceived as occurring in some way beyond the *self*, including on an elevated level to other people and living things.

Mystical experience is also associated with a sense of calm and transcendence. This isn't just a feeling of refuge or quietude, relaxation or emptying out. The person seems to have moved beyond emotion and need as though going to a place of serenity and peace within. The keyword here is *beyond*, to a space where there is no body or mind, attachments or ego, where the individual feels separated off and protected from the reactions of the senses and disruptions of the outside world.

Finally, spiritual experience is associated with the perception of harmony and integration as though everything has a place and fits together seamlessly on many different levels. This may result in a sense of Absolute Truth, which feels "written" and untouched by human interpretation but may be manifest in the real world as a conviction or clarity about a general or specific issue. Perhaps, the person has a profound feeling of certainty as to the existence of God or that this is the right person to marry or the right thing to do. There may be received what seems like an irrefutable answer to a personal question or ongoing dilemma.

Like everything else that goes on inside our minds, spiritual feelings tend to wax and wane. They occur in varying intensities just like the more typical psychological and physical feelings. This is true even for people who are strongly spiritually committed. We may be *spiritual beings* but live in *physical* bodies and within a *human* world. For most of us, spiritual awareness is very much in the background most of the time. Yet, since we are *spiritual beings*, the opposite may also apply. Even those who are not oriented to faith may receive hints of spiritual reality, whether they consciously believe in this or not.

An example is involvement in some of the spiritual practices that do not involve a traditional belief system but result in some degree of expanded awareness. Practitioners may report a sense of the opening up of consciousness and new and unusual feelings and perceptions *(in line with the types of experiences that have been described)*. This is why people become hooked on meditation or yoga class or personally meaningful rituals. It *feels* good and creates a sense of belonging to a greater vision, at least for the period of time in which the person engages in the practice.

Even those who do not believe or practice have likely experienced such perceptions although they might not think about it. There are junctures and situations in life in which we feel a deep joy beyond words, an indescribable wholeness, an attachment to something greater and true. We *feel* these things when we behold the majesty of nature… have wondrous moments of life and family *(like the birth of a child)*… in the midst of concentrated or creative endeavor… become enmeshed in personally meaningful art or music… or participate in activities that have a higher purpose. The transcendent overtones may seem most evident in times of trouble or on sad occasions.

For example, when participating in the funeral of a close friend or loved one, a person may recite or attend to the Lord's Prayer, even if he or she is not Christian or does not believe in God. The words may have no meaning to the individual and may even contradict personal philosophy. But the process of joining in prayer with others does feel momentarily transforming. There is an elevated energy about it that seems to create a reverential space, in which the individual may feel actually connected to the loved one who has passed, to the other mourners, or to a unified presence or harmony at large. During or after the prayer, there may be a sudden emotional shift so that the person is more at peace with his or her own grief. This would not have happened without the prayer. There may be real bodily feelings of warmth or relief.

Another example of the effects of spiritual experience is how people respond to sacred writing. Holy books, such as the Bible or the Koran, are never read just once or absorbed logically and directly. You can never know a holy book fully or finally in the sense of completely absorbing or understanding the material. These scriptures are read and re-read, typically in small passages, which can be turned over and over in the person's mind and pondered and digested. The meaning is always much greater than the words on the page.

Even when we get it, we often discover another meaning in the same passage later on. The words never mean the same thing each time you read them. There is an emotional transition or the perception of sudden insight, resolution, or release. This is why scriptures tend to be read with the purpose of ongoing guidance and inspiration as each time the learning that occurs is different than the last. It's certainly not just information or even versions of Truth. There is a vitality and real energy to the words that have the power to connect with our immediate experience. We don't only seek to understand the words, but they transform us. They take us from one place to another in our subjective lives.

It is always the experience that we find so compelling. Without experience, belief alone tends to leave us cold. The problem is that beliefs are ideas, which are never as enthralling as feelings. Even the most cerebral among us can be thrown into an emotional tailspin because of a trauma, obsession, or unresolved issue. Intellect is a powerful tool for mastering the world around us, but we live in our bodies and hearts. For many, it is only after they have opened to spiritual awareness that the beliefs become meaningful. It is the feelings that make the ideas ring true.

It is the *experience* that connects us to God.

6 Random Pieces of Soul?

When I was seventeen, I had a vivid nightmare so immediate and intense, it felt like I was really there. The car jackknifed, spinning around, and skidded across the road, explosively smacking into a telephone pole. A loud crack of metal on wood. I saw the driver lurch forward, some blood, and then horror. It was my father's face. He seemed to be looking at me intently although I wasn't in the scene. He didn't show anger or fear at what had occurred but only a look of immense longing towards me. Suddenly I felt very close to him as though I was in the car and he was holding me in his arms as he did when I was a small child. Then he slumped, eyes closed, over the steering wheel. I woke up screaming.

It was 6 o'clock in the morning. I couldn't sleep and lay awake, watching the clock for the next hour. Throughout the day, I felt oddly suspended. I tried to call my parents who were 400 miles away *(I was in school)*. It was late afternoon when I heard the news that my father and youngest sister had been killed in an automobile accident earlier that morning around 6:00 A.M. In my shock and confusion, I remember murmuring something about my father losing control of the car and hitting a telephone pole. My mother seemed taken aback despite her stunned and anguished state, "Telephone pole? No. They were struck by a driver going 90 miles an hour in the wrong lane." That driver also died.

For me, the dream has always been a source of comfort. Over the years I've learned this type of experience is not that uncommon. I have repeatedly been told of similar dreams occurring at the time of another's death. The details may not be exact *(my sister was not in the dream)*, but there is always a sense of reality or visitation. It is as though the dying person is trying to communicate something before leaving, maybe just to express love and to say good-bye.

Often it is a loved one or family member to whom the communication is made but not always. I have also heard of this same type of experience occurring during the waking state. This can range from a full vision to what seems to be a telepathic message or an apparition in bodily form. Sometimes the image is partial or subliminal, such as the face of the deceased person flitting across the mirror while the other is shaving. There may be a fleeting sense of the dying or deceased person's presence or a quick related memory or thought *(perhaps for the first time in years)*. Usually these encounters are perceived as loving or reassuring, once it becomes clear exactly what has occurred.

I know it sounds strange, but I have heard these stories over and over again. Sometimes there may be peculiar or intense experiences that have no direct connection with a deceased individual and most likely would not even be remembered until it is learned that this happened around the time of the other person's death. The receiving individual may become very upset by a song or instantly feel desperation, overwhelming loss, or impending doom. There may be an outburst of tearfulness for no apparent reason. Sometimes the feeling just hangs there for hours, or it may disappear. Later, the individual learns that the other person died exactly at or around the same time. It is then that it all seems to make sense, like the last piece in a jigsaw puzzle but on a feeling level.

I recall one woman relating how she had been sitting in a room with a group of friends when a frightening wind came through and wafted over her. This wasn't that remarkable. The windows were open, and there were often breezes. No one else seemed to notice. Why would this have caught her attention? Or even be remembered? She couldn't shake the ominous feeling that had descended over her with the wind until hours later she learned a cousin had died around the same time. Later the memory of the wind experience had become so comforting to her since she had felt communicated to by her cousin and that this was an act of love by his doing so. Another part of her discounted this feeling as ridiculous, so she had never shared it previously.

Experiences like these surrounding death, premonitions of death, or witnessing others die are almost always emotionally gripping. They speak to the great unknown and inevitability about which we can all agree. We all die. On some level, what happens after death should be of deep concern and curiosity to each of us since whatever happens is going to happen to us. The mystery of death also raises questions about the meaning of life and the human condition. What's it all about? Are we part of a larger picture and greater order? Is there something beyond life? Even taking death out of the equation, is there something other than the physical plane while we're alive?

People who believe in God or an afterlife are often ridiculed as needing this fantasy as some type of reassurance. It's looked upon as an infantile wish and ultimate denial *(i.e., it's not death at all, only the beginning of something better)*. This caricature never made sense to me as it assumes that faith is always through rose-colored glasses and that believers are conjecturing an idyllic situation through their belief. Yet, even when religions describe a blissful heavenly state after death, many devout people don't know if they are going to get there. It's not as easy or childlike to hold such beliefs as is usually portrayed. Allowing that God, a spiritual reality, or afterlife exists *(even just being open to the possibility)* is no guarantee that what lies beyond is positive at all, including for religious people. They may choose to maintain their belief that it is, but that's faith, not a guarantee.

For many spiritually oriented people, to categorically deny the existence of God or an afterlife would seem to be the ultimate cop-out or denial. Once you say something doesn't exist, you don't have to deal with it. No one knows for sure. It is a matter of faith, but faith also maintains the spiritual is beyond physical exploration and human understanding. If people had proof of Heaven or Hell or even that we travel for eternity as little bubbles or magnificent stars, for that matter, wouldn't that change or direct things in the here and now? I've often heard the precautionary logic that, since we don't know, it's probably wiser to hedge the bet on the side of God. Wouldn't it be safer to live your life as though God exists and then find out you were wrong, rather than the other way around?

The modern scientific assumption is that it's all about biology and the workings of the physical world. We're born. We live. We age *(if we're lucky enough to keep living)*. We die. The End. Bye-bye. In this view, it is presumed that everything can be reduced to physical elements and explanations. Telepathic and paranormal phenomena ultimately can or will be explained through natural mechanisms. It's just a matter of time. Maybe it's energy waves that can account for spiritual perceptions? Perhaps, we just don't know. Yet. We might not have all the data, but the assumption is that there are entirely rational explanations just waiting to be discovered.

There is always great glee and a roar of laughter from the audience when futuristic films lament the backward medicine and technology of the 20th or 21st century. As human beings, we seem to instinctively know our own fallibility as well as potential. There is no doubt a lot of factual knowledge still to be learned, but traditional belief systems assume that human knowledge has its limits. This gets back to the core principle of the existence of God and a truer spiritual reality *beyond* the physical. *Beyond* the physical does not mean an extension of or at the outer limits, and we can keep pushing further. *Beyond* means another dimension or reality entirely. Spiritual Truth can never be reducible to physical elements and natural laws. It is unknowable, at least in its totality, to human beings on the physical plane.

The bias of our culture is undeniably towards physical explanations for everything and the ability of humankind to find them. It teaches to discount, not only spiritual ideas and explanations, but paranormal ideas and the individuals who have them. Either an attempt is made to explain such phenomena scientifically or in rational terms or the credibility of the report is questioned *(i.e., "You just thought you saw that"… "It's only wishful thinking"…)*

I learned this so well when my father and sister died. At the time, I considered myself an agnostic, and my dream didn't change that. I was also young and lacking in the seasoned *(or cynical)* discrimination that many adults seem to have. So I was more open despite my attempts to appear intellectually polished. For me, the dream seemed connected to that intuitive rhythm in life that I had always perceived beneath the surface of things. It was also soothing. Since as long as I could remember, I had also been interested in all things psychological *(whether normal, not so normal, or paranormal)*. When I selectively decided to share my dream, it was with the idea that this was an important piece of data of what can happen to people. How surprising to find that others didn't think so.

The most common reaction I got was that it was simply coincidence. All that occurred was that I happened to have a nightmare *(nightmares of loved ones dying aren't that uncommon)* on the night that my father and sister died. Sheer happenstance.

"It was at the same time," I offered.

"Doesn't matter," I was told. "Even if the time was right…"

("But I was watching the clock…")

"… No, it was one of those chance things that just happens."

It was also pointed out that the dream got the actual facts of the accident wrong, which I readily admitted *(again, my sister wasn't in the dream)*, although I had the feeling that if it had been an exact carbon copy of what had occurred, I would have been discounted even more.

People do dream of loved ones dying. I've had other such dreams, although extremely rarely, and the person did not die. I've never had any other dreams of my father or sister dying, either before or since. This was so ludicrous to me and still is. Look at the numbers. If I was seventeen at the time, and we allow that I was too young to really understand what a dream was before the age of five, this still leaves approximately twelve years from the age of five to seventeen. That is 12 years of 365 nights of potential dreaming *(not counting Leap years)* or 4,380 chances for a similar dream to occur. It didn't. *(I won't even begin to compute the years of potential dreaming since that time.)* I still get the random coincidence explanation to this day.

Another reaction was that it didn't really happen. I just thought it did. No one ever accused me of lying. The impression that I got from others was that they believed that I believed that it did happen. Yet somehow, unconsciously and in retrospect, I had embellished in my mind what had occurred because of my underlying emotional needs. Maybe the motivation was wish fulfillment. After all, the dream did give me consolation. Like many people, I am just hoping that such things are true *(Who doesn't?)* and that I will see my father and sister again someday. Perhaps, the idea of my father appearing to me made me feel special or loved or still connected *(I'll admit I was a Daddy's girl)*, and this helped me deal with the grief and horrific loss. In other words, the dream, as remembered, was nothing more than a psychological coping mechanism.

Sometimes the implication was more emotionally damning. It's not just that the dream could be explained as my way to deal with tragedy at a relatively young age. My fascination with the dream and insistence that it occurred suggested something in my personality might be awry or out of balance, too willing to grab onto supernatural reasons, too enmeshed in imagination and not a rational approach. My profession might agree. To really take such things seriously suggests a person could be out of touch with reality, implying some type of psychosis. Even if the reality orientation is determined to be solid, paranormal pronouncements or too much interest in such matters tend to be seen as going over the line in terms of appropriate and logical behavior.

On the other hand, so many people have such experiences and, as in the case of mystical phenomena, they seem so real. I have been surprised by how many normal-appearing, even straight-laced, folks share strange but persuasive occurrences that seem to give evidence of a *higher* consciousness or realm beyond the physical. This might include an out-of-body experience or seeing a nonphysical entity *(sometimes demonic, sometimes angelic)* or again, the mystical perception of feeling the presence of God. More common are reports of seeing ghosts or being contacted by people who have died.

Often the person reports one or two incidents that have stood out. It's not as though this kind of thing happens a lot, although it can, perhaps during specific periods of an individual's life. Usually these experiences are so striking, even if momentary, and the person may have difficulty describing in words exactly what occurred. There may be some anxiety attached, as what was witnessed was beyond rational possibility, although simultaneously we see that steadfast conviction that what happened was real. The individual may struggle with this experience because it was so outside the accepted norm and typical way he or she approaches life. Many of these people have no particular religious or metaphysical interest. They have tried to explain or rationalize, minimize and repress, but they just can't.

One of the most extreme paranormal phenomena is the *out-of-body experience*. This occurs when personal consciousness is reported to leave the body. Usually the person has the perception of elevating above or outside bodily form and can look down and see his or her own body below. This is different from the classic mystical experience, in which the individual has the sense of having permeated some membrane of awareness and is briefly immersed in or merging into a Higher consciousness. In the out-of-body experience, the individual describes the awareness of remaining intact as a separate being in consciousness but traveling outside the physical bodily form.

Sometimes the *spirit* may be experienced as traveling in another dimension, or there is the sense of being transported to a completely different realm. Sometimes the individual describes being outside the body but on the physical plane. People may report minute details of what was said or observed, such as in the next room or during surgery when they see themselves on the operating table below with the medical team gathered around. Generally, they describe being in a lucid state as the experience is occurring, and the descriptions are also remarkably consistent from one person to another as to the sensations and perceptions associated with this state. In serious attempts to scientifically validate these experiences, the individuals studied are noted to appear fairly normal overall.

Among out-of-body phenomena, one of the most publicized is the *near-death experience*. This occurs for some people after having been pronounced clinically dead or otherwise extremely close to death and then subsequently revived *(although this can occur in association with non-life-threatening events as well)*. Classic descriptions include the perception of traveling, sometimes through a tunnel, towards a white light or spiritual presence. There may be waiting, welcoming relatives who have passed on. There may be a review of one's life with a religious figure. Typically described are overwhelming, extraordinarily positive feelings *(such as an infusing, blissful warmth)*, and the person seeks to keep moving towards the light but may be stopped from doing so, even hearing that it's "not your time." Because the feelings are so intense and beatific, there is often sadness at turning back and having to return to bodily form.

Consensual reports of such experiences have occurred throughout history and different cultures. Even children who were too young to fully understand what they had experienced have drawn pictures with these same elements *(i.e., the light, a tunnel, religious figures, or relatives who have passed on)*. There have also been reports of some hell-like near-death experiences of absolute horror as well as the overwhelmingly positive ones. In these hellish accounts, sometimes the individual is given the choice to repent and essentially a second chance in returning to the body and human life.

There are a lot of theories regarding parapsychological phenomena, including from a scientific perspective. As always, there is strong motivation to find a way to explain these occurrences in *physical* terms. For example, in near-death experiences, one hypothesis is that the *biological* process of dying causes a *psychological* reaction that involves extreme images, feelings, and sensations *(i.e., a kind of a pre-death altered state)*. Since death is a part of our inheritance as organic creatures, this biological process would be the same for everyone. This would explain why the descriptions are so similar from one person to another. The idea is that there may indeed be a kind of beautiful and soothing hallucination, caused by the release of chemicals as the brain physically begins to shut down. According to the scientific perspective, this hallucinatory state has nothing to do with a *crossing over* or a spiritual reality at all. It's an aftereffect... *not* the afterlife.

Like the awe-inspiring mystical states, out-of-body and certainly near-death experiences are very rare and could be expected to affect the person in a major, mind-shattering way. The implications are tremendous. Similar to transcendental mystical episodes and visitations from dying people, such exceptional experiences give the impression of opening a window onto another larger reality or order beyond the consensual physical domain of our senses. Definitely, this holds the potential to rock one's world. In some way, the individual has to come to terms with what he or she has experienced as well as the philosophical implications.

It's amazing how many people manage not to. The twin masters of what one has been taught is real and the fear of mental illness are very powerful. Many engage in a process of *experience nullification*, that is, they end up rewriting history or erasing from memory what actually occurred. Through all sorts of psychological maneuvers *(discounting, denial, rationalization, and repression)*, the person manages to deny, ignore, or reframe what was originally perceived, similar to what I did with "the Peace of God." Through *experience nullification*, even the most extraordinary spiritual or paranormal phenomena can be rendered meaningless and entirely trivialized.

However, some experiences appear so outlandish that we are almost forced to make a choice. Do we believe it or not? Was it real or not? Thinking you've seen a ghost or traveling outside your body is fairly clear-cut and far out, if not downright freaky. There is usually some mental need to come to terms with what has occurred one way or another. There are also everyday experiences with spiritual or paranormal overtones that are quite common although subtle and ambiguous. Vague coincidences or feelings of being led are just not that outstanding or defined. The person doesn't really have to pay attention to them and forgets what occurred almost immediately or within a short period of time. The potential meaning of such low-level paranormal events does not have to be confronted directly. Such underlying phenomena can be naturally catalogued as a random occurrences if the person is so inclined. *Experience nullification* is easy or not even necessary.

There are also those who may look towards such paranormal occurrences, not only as corroboration that there is something happening *out there (i.e., beyond the physical),* but as possible signs or communications, which are supposed to be taken as guidance. For example, many have incidents of *mental telepathy*. Seemingly out of nowhere, the image of a person from your life or past comes to mind along with a disturbing feeling. This doesn't only occur when death is involved. You call and find out this person is ill or getting a divorce or somehow in trouble or even was just thinking about you and wanted to talk. It almost seems as though you were called to call.

There may be instances of *synchronicity*, such as when friends living on the East and West Coasts suddenly call each other at the same time. Telepathy may occur in dreams that in a direct or symbolic way turn out to be prophetic, either on a large or small scale. The dream may provide direction in a person's life or an answer to a question. Sometimes the dream seems eerily psychic, foretelling future events that do come true. There may be the sense that the dream was not really a dream as occurred rather dramatically with the deaths of my sister and father. While dreaming, there may be a feeling of actually traveling through consciousness to connect with another person although no perception of going out-of-body is reported.

Like dreaming, *intuition* is another phenomenon that raises the question of a greater meaning or underlying, unseen reality. In the mainstream, intuition is commonly recognized although usually in a purely humorous or colloquial way. Intuition is that "sixth" sense or hunch or gut feeling and, in serious reports, can involve a real sensation in the stomach area. Sometimes genuine intuition seems to arise solely from within. There may be a strong internal sense of motivation or foreboding. This can be an idea, a sudden insight, a sense of rightness, or urging that seems to come out of nowhere. Intuition may also appear more external as though the individual is picking up or reading cues or vibes from the outside world.

Sometimes aspects of intuition can be rationally explained. It is pointed out that intense, mysterious feelings about other people could come from observing nonverbal cues *(e.g., shifting eyes, facial expressions, body posture)*. There may be subliminal information to which the person is responding *(e.g., the old "gun bulge" in the jacket as depicted on detective shows... or the undercover agent wearing "cop shoes")*. In these cases, we are processing actual data without being aware of doing so or having an unconscious emotional reaction to something objectively real *(i.e., there is nothing psychic or paranormal or even "intuitive" about this at all)*.

It may also be that what seem like intuitive feelings could reflect some physically explainable process that is not yet understood. Even scientifically oriented people would allow for the possibility that human beings literally do have a "sixth" sense *(based on energy waves perhaps?)* that lies still undiscovered. The spooky phenomenon of animals leaving an area before an earthquake or flood is pointed to as evidence of some underlying biological process or mechanism, a kind of ultra-sensitive radar, that may be playing out in the natural world.

Intuition has become more accepted in recent years, to some degree because some very successful businessmen have acknowledged it was a wacky hunch that started their billion-dollar dynasty in the first place. Intuition may be glamorized as akin to creativity or touted as the source of inspiration in general. This seems to reflect some recognition that to be in touch with one's intuitive capabilities is a resource that expands both professional and personal horizons.

Nonetheless, in the modern mindset, to depend on intuition too much remains suspect and is typically viewed as a slippery slope. It's considered okay, even kind of intriguing, as long as this remains relegated to the realm of the quirky or creative. In contemporary life, logical reasoning and rational thought are usually preferred. Plus, at some point, intuition blends into a feeling of being led or "supported" or precognitive *(i.e., reflecting future events)*. All this gets into the weird and irrational once again because it does suggest that something else might be going on in another realm.

When it's inspired ideas or compelling internal feelings, intuition is easy to explain away because it is so subjective. No one can verify what goes on in another's psyche one way or another. Whatever a person comes up with can always be diminished as imaginary or overblown or arising out of unconscious needs. Yet sometimes intuition does suggest a kind of sensor for picking up actual patterns in the external environment *outside* the individual's consciousness. This raises the question: Is there another reality *out there*?

An example is the intuitive perception of a *negative* or *positive* force or energy about a person, a place, or particular period of time *(e.g., the "vibe" of a Friday night, the full moon, a neighbor, the vacant lot on the corner)*. At times this has more of an emotional quality. A certain part of the city or a specific house or room may be described as having a *creepy* or *sad* feeling about it. There may be felt an *angry* vibration or cast to the day, which seems to be echoed in the noises of the animals in the neighborhood, the palpable frustration on the freeway, the tension in the air.

What is interesting is that often there is consensus among numerous people, including nearly everyone that is asked, as to what the predominant vibe or energy is about a particular individual or place or period of time. This implies that such impressions are not just an extension of the intuitive person's mood or emotional issues or a figment of imagination. Something real and objective is being apprehended and understood by a number of people.

Beyond discerning various types of energy, intuitive individuals may describe feeling the *rightness* of things. This can mean anything from it feels *right* to take the freeway *(possibly avoiding a dangerous accident on the side streets)* to finding "the One" *(whether a car or the perfect mate)*. There are also stories of people who refused to get into an elevator or scrambled to get off an airplane and ultimately avoided death by doing so because of a sudden and inexplicable feeling of *wrongness* or danger.

What is going on with these feelings of *rightness* or *wrongness*? Is it a protective spiritual force? The hand of Fate? A guardian angel? Random incidents *(as the Coincidence Crowd loves to proclaim)*? Many of us do have the sense of being guided in our lives by unexplainable feelings and odd events. Sometimes strange circumstances lead us to choose a certain fork in the road or may force us, without choice, to take a clear or unanticipated direction. Looking back, some of these events were so pivotal, true turning points in the course of our lives. It is natural to ask if they were destined in some way.

Is there an individual fate for each of us? Possible multiple fates and we choose through our actions? This is the idea that "There are no accidents." In contrast, the opposite view is that it all occurs by chance. It is pointed out that the major events of our lives may seem predetermined, but this is because they have become so personally meaningful. Because of our emotional investment, they have taken on some greater cosmic aura or implication, which simply isn't real, and originally were random occurrences.

There is also the conviction of *being led*, which takes the idea of personal destiny one step further. *Being led* goes beyond intuition, which can only provide guidance through clues or insights. Intuition involves being given information, but it doesn't force the person to necessarily do anything with it. From getting off a plane because of a feeling of danger to deciding which car to buy, in intuition, there is still personal choice. The individual gets to decide whether to act on the intuition or not. Sometimes that action takes courage or at least the willingness to go against a very strong tide of other more rational people and naysayers, Still, it's up to the individual as to whether to listen to that inner voice and to heed whatever inklings or warnings have been presented.

When intuition crosses the line into *being led*, this is a whole different deal and takes personal choice out of the equation. *Being led* involves a perception of feeling moved towards a place or person or opportunity by a series of seemingly unconnected and odd events. These occurrences, in retrospect, seem to have pushed the person in a specific direction while logically it doesn't make sense. At the same time, what happened seems too coincidental to really be coincidental. There appears to have been some kind of greater purpose or intent, almost as if an imperceptible but more powerful force was moving pieces of the world around, as though on a chessboard, in order to position or influence the individual.

Almost all of us have had the experience that we mistakenly took the wrong turn, were compelled to take a different route altogether, or were held up in traffic, only to later see that this resulted in an opportunity or meeting someone important or avoiding a calamity. We may feel protected, from an embarrassing run-in with someone we didn't want to see to a life-threatening injury, through mysterious occurrences and what appear to be cycles of Fate that are bigger than we are. I have heard of people who felt abruptly compelled to turn their car around in mid-traffic or to stop the car and go into a store for no apparent reason, only to meet someone who was to become of central importance in their lives. In this same manner, sometimes we are led to things that are uncomfortable or painful but were necessary, a turning point, or something we needed to know.

Sometimes such situations, negative or positive, are accompanied by strong but strange physical feelings as though the individual is being propelled or called by some external force. What may be described is not being able to stop one's self as if actually pushed or pulled along by the strong hand of Fate. The legs and body are going in one direction, but the mind is confused, saying, "Whoa, what's happening? What's going on here?" People may describe what seem like strong barriers of energy coming down to block some action. They want to cross the street, which is empty, but they cannot almost as though there is an invisible wall. There may be a sense of being gently held or caught up in or guided by a soft but imperceptible breeze-like energy.

A sense of *being led* is powerful, particularly when people look back over their lives. In addition to distinct events or interactions that *feel* fated, many have the overall impression that life just doesn't seem random, whether this involves paranormal experiences or a sense of personal destiny or being so specifically attracted to certain other people. Clearly, we are presented with choices and may seem victims of circumstance at different points in time, but there is also an overarching sense or tapestry to our lives and experience. This goes beyond a self-fulfilling prophecy, based on goals and psychological issues or the playing out of patterns recreated from our past. There's a feeling of totality and wholeness as though all the different parts in our lives are integrally connected in a purposeful way.

This is why, for so many, commonsense would indicate something else is going on – *beyond* the purely physical world.

7 Faith May Not be so Blind

There is a great divide between those who have faith and those who do not.

Several years ago I was contacted by a friend who had known me long before I had any interest in spirituality. As so often happens, out of grief, she had been drawn towards faith but was going through what she termed a "crisis of faith." We had lost touch although she had been to my website and had some idea of the direction I had taken. She seemed intrigued that I appeared to have faith but lamented that she could not without some proof. She seemed to be reaching and hungry but could only go so far.

This made me reflect back to my own awakening. My friend came from a part of my life long before I ever thought about God. I was living in a different city. We were younger then. At the time, she had dabbled in Eastern spiritual ideas although never practiced any formal religion. I hadn't been interested in anything spiritual at all. Now twenty years later, philosophically she seemed pretty much in the same place. There was an interest, but spirituality just hadn't been an important part of her life. I had done a 180 degree turnaround. Faith had become a central pillar of mine.

As we reminisced a bit, I was flooded by the awareness of how much happier and grounded I was now. It's always interesting to see the trajectory of lives... what happened as opposed to what was planned, hoped for, or wondered about. When it's your own life, it also takes you aback, knowing that it all could have gone in another direction. Or could it? It wasn't that I had been unhappy then, but I was lost.

When I think back to before I had God in my life, it's always a lost and unanchored feeling.

It was when I opened the door to faith that everything shifted. It was like a switch had been flipped, and some dynamic force began to transform me in a huge way. This progressed softly in a silent wave of change that I barely was aware of on the surface. At the time, I knew I felt differently and was thinking and doing things I never had before. But I was old enough to have gone through numerous transitions and phases, so this wasn't unusual. Life is a constant evolution of interests, goals, even relationships.

Once awakened, I also became so immersed in my new mindset and activities that I stopped thinking about myself or where I was headed as much as I used to. Somewhere along the line, I did pause to reflect and was astounded at how altered everything had become. There had been a major turning point, a watershed, and reorganization. Even now, so great is the metamorphosis in my identity and experience that it seems beyond myself, a miracle or gift not of my own doing, but it is solid and real.

Opening to God was the obvious miracle and catalyst in my consciousness. It all hinged on that willing awareness that I held within. My newfound faith also reverberated out into every aspect of my existence. Somewhere along the way, I seemed to have crossed a line from primarily experiencing myself as a *self* or a *psychological being* in a *physical* world... to a *soul* or a *spiritual being* in a *spiritual* world. Ironically, it was from this *spiritual* vantage point that I found the most effective tools for coping with *psychological* problems.

What do we mean by faith? Of the dictionary definitions, the most general involves strong confidence in a person or thing. Taking this one step further, faith can mean a belief that is held without proof. Even more specifically, faith may be a belief in God or the doctrines of a religion. Finally, faith can refer to religion in general or to specific religions *(e.g., Judaism, Buddhism, Christianity, Islam)*.

What all these definitions suggest is that faith involves a condition of *trust* that goes beyond mental belief. It is not simply intellectual assumption or opinion or analyzing the pros and cons as to whether a person or situation deserves one's confidence or not. Faith is a belief *in* something, not a belief *about* something. Faith involves an emotional truth, which is compelling to the individual and arises out of conviction or instinct, not rational analysis.

Among spiritually committed people, faith is associated with a belief in God and tends to be viewed as all-or-nothing. You either *are* a believer... or you're *not*. Logic dictates you can't both believe in and not believe in God at the same time. That being said, even when the belief is present, there is a range as to how strong that belief is and whether or how greatly it affects day-to-day life. For some, a belief in God may be real, even profound, but remains a distant philosophical abstraction with little or no impact in terms of the substance of daily living. At the other extreme are people for whom the relationship with God is a central, ongoing force. Theirs is a *living* faith.

Generally, when believers speak of faith, this also does not mean a vague, half-hearted notion of God but acceptance of an omnipotent God with real presence in their lives. While each person's experience of God is unique, for believers, God and faith are never relativistic concepts to be defined and redefined ad infinitum, based on one's background or situation or personal need. God is Absolute, and traditionally faith is absolute belief in God. You either believe in God as an actual Supreme Being or true Higher Power, or you don't.

This is why traditional faith is so powerful, both in the head and in the heart. Mentally, faith is the conviction that there is a loving, all-powerful, and omniscient Higher Power, always beyond human understanding but with ultimate influence over our lives. For people of faith, God becomes central in their personal belief system with regard to understanding life, themselves, where to find meaning and value, what is Truth, and standards of right and wrong. On the *intellectual* level, faith provides a way of looking at the world as well as a comprehensive reference guide for optimal behavior.

Experientially and *emotionally*, faith leads to a sense of inner, loving connection and guidance always available. The power and love of God are not only ideas but play out in the individual's life. The more spiritually committed a person becomes in terms of living according to the *intellectual beliefs* of faith, the more apparent will be the experiential and *emotional benefits* of faith. So the stronger the spiritual commitment, the closer the relationship with God becomes. God is the Highest authority but also the loving caretaker and support, the teacher, a friend, and companion when needed. As I discovered when I opened that door, faith provides a new emotional source and resource on a very personal and experiential level.

Like so many before me, faith presented an entirely new start, a fresh perspective, a sense of being reborn into a more authentic identity, and so much more. Once that door of faith had been opened, it was like entering a new world. People of faith often describe a recognition or *awakening*, a moment or period of time, during which they came to a realization of spiritual Truth. Again, this usually isn't only an intellectual decision that a Higher Power exists but is multilevel, involving emotional and perceptual shifts, with an awareness of the presence of God. The person now understands that spiritual reality *is* real, and it seems almost impossible to walk back this perception although some may try. The envelope has been pushed, the bell has been rung, the milk has been spilt, the horizon expanded.

For the spiritually committed individual, faith is a turning point and new beginning. It is also a journey. There are really two parts. The first is opening the door *to* faith *(not always easy to do)*. Once the person opens that door and has faith, then there is the opportunity to live *in* faith *(also not easy)*. This is a confusing dynamic, but basically faith can be conceptualized as having two stages: *awakening* to faith and *maintaining* faith. First, you have to awaken, to open that door to the brighter horizon and new frontier. Second, there is a new life waiting for you on that frontier, but you have to maintain faith to have that life. Both *awakening* to and *maintaining* faith are the choice of the individual and involve an ongoing commitment.

Obviously, faith isn't passive and is often described in terms of movement towards or being in a different existential place. The individual may be portrayed as making a leap, crossing a bridge, or again, opening a door. Like the abrupt divide in conversation when it becomes apparent that two vastly inconsistent concepts of God are being discussed, traditionally the idea of faith is akin to crossing a river of demarcation with people living in two qualitatively different realities on opposite sides. People of faith may also conceptualize their lives as separated into two distinct periods, *before* and *after* a relationship with God.

What does this mean from a practical point of view? My own transformation after awakening is a real world example. *Before* God, I was a creature of culture, not that I ever thought about myself that way. Like most people, I was just instinctively utilizing societal norms to understand and guide my experience. This didn't mean my life was organized around social approval nor that all norms are negative.

Many are quite useful, as they allow us to participate and thrive in the society in which we are born, which most of us want to do. I was also in the fortunate position of having studied psychology, which is the accepted foundation of knowledge regarding human nature in the modern, secular world. So I should know what makes people happy.

Did I? All of us develop a personal truth, based on our experience, what we have been taught, and who we uniquely are. *Before* God, relying on my personal truth didn't always work out that well, even with all my expertise. Sometimes it did, but there was a lot of room for improvement. My sensitivity *(such an essential aspect of who I am)* at times felt like a burden, and I even intuitively suspected that the way I was interpreting a lot of my reactions as low self-esteem was probably digging that hole even deeper. Sometimes there seemed a conflict as though what I was striving towards and who I was trying to be were at odds with another, most important part of myself.

Like most people, I couldn't help but measure who I was and where I was headed in relation to the attitudes and standards of my peer group, a subset of society at large. This was a quandary. The goals and values which appeared to be the agreed upon formulas for happiness often seemed so empty, superficial, or just plain wrong. I wanted to be accomplished, and money is always a necessary means to an end. Yet all the materialism and competition this seemed to breed felt hollow and antithetical to more meaningful, even exciting, aspects of living. The harshness also felt cruel at times, making me morally queasy.

I also never was comfortable with professional politics. I had gone into psychology out of curiosity about people *(including myself)* and wanting to help others. But the business of success and career advancement in general *(advertising and networking, even with other psychologists)* involved the hyped-up selling of one's expertise and a degree of self promotion that I had found difficult. On the other hand, it was clear. If I wasn't willing to play, I wouldn't get the reward. In fact, I might not even get out of the gate and have any career at all.

This was my predicament. If I didn't follow the program, some professional and personal opportunities were automatically cut off, and I could veer into feeling a "loser" or being very much alone. So I tried. I learned to "talk the talk" and could "walk the walk." There were even times when I would convince myself that these societal values were my own. Then, in my heart and the more honest depths within my psyche, I would acknowledge that I just couldn't get fully invested in many of these things. *(As Zippy, the Pinhead would say, "Are we having fun yet?")* So I would feel insincere, false unto myself, and bored, sometimes hypocritical. It was a vicious cycle.

Personally too, there were pressures as I wasn't getting any younger. Was I about to miss the boat of bliss as well? Often I was reminded that I needed to be realistic, find the best available mate, grow up, and settle down. Always out of the best intentions, friends and associates ran the stats of single men by me, like applications at a job fair, amid fear-producing remarks, which established the hourglass of romantic happiness was running low by one's mid-thirties. Usually I would go along, but so often there was frustration and disappointment on all sides. This was a tough one. My sensitivity just didn't jive with the brutal dating scene, not only the risk of getting hurt and rejected, but I also hated the idea of doing that to someone else.

I actually had been married when I was younger to a very nice young man, and we set up a very nice young life although we weren't right for each other. It also had become regrettably obvious to me that it was my seeking society's Golden Formula of perfection that had me pushing for that marriage in the first place and then wanting to end it when the formula became stale. I also had come to understand there had been a desperate underlying motivation to that marriage, in that I had been trying to put myself back together in the aftermath of my father's and sister's deaths, by trying to create *(and pretending to have)* the unblemished life.

I didn't want to do that again. Not only was it unfulfilling. Through my inauthentic existence and being dishonest with myself, I felt what I had done was wrong and unfair and had caused a lot of pain, even if unintentional. So this was one area I didn't want to compromise. I staunchly held to the ideal that people can find the right relationship and true romantic love. I knew a number of people who had. But I was often cautioned as to being juvenile and possibly self-sabotaging through my wide-eyed fantasies *(and the hourglass emptied further)*.

After God, everything changed. How could it not? In faith, one is essentially inviting the presence, love, and authority of God into one's psyche. Instead of relying entirely on my personal truth, there was now Absolute Truth as a guiding input and force. The cultural norms and standards seemed to take a backseat. I was still a functioning and productive member of society, maybe more so. I was still living through the prism of psychological experience as we all do, even after becoming spiritually aware. I still had all the emotional and human needs I always had and always will. So what was different? There was a new authenticity, clarity, and resolve to my choices and the way I was pursuing my life. This was both gratifying and freeing.

Quite unexpected was the new source of unconditional love and nurturance that I experienced in my developing relationship with God. I felt filled and cared for in a way I never had before. This helped to center my emotional existence and to deal with the ups and downs, particularly those disappointing or negative interactions with others.

In short, I was less needy. When one is filled up, emotional reactivity and the pressure of self-esteem become less paramount. I was better able to reason and focus and to make better choices from a more meaningful and controlled internal place. There was also a mellow, satisfying backdrop of wholeness and tranquility, adding to the sense of security and calm.

My relationship with God also became such a prominent resource in terms of direction and guidance. This seemed to be providing an outlook of hope, instead of anxiety or desperation, given that the future is always unknown. I was willing to take the time and no longer worried so much about what I might be missing or who I was in terms of society's norms... or whether whoever I was made me a "winner" or "loser" in the march of life. Rather, I began to see my identity more in terms of an unfolding of purpose and growth that occurred in the process of living moment to moment, the ultimate schedule and destination determined by God. At the same time, it also felt as though I was being encouraged in the direction of my greatest good, whatever that means.

It was with this mindset that I was able to develop my painting so fruitfully and blissfully for a period of time. Instead of trying to maintain a balanced but frenetic lifestyle, forever vigilant to all the opportunities I might be missing and that life was moving on, I allowed myself to take time out and be consumed by this very private and personally absorbing endeavor, my artwork. This also proved to be a gateway to immense self-discovery and sense of accomplishment down-the-line *(which did lead to other opportunities)*.

In an honest relationship with God, I was also better able to have an honest relationship with myself. Not only did I feel generally loved and led in a way that seemed right and personally meaningful, but I was beginning to appreciate the importance of absolute spiritual values. These were becoming a reliable compass and anchor in the day-to-day. It was no longer about personal goals first and *maybe* managing to do the "right" thing in the process. It was now about *always* trying to do the "right" thing, to the best of my personal understanding, in whatever I was doing that had become the goal. I had discovered that moral choices were preeminently important and there was a yardstick of Higher Truth. I began to seek integrity and wholeness in what I thought and did and felt instead of focusing so predominantly on my own needs, self-esteem, and emotional reactions.

To many nonbelievers, the changes I just described would be categorized as delusional or childlike, the cravings and foolishness of a "true believer." The popular stereotype of people of faith is of irrational and dependent followers, who have turned off intelligence and *(like lobotomized robots or docile sheep)* blindly allow God to take over their thoughts, emotions, and lives. For the spiritually oriented person, it is clear that the nonspiritual person just doesn't understand what faith actually involves. Faith doesn't derive from stupidity or need but is a matter of choice. One can always choose to deny the presence and power of God in one's life.

Why is it unintelligent to believe in God? To many, the idea of a Higher Power is simply an irrational concept because this is not based in physical reality. Here again we see the most common and quintessential argument of skeptics that there is no *objective* proof. This may be conclusive to nonbelievers, but people of faith say so what? Faith is necessarily without proof. That's a given. It's a *subjective* experience. We can't observe spiritual reality through our senses. We can't fact-check it or measure it. We can't prove it. Just because you can't prove it doesn't mean it isn't real or isn't so. There are a lot of things in life we can't prove. The basic assumption is that God and the

Truth of God are beyond human comprehension. Faith goes beyond mental belief and isn't about weighing factual data. It's about *trust* in a mystery by definition. It's the willingness to surrender control to that mystery and to put one's self in the hands of God.

The nonspiritual person may find it ridiculous that people of faith give so much power to God. The person of faith may find it equally senseless that the nonspiritual person would put so much trust in human beings. Without question, there are aspects of the human condition that are beyond our comprehension, such as death. How do we know for sure there isn't an afterlife or other phenomena we can't observe but do affect us? Maybe what seems so negative at this point in time, like death, really isn't in terms of the bigger picture or down-the-line. The same would be true for what seems so positive as well.

We just don't know. We don't have any more proof that there isn't an afterlife than that there is. We all live with lack of certainty about many things in our human lives all the time, but we don't denigrate or ban them as silly. What about love? We feel it in all shades and forms, but what constitutes proof of love? There are definitely times in our personal relationships when we may wonder if love exists, but we don't walk away just because objective proof is lacking. We make decisions based on our subjective impressions. Why then is the subjective considered so irrational when it comes to God?

And what about even more concrete and physical phenomena such as how and if medicines work? Often we don't know why *(there's no definitive proof)*, and the scientific evidence we do have of benefits or side effects easily changes with the next research study. As the saying goes, we don't "throw the baby out with the bath water." We try to make the best decisions we can, based on the information we do have, even if limited or contradictory. To pretend that mystery or uncertainty doesn't exist... or to discount types of experience that might support things for which we have no proof... makes as little sense to the person of faith as belief without proof makes to the nonbeliever.

People of faith will readily agree that modern science has come to know a lot about the physical world; the operant word being *physical.* Yet why should we assume that this type of knowledge generalizes to all aspects of human experience and the cosmos at large? The spiritual point of view is that it is hubris to think that it does. It may even be looked upon as ironic that people who don't believe in God tend to assume that human beings are nothing more than the result of chance organic evolutionary adaptation, but they seem to think these same human beings *(i.e., chance organic accidents)* can know everything.

Is the insistence on proof as the absolute standard an attempt to maintain the illusion of personal or human control? Faith oriented people may be considered stupid by nonbelievers because they seek to yield to God's will. Still, given all the unexplained mystery in human life, couldn't nonbelievers be considered even stupider still *(or at least taking a big risk)* in their arrogant demand for proof as though auditioning God? For the spiritually committed person, it seems riskier and more of a leap of faith *(in the colloquial sense)* to not make the leap of faith *(in the spiritual sense).*

Of course, for most people of faith, it's not the theoretical arguments that are so powerful. It's the *experience.* Even on the level of personal consciousness, it would seem there has to be something more than what we can account for physically. There is such richness and fullness, which goes so deep and on so many levels. The boundless landscape of our consciousness and dreams... the intricate, multilayered movie inside our mind... the tapestry of our life story... the strength of our relationship bonds *(such as in love or motherhood)...* the intensity of

FAITH MAY NOT BE SO BLIND

our emotions, even the painful ones. To categorically reduce this to biological mechanisms or strictly physical processes would just seem to be an oversimplification.

In addition to the richness, wholeness, and depth of our experience *(which again feels too meaningful to be random)*, when people become more spiritually aware, there seems to develop an attunement to another level of experience *beyond* the physical. From our subjective vantage point, this goes further than intuitive feelings. As I perceived from the time I was a small child, it just seems that something else is going on beneath the surface of things. As we live our lives moment to moment, there seem to be configurations of *spirit* playing out in what we do, where we're led, who we meet, and in our interactions with others. Spiritual people may perceive patterns or layers and connections as though immersed in a vital spiritual reality.

Not only is there the overall sense of connection with and guidance from God. People of faith feel potentially and meaningfully bonded with other people and living creatures on a *spiritual* level and that this plays out in their *human* existence. They do feel their lives have a purpose, an integration, and greater meaning and that they are specifically led in the direction of their greatest good although what this is and how this will play out are not entirely knowable, even while in the midst of it. There is also the impression that all of us have a part to play in the grander spiritual dance or design.

The person of faith also begins to see the work of God in his or her life. The more one is open to being led through faith, the more aware the person becomes of signs, synchronous and meaningful events, and what seem like subtle guideposts in how life begins to unfold. There may be a feeling of correctness or the fate of things. People of faith feel this is the plan of God.

Usually there develops a feeling of wondrous occurrences and actual miracles, both great and small. Money may show up when needed, maybe from odd sources, such as a neighbor just at the right time asking to buy an old car you've been thinking of selling but never put on the market. There may be a trail of information that seems to unfold. The individual may keep running into people or events that appear in the manner of messengers, as they echo in some outwardly unrelated way an issue the person is dealing with, ultimately leading to an answer or resolution.

For the person of faith, it also becomes increasingly apparent how wise it is to trust God, who seems to know us better than we know ourselves. Spiritually committed people learn over time that reward and happiness are found in unexpected places and sometimes by first having to give up what we thought we wanted, only to later discover there was something better in store. There develops a sense that God does take care of and fulfill us to a degree that is greater than we ever thought possible and in ways we never could have imagined.

Evidence that we are living a mysterious truth may be seen in the paradoxical nature of so much of human experience. Our human perspective is relative and overall limited. Things may not be what they seem. This is why spiritual knowledge is accepted as beyond our comprehension. What starts out as a negative may not be down-the-line or in the bigger picture. Often it is the most painful events that are the turning points and end up having so much purpose and meaning in the story of our lives. Sometimes the change is positive *(from our human perspective)*. Sometimes not, but we learn something of great value that we wouldn't have without the pain. Wisdom is hard won and there for the taking, but wisdom is not just a bitter pill. It teaches us how to live our lives from this point forward. Plus, with God, there is always hope and the potential for love, even at the end of life.

For those who have crossed that bridge of faith, there arises the conviction that faith works, at times much to their surprise. However challenging and difficult to maintain, the new way of faith trumps the old. It becomes the reasonable choice by far. Like myself, once awakened, people may look back and remember their way of being in the world *before* God with marked discomfort because the contrast with the new and preferred way of being *after* God is just so strong. The choices made, the opportunities that appear, the feelings of well-being and loving connectedness to others, not only seem greater and better, but qualitatively different from whatever went before. With every passing day, people of faith tend to report the ever deepening realization that they are in far more capable hands than their own.

In other words, faith may not be so blind. For many, given their experience, faith just makes sense and offers better explanations. There may not be *proof* of God or of a spiritual reality beyond the physical, but there may be *evidence* within an individual's experience on so many levels. The human condition is replete with mysteries and ambiguities. For many, the existence of God is a far more reasonable and complete explanation of all these phenomena than the so-called rational scientific explanations, which can seem insufficient or convoluted, like fitting a square peg into a round hole. For the person of faith, there may be the sense that for people *not* to believe, they must be missing something.

In terms of *awakening* to faith, there are two common scenarios. The first is when a person comes to God for the very first time. As was true for me, religious background or exposure to spiritual principles may have been sparse or nonexistent. There may have been little interest previously or agnostic, even atheistic, views. In this case, what occurs is a massive revolution in worldview in addition to all the existential and lifestyle changes that have been described.

The other scenario is the person who was brought up in and perhaps practices a religion and may have always believed in an all-powerful God. In this case, there is not technically an *awakening* to faith, but what is experienced is a marked *deepening* of faith and the relationship with God with a greater commitment to more consistently and fully be guided by spiritual principles in everyday living. In doing so, often the inner experiential transformation is so great that there is the sense of a qualitative shift, of *awakening*, of crossing a bridge from one way of being to another.

Almost all religions hold a belief in a Higher Power or Consciousness as a basic tenet. Does that mean that all religious followers have faith? In one sense of the definition, it does. Whenever we speak of faith, there is always the question of religion. Devout people truly believe in God, and those who practice or identify with a religion presumably accept the fundamental premise of God's existence. But, for some, it does appear that their religion has more to do with social or psychological identity *(i.e., being Catholic, Muslim, Jewish, born-again Christian)* than it does with God or genuine spiritual concerns. These people may talk a lot about their religion and its rules and doctrines. They may even talk a lot about or constantly refer to God. Yet, to the outside observer, it would appear that God and Absolute Truth are missing in action in terms of how they actually behave.

The prevalence of hypocrisy and extremism throughout religions is well-documented. Skeptics like to point out that religion has likely caused more wars and carnage than any other factor in human history. All this is well known, and we can see it everyday on the world stage and sometimes in our personal milieu. "Do as I say, not as I do" is a staple of human behavior, whether religious or not. Suffice it to say that all this says something about human beings, *not* about God.

What is not stressed, especially in our secular age, is that religion can be a beautiful vehicle for spiritual growth and expression. Throughout history, religion has provided the language and roadmap for encouraging spiritual experience and living a worthwhile and meaningful life. For many religious people, this continues to be true. Their faith is a positive force, a source of healing and joy, and fosters a personal connection with God. In both its doctrines and practice, their religion provides emotional nurturance and critical guidance, often under the direction of the priests, pastors, clerics, and rabbis who have genuinely devoted their lives to the service of others.

For others, religious faith does appear more external and on the surface. They may truly believe in God as the Supreme Being, and their faith may serve as a kind of manual or reference guide, through which to understand the world and how to live a good life. But an emotional connection with God seems to be absent or is experienced only occasionally, such as during times of trouble. The rest of the time they are so fully caught up in the ways of the mainstream world that any spiritual considerations seem to be lost. These people don't appear intentionally hypocritical and may not be hypocritical at all. They may want to live spiritually devoted and virtuous lives. It's just, in the bulk of their lives, the societal values prevail.

There are various explanations why this is so. Again, the influence of the culture is so pervasive and often unconscious. Secular values seep into our psyches through media, advertising, and just being alive in this day and age. It is easy to see how anything truly spiritual, including a sense of the presence of God, could get obscured or compartmentalized, even without awareness that this is happening.

There are also those who seem unmotivated to seek deeper spiritual experience. Again, they may absolutely believe in God and want to be good. Yet they are fairly satisfied with what life has to offer, or they are complacent or so extroverted or "in the box" type of thinkers that there is simply no impetus for them to turn inward or to question or explore their inner or outer world. They go along with the program *(religious or cultural or a combination of both)* and don't rock the boat although this can change quickly if their boat gets rocked by someone or something else.

Many religious congregations do recognize their truly spiritual members and applaud them as being particularly dedicated in living their faith. There is also the idea that faith may become stronger when one has had doubt because this means the person has really thought through what that faith involves. The commitment to faith is a process, through which the individual has arrived at a sincere conviction and personal affirmation of the truth of their religion, by addressing and working through the doubt. Otherwise, there may be only superficial acceptance of what the person has been told. This runs the risk of a kind of servitude to the religious doctrine instead of true commitment and service to God.

For some, religion is extremely helpful in understanding and guiding spiritual growth. For others, it almost appears to be a strategy for avoiding real issues *(i.e., if you just follow the rules, you don't have to look within)*. For still others, religious doctrine and practice seem to get in the way of deeper spiritual experience and expression. A friend of mine likes to say he cuts out the middleman. While he previously went to church regularly, his faith now exclusively involves and is primarily expressed through his direct relationship with God.

This would seem to be a central and pivotal issue in addressing faith. It is the emotional bond that makes faith so powerful, mentally and experientially. How this is engaged in will vary from one individual to another, but it is when the person enters into an actual and active relationship with God that there is a sense of *awakening* to faith. For some, religion facilitates and enhances this relationship. For others, religious doctrine or practice may feel too constraining and even seem to get in the way of the spiritual bond. In this view, it really is a matter of personal choice how one connects with God. The important thing is that the connection is sought and nurtured.

No matter what the specifics of the belief system, the individual tends to find in faith a perspective of wholeness. Within a spiritual context, life intuitively makes sense. Nonspiritual people are quick to point out that faith is only seeing what one wants to see. People of faith respond that the nonbeliever is not seeing the total picture and is in denial about a critical dimension of life.

These are the two sides to the proverbial coin. To the nonbeliever, the idea of a *spiritual* order is an irrational concept – because it is not based in *physical* reality. How could there be anything more?

For the person of faith, it is just as reasonable to ask: How could there not be?

8   Fear and God-Fearing

When I first woke up and heard the rattling, I assumed it was the couple downstairs. I thought they had moved out the day before. For months they had been arguing loudly and throwing things to a degree that the landlord had given them notice. For the past two weeks, the tone had become ugly and angry, and the outbursts had been a nightly ordeal. I was concerned all this fighting would escalate into violence. It was a helpless feeling, so I had been relieved that day to see them move out.

Now... what the? I shot up in bed, more in anger. They were back? Enough. This was outrageous. The crashing was so intense it seemed the house was rocking. Then I realized it was, jerking viciously from side to side. This was an earthquake. A large snap and I heard dishes falling from the cupboard, an angry cascade of smashing glass in the next room. As I slunk down beneath the covers, the shaking room seemed oddly suspended as though the supports below were about to give way. When the movement suddenly calmed, I took a breath, wondering what should I...? Then a huge, violent jolt ripped through and, like falling dominoes, a series of whopping crashes from beyond my bedroom door. It felt like half the building had fallen away.

It was at that moment I realized I could die. A flash of sadness and my chest became immobilized, my heart paralyzed in fear. I had brief flashes of lamenting why had I moved to California... that this must be the Big One... that maybe I was going to die. I could feel my body tautly coiling, like a defenseless animal, in anticipation of the final strike that would collapse the building and possibly be my last awareness. All this took place within a matter of seconds.

At some point, I began to recite the Lord's Prayer. "Thy will be done…" Suddenly this had an immediate existential reality. And then somehow... I gave it up to God. I still don't know what that means; I just know that I did so. It was like a mental release of acceptance, and something had been let go. Instantly, there was a calming in my heart area. Uncannily, it seemed that I no longer had fear although I was still afraid. The shaking continued for a few moments but more on the periphery, finally stopping altogether. Gingerly moving to my bedroom door, I fully expected to open it onto fresh air, the room teetering on the second story frame. It wasn't. It had been the bookcases that had fallen over in the other room, smacking onto the hardwood floor.

The Northridge earthquake was the only time that I really thought I might die and had time to think about it. I'd been in close calls, swerving quickly on the freeway to avoid an accident or choking for a few harrowing seconds. There wasn't time to think of what might be happening, and then it was over and forgotten.

During the course of our lives, we never know. Walk out the door in the morning or go to sleep at night. Life can be irrevocably altered or end at any moment. Sitting helpless in the ER or waiting for the biopsy results, we flip-flop from catastrophic thinking to bargaining with God for another chance. We are lucky when we only have to deal with the possibility, and nothing happens. At that point, in the midst of waiting, it is profoundly clear as to what is truly important in life. We have learned our lesson. Do we remember it? Too often only when it is too late.

Atheists ridicule people of faith but also seem mystified. They argue, not only is there no objective proof of God, but how could anyone believe in such a cruel God, who would create a world with death,

FEAR AND GOD-FEARING

evil, illness, and such unhappiness? Bad things do happen to good people. There's no denying it. Life is harsh and then inevitably lost. The nonbelievers' logic is: If truly the Creator of it all, God would seem to be extremely angry and punitive towards human beings. They acknowledge there are wonderful things in life and about the human condition. Still, look around. In their view, to assert that God is a just and loving Authority or Creator simply seems absurd.

For many nonbelievers, to have faith *(i.e., belief)* is stupid enough. To be God-fearing *(i.e., yielding to a punishing or unfair Supreme Power)* is truly off the deep end. Karl Marx' famous quote is that religion is the "opium of the people" *(Critique of Hegel's Philosophy of Right, 1843)*. The implication is that faith is a coping strategy to deal with the misery and inequities in this life by imagining an idyllic state in the next. Freud also saw religion as a wish-fulfilling defense mechanism, a childlike way for the individual to deal with underlying issues, at the same time providing structure and control in society at large.

What do we mean by God-fearing? The term evokes an image of dogged stoicism usually during a time of hardship and futile suffering on a grand scale. The worn and weary but enduring faces of the 1930s Dust Bowl or Great Depression. The eyes, like steel, stare out in resigned tenacity. There may also be the caricature of upright *(or "uptight?")* living and repressive propriety, such as in the *American Gothic* painting by Grant Wood. We see the older Midwest farmer with the pitchfork, rigid in his austerity. A dour, buttoned-up woman by his side.

The modern connotations of God-fearing would speak to a ridiculous situation if taken literally. The depiction is of a vindictive God, who has created for too many a life of adversity and affliction. Basically, an individual who is God-fearing is portrayed either as a victim of

Stockholm syndrome, in which a dependent bond is formed with the captor and abuser *(i.e., God)*, or the person of faith is seen as similar to a frightened child, who is trying to be passive, quiet, and good enough to avoid upsetting the harsh and abusive parent *(i.e., also God)*.

For spiritually committed people, this point of view shows a lack of understanding of what faith and God are really about. Some of the modern anger at religion comes from the assumption that it controls people or numbs them to the realities of life because of some vague promise of intangible gifts, particularly down the road. Spiritual people assert the gifts are real, including in the here and now.

What are the gifts of faith? First, there is an actual feeling of being loved when one embraces a relationship with God. Second, through *spirit*, there is a sense of being led as well as supportive connections with other people. Third, there is an awareness of the importance of Absolute Truth, including the gift of the higher spiritual values. These offer a moral compass, so that the person receives guidance as to how to best approach life, whatever the circumstances over its course. In short, faith provides another source and resource for dealing with the challenging realities of physical and psychological existence.

In essence, God-fearing means the ongoing acceptance of God as the Higher Power. If *awakening* to faith is acknowledging the power and presence of God, *maintaining* faith is putting one's self in God's hands and yielding control to the greater wisdom, Higher Authority, and spiritual Truth. When people accept faith, especially when they commit to *living* their faith, they are essentially deferring to God as knowing all and knowing best.

The spiritual relationship with God, while reciprocal, is not equal. It is like that of a loving parent and child. God is *not* the harsh or abusive parent described by skeptics but one who has the child's best interests at heart. The good parent always has the authority and greater knowledge but nurtures and teaches the child in the direction of optimal development and growth. Being God-fearing is respectfully abiding by the rules set forth by the Higher Power or Divine parent in this caretaking relationship. In faith, we come as children to God. It is a stance of humility that says "I'm not in control of everything."

For sure, this is never easy. It is one thing to accept the mystery of life and defer to God within the larger, abstract philosophical picture. To be God-fearing can also take on a more intimidating meaning in that we must be willing to accept whatever God has in store for us individually. At any moment, we may be called home or faced with a lesson or circumstance or opportunity that is out of our psychological comfort zone, possibly involving loss and significant emotional pain. We may also be called upon to step up to the plate for someone or something besides ourselves or for the greater good, including at tremendous or ultimate cost to ourselves.

From the human perspective, the mystery of God is fearsome. "God giveth and God taketh away." We can never know why or what we will be called to do or confronted with over the course of our lives. The God-fearing individual expects to be called upon or used for a higher purpose, which does give meaning and joy on a deep level. People of faith seek to serve God. This is what they signed on to do when they committed to faith. But it is certainly easier when how God uses or calls upon the individual is non-threatening or life-enhancing from a human perspective. It is a jarring and humanly frightening scenario when what is asked is at odds with personal comfort and desires. What happens if we are called upon *(or forced)* to change or leave the life we know or the people we love? Since we all age and die, this is the human reality we all face eventually.

There are the old clichés. "God's time is not our time." "The Lord works in mysterious ways." It can be very unclear exactly what the spiritual opportunity or lesson is or why the person is faced with such a formidable situation, especially when others may not be, including those who seem less deserving. From the human perspective, it can seem so unfair. The inexplicable mystery of it all can be even more anxiety-provoking and never resolves. For all human beings, spiritually oriented or not, there are unanswerable questions that weave throughout our lives. The person of true faith has to deal with this unknowable reality but still chooses to defer to the greater authority and will of God.

When it comes to God-given lessons and opportunities, sometimes it seems we don't have any choice in the matter. Sometimes we do and may choose *not* to step up, to reject the opportunity we have been given, or we decide *not* to approach the challenge in a faith-based way. It is said that God never gives us anything we cannot handle, but some of the lessons or tasks and challenges, with which we are confronted, can require sacrifice, extreme courage, or endurance and seem to irrevocably alter our world in a negative way.

Maintaining faith can be extraordinarily difficult. It is easy during the good times, but commitment to any relationship means sticking it out during the tough and uncertain times as well. In terms of a relationship with God, we build and maintain trust through faith. From the human perspective, like any relationship, the connection to God does not always appear clear, smooth, or accessible. We may feel let down by God in terms of our own desires. When faith is low or things are hard or upsetting, it is not uncommon for even a strongly spiritually committed person to become angry or question the relationship. Of course, from a spiritual perspective, the bond with God can always withstand such questioning and remains available as long as the individual is open and willing to stay committed and engage in that relationship.

Maintaining faith requires discipline and perseverance. Many belief systems warn that, when people first find God and experience the joy of spiritual awareness, they form the mistaken impression that the blissful feelings and sense of euphoric, transcendent connection are what faith is all about. It just *feels* so good. A kind of dreamy, ecstatic high on life state that is truly wonderful. The reasoning seems to be "Since it's so spectacular, it's got to be God." Then, similar to human romance when infatuation plummets or the fires of passion begin to fade, with the first sign of difficulty or that a spiritual relationship does not guarantee wish fulfillment and 24-7 elation, the newfound faith collapses and may soon be discarded.

Some of the modern, particularly commercialized, approaches to spirituality seem to focus on the bliss and empowerment features *(it's all about feeling good)* to a degree that would suggest that spiritual awareness is the newest designer drug on the party scene. The God-fearing aspects of faith are avoided, even denigrated, as emblematic of an outdated and repressed time when "authoritarian" religion but not "creative" spirituality maintained control. Some modern approaches even advocate, for an immediate blast of pleasurable feelings and personal power, all one has to do is affirm and believe.

Still, how deep does this go? How well does it work over the long run? Sure, you can probably will or soothe yourself into a relaxed and pleasant state... but how valuable is superficial felicity in living life? Through positive attitude alone, you can probably talk yourself into doing something you needed or wanted to do, which is a wonderful thing, but little *(or even big)* bursts of courage or self-actualizing effort do not address or sustain the totality of one's existence.

For the traditionally spiritual person, there is a lot more involved. It's the entirety of life, in all its vicissitudes *(positive and painful)*, that is the playing field, and faith can always become greater. A God-fearing faith means sticking it out, acknowledging and working on our human frailties, while surrendering control to God, no matter what our personal circumstances. As codified in the human marriage vows, the true power of love is evident in commitment over the long-term, through sickness and in health, for richer and poorer, in good times and in bad. Similarly, we commit to the entirety of life in our relationship with God.

In retrospect and over the long run, people of faith do tend to endorse the spiritual path as worth it, right and true. Usually they are exceedingly grateful. Faith is viewed as the ultimate gift. Yet, in the day-to-day, faith is not easy and can feel burdensome if the individual wavers in trusting God. Even if someone does surrender mental control and, like so many people of faith, avows that "God knows me better than I do myself," there is still the painful reality of the finite nature of physical existence. All human beings have to come to terms with their own limits, no matter how blessed by God they may feel.

Spiritual people agree that the finite aspects of life and the human condition are very difficult to accept. For everyone. No one likes it, but that's the way it is. We don't know why. This is part of the greater mystery and wisdom of God. We all have fear. All of us are up against our own mortality. Nonspiritual people may reject God but have the same existential issues and their own Higher Power to deal with. It's called Nature. As organic creatures, we all die. None of us know whether we will wake up in the morning and, if we do, what the day holds in store. At any moment, whether we consider it random or Divine design, our fate may be revealed, for better or for worse, and at some point our life as we know it biologically does come to an end.

FEAR AND GOD-FEARING

Why be angry at this? It is what it is. People of faith are often stymied as to why nonspiritual people would anticipate life to be any different and then repudiate God for not delivering a more humanly palatable model of earthly existence. The skeptic seems to be bitterly focusing on the difficult aspects, like a thwarted child. Why exactly? Because we experience pain and restriction? Because life is unfair or wasn't created in the desired image of human beings? Why should we expect it to be? The person of faith is motivated to accept this reality and get on with it and then focus on the positives. This isn't denial but a realistic assessment that there are both negatives and positives from our limited perspective as human beings. Faith is the commitment to remain optimistic, to see the glass as half full. In contrast, nonbelievers often appear cynical, pessimistic, and angry to people of faith.

On the other hand, there is a difference between believers and nonbelievers in that believers assume there is something more in God's Authority and greater wisdom. Even taking out of the equation the possibility of an afterlife *(which believers tend to accept while nonbelievers do not)*, why we are living and how best to do so are approached differently by those who have faith and those who do not. For those of faith, what happens during our tenure on earth is looked upon as purposeful and planned, at least to some degree, whereas nonspiritual people see random luck or circumstance. Both ascribe some measure of choice to the individual. The spiritual person believes it is the best choice to allow one's self to be led by God and to defer to the Higher Power and Authority. The nonbeliever assumes that the best choice is to rely on human intelligence *(including the greater body of intellectual knowledge and expertise)* to make the best decisions in living.

This may be the key issue with regard to being God-fearing. Who should have control? The spiritual attitude is that we should respect and defer to God's greater wisdom. As human beings, we are not in control, either personally or collectively. Why should we pretend that we are or try to be? The spiritual point of view is that, as human beings, we need to accept this and the finite reality of life.

In contrast, nonbelievers assume that God is a fictional character. In their estimation, to defer to the higher intelligence and wisdom of God, essentially a figment of imagination, is preposterous. The natural world is regarded as the only valid frame of reference, and within that world, *Homo sapiens* is the controlling species and reigns supreme. Nonbelievers acknowledge there are many adverse circumstances that seem beyond human reach, at least for now, at the present time. Nevertheless, it is assumed that human intelligence is the best chance we've got to conquer adversity, both in our personal lives and for the planet at large.

Spiritually oriented people will agree that human intelligence is remarkable in many respects but also limited and biased. Not only is God wiser, but there is always a potential conflict between the intelligence of God and that of human beings, even those of faith. As *spiritual beings* within *physical* bodies, often the *spiritual being* and *physical* body just don't mesh very well. The *physical* body includes all our biological needs, urges, and sensations. By extension, it also includes our *psychological* experience *(all our thoughts and emotions, impulses, desires, dreams, passions, and reactions to others)*. In other words, the human condition is inherently messy. When human beings deal with any issue or problem, either individually or collectively, the likelihood for disarray and discord is tremendous. It's a veritable minefield, both within and outside ourselves.

For the God-fearing person, this is where the absolute spiritual values come in and why they are so important. These higher values are derived from the Absolute Truth of God and provide guidelines as to how to have a life of worth and wholeness. These values are universal and nonnegotiable. They transcend the intelligence of any one human being or culture or collective human knowledge. Spiritually committed people accept such values as a gift. They know that they need God's guidance and are thankful for it. As human beings, we all have our vulnerabilities and frailties, all those potentially out of control emotions, biases, impulsive actions, excesses, and ego needs that accompany a biological and finite human existence. These can get in the way and cause hurt for ourselves and others, even unwittingly.

Again, we see how the attitude of God-fearing faith is similar to the trust that a child has in a loving parent. Although children love their parents and may respect their authority overall, they are, after all, children. They want what they want. They likely resist and try to manipulate around all the rules and discipline and warnings about what's good for you. Children do not have the judgment or experience in living to foresee consequences or the bigger picture. They don't comprehend the fallacy of eating only dessert or having nonstop playtime… to never have to take a bath or go to school or comply with a designated bedtime. Once grown, the adult often looks back and is enormously thankful for the discipline and lessons that were so infuriating as a child.

As children of God, people of faith appreciate the guidance that the higher absolute *spiritual* values provide in living a *human* life on the *physical* plane. These values provide structure and teach discipline, which is entirely worthwhile in the bigger picture and down-the-line, however difficult or burdensome adherence to such values may sometimes seem. As with children, this is not just a matter of being docile or rule-abiding. We learn over time that these values do lead to a more meaningful and fulfilling existence in the long run.

What are the higher spiritual values? All belief systems have rules and regulations about how a devout person should live and behave. Often these are demeaned as showing the rigidity of formal religion or minimized as nonsensical, insignificant detail. Some of these rules and regulations can seem rather trivial and may have more to do with customs or habits *(such as what to eat)* or the traditions of the culture, in which the religion arose. While there may be a higher spiritual reason behind the rule or requirement, sometimes the meaning now seems more historical than anything else.

There are also rules and regulations that are obviously spiritually important. These are the abstract, philosophical, and generalized moral assumptions that appear fairly universally in belief systems in one form or another. Their understanding ultimately goes beyond cultural influences or personal experience. They provide tried and true guidelines of what is "right" and have existed throughout the world and recorded time. Generally, these values involve how to treat other human beings and honor God and the gifts of God *(such as a human life and the richness and beauty of the natural world)*.

Compassion. Kindness. Charity. Forgiveness. Respect and acceptance of others. Honesty. Loyalty. Balance. Diligence and responsibility. Discipline. Humility. Harmony and peace. Courage. Love. What all these have in common is that they speak to the exemplary ideals of human existence and a *higher* level of being, at the same time containing and keeping in check our *lower* human vulnerabilities and frailties *(again, all those emotions, biases, impulsive actions, excesses, and ego needs)*.

For the person of faith, these higher absolute spiritual values can be conceptualized as the *God rails*, that is, God's guardrails. By both following and living within them, we are led to a better life. The *God rails* keep us in check and also provide ideals to strive for. They offer inner direction and a moral compass, and they instruct us to uphold standards of worth and value beyond our own ego desires. Living up to such standards typically results in a sense of honor and integrity, which is much more meaningful than the success of any ego agenda or self-esteem.

The narcissistic values of the mainstream culture are plainly at odds with the *God rails*. In modern society, there is even somewhat of a condescending attitude towards the idea that human beings need rails at all. Even when baser instincts or the cruelest emotions are predominant within an individual's personality, as we've discussed, this is looked upon as dysfunction, not moral transgression or "wrong" or evil. It is assumed we should try to understand or fix the problem, not hold the person fully responsible. For the adequately functioning individual, who is trying to live a fulfilling and successful life, societal norms advocate self-indulgence and self-aggrandizement without culpability. In this atmosphere, it is easy to see how the higher values represented in the *God rails* would be viewed as rigid and repressive.

Nonspiritual people also point out that one doesn't have to believe in God to have good personal ethics. Surely, this can be true, and many nonspiritual people do acknowledge moral ideals that are the same or similar to the *God rails*. Naturally, they view them differently, not as Absolute Truth coming from God, but produced through evolution and likely embedded in our genetic code. Presumably, it was adaptive for human beings to act with cooperation, restraint, harmony, and responsibility, and out of this survival advantage, morality was born.

In contemporary society, it is usually agreed that justice and not hurting other people, at least in the greater social context, are higher values. We also hear a lot about compassion and serving the greater good. All this is admirable, but the secular approach to morality is not only relativistic but can be emotionally distant or arbitrary. Without the Higher Authority and overarching standard, moral behavior is left to the discretion of the individual. Where is there personal stake or responsibility? Morality becomes whatever one wants it to be and is invoked only if and when the desire hits. This mindset runs the risk of trivializing or reducing moral behavior to what is occasional or superficial. However well-intentioned, serving Thanksgiving dinner at the homeless shelter or weekly recycling is not the sole measure of an ethical person.

Plus, even if motivated and well-meaning, can human beings be trusted to know ultimately and consistently what's best for themselves? To do the right thing? To truly act in the interest of others and the greater good? Given human nature, do we need the fear of the greater authority in the relationship with God to even be motivated to seek higher values in a meaningful way? Is it the *fear* in God-fearing that keeps us in check? If we continue the analogy that the relationship with God is similar to that of a parent and child, can the child be left home alone and *not* run the risk of burning the house down? There are those who would argue that this is exactly what has been happening as God and the higher values have become less prevalent in the mainstream culture.

This is a predicament of the human condition. When other human beings decide for each other or even for themselves, it gets unruly and subjective and often doesn't work. We tend to focus on those things socially and psychologically that would seem to get us what we want, but typically the formulas are shallow. The most successful people or those who would seem to have it all at the same time seem to be missing something beneath the surface. Look at people who have had years of therapy to learn about themselves or those with the highest education. They may be luckier or more insightful but not necessarily happier than other people and may be more unhappy.

Without the *God rails*, it is just not as clear-cut as to what is of benefit, let alone "right," in guiding one's life. Nonspiritual people may say they feel in control and independent, but often this seems like a façade. From the outside looking in, there appears to be a lot of confusion and negative emotion, such as anger or fear. As our world has gotten more secular, so many seem to have lost touch with some essential part of themselves and life experience. In fact, after all the psychotherapy, medical progress, self-help, and modern conveniences *(which should allow for greater quality time to fulfill and advance ourselves)*, people still seem to be as unfulfilled, aggressive, bickering, and scrambling as ever. Even beyond intelligence, can human beings be trusted to make wise judgments and positive choices, even when well-meaning? Can they even agree as to what those positive choices are?

I was at a dinner party one night where the wine was flowing. The conversation turned into a whimsical fantasy of what would it be like if the average lifespan was 800 years. Everyone started to jokingly spin out various scenarios. Not one, among the dozen or so people at the table, all of whom were in their 30s and 40s, considered that the years of being elderly, dependent, or infirm might be lengthened as well. After all, this was a game about the possibility of an extended lifespan, not of limitation or decline. Knock off 20 years at the beginning for growing up and maybe 10 at the end for old age, which left 770 years of vibrant, in the prime of life, adult living to spend in whatever way one chose.

This was exciting. The ideas were popping around the table. Would people change professions every 100 years? What about relationships and marriage? *(Till death do us part? Could even soul mates really withstand so much familiarity? How many serial monogamies could you fit into eight centuries?)* How long would the TV season run? Think of all the reruns... and reruns... and more reruns. How many grandchildren and great-grandchildren *(and great, great, great+.... grandchildren...)* would you have to love... and love you back? To gather round on holidays *(...and buy presents for)*? Would there be a midlife crisis during your fourth or fifth century? How many remakes of *Psycho*? *Godfather, Part 43*? Definitely, there would be no excuse *not* to see the world several times over... to *not* accomplish your goals and pursue your dreams, dozens of them. The horizon seemed limitless. With 800 years, life would be an endless vista of roads to travel, adventures to explore, people to encounter, visions to fulfill, experiences to satisfy...

But what if people just remained locked in complacency and security-driven stagnation? The more the game played out, the more exhausting, alternately boring and frightening, this new and extended life seemed to become. How many years would you have to work before you could retire? And what about resources? Could the planet support such crowding and all those mouths to feed? With centuries of marriage, could you really expect a spouse to be faithful? The enthusiasm began to wane and sour around the table. Would anything really be any different? Or would it be just 800 years of more angst and complications with long, tedious expanses of time to be filled, jaded hopes, underlying anxieties, and nothing changes? Then someone asked, how would you feel when you turned 750? Would we be hoping they'd find a way to extend life another 800 years?

9   Hole or Whole?

It was one of those beautiful California mornings when the sun bathes everything in a wash of crisp, bright light. There is a promise to the day before noon and the dry, baking heat takes over. As I started across the empty parking lot, a woman came out of the grocery store and headed in my direction. Clearly, she had been or was extremely sick. There was the telltale scarf, wound tightly around her head, but it was more the ravaged emaciation. Her clothes hung so loosely although at the same time seemed to be providing needed support. Stalwart in her shuffling, she moved slowly while clutching a small plastic bag.

Her eyes were piercing but far away, wise and a little frightening in their intensity... or maybe I just projected because of what could so easily be imagined she had felt and seen. At the same time, there was a solid calm in her gaze, which seemed to be the steadying force and anchor for her frail body. Suddenly a youthful playfulness flashed across her middle-aged face that was unexpected and striking. As I walked past and began to smile, she startled. I thought she had seen me, so penetrating had been her focus and there was no one else around. It was then I realized she was intently drinking in the warmth and glare of the sun. There was a transfixed and transcendent quality. She seemed to smile but looked beyond me. It appeared to be the day and the warmth with which she was communicating.

After passing, I kept walking and didn't want to stare. Not that I sensed she would have let me, since there seemed to be an invisible barrier between us, as though she had grown weary of the pity and fear in the eyes of others and now refused to engage anymore. At the entrance of the grocery store, I felt compelled to look back. Eyes closed, a look of blissful appreciation on her face, she had her arms raised to the sun and had begun slowly twirling around in the empty parking lot, as though dancing, absorbing every sensation and molecule the day had to offer.

I didn't know this woman or what happened to her. I don't know whether she was spiritually oriented or not. It did seem she was doing life proud. People who have faced or are facing death often have a changed perceptual basis and attitude towards life, no matter what their philosophical orientation. With the possibility that they have few moments left, they experience joy in the moment, a cut to the chase insight into what is meaningful and worthwhile.

People who are close to death may have a truer and more meaningful perspective that cannot be attained in any other way. Many cultures equate wisdom with age. The older we get, the wiser we are assumed to be due to having so much experience in life. But could this be backwards? Does wisdom arise, not so much from the perspective of having so much experience accumulated, but rather from the stark realization of *not* having much experience left?

From a spiritual viewpoint, the transitory nature of life has one very positive psychological outgrowth. Spiritual teaching emphasizes the importance of thankfulness. Faith specifically teaches not to be resentful about death's inevitability. Death is a part of life, which is given by God. In fact, once we face the actuality that our human existence is time-limited, life then becomes a precious gift. The message is: Don't waste it. The length of life is up to God. How we spend it, whether we cherish or trash it, is a personal choice. Still, just as we would honor and take care of a special gift from someone we love, the spiritual directive is to honor and take care of this gift of life from God.

This is the silver lining of being God-fearing. Life can stop or fall apart at any time and will. Those things we cherish in life can disappear and will eventually fade. Health... beauty... intelligence... loving relationships... earning capacity... sight, taste, smell, and sound. We need to enjoy and use constructively whatever gifts we are given for the time that we have them. We also need to appreciate those gifts that we do have, even if *(from our human perspective)* they are not what we wanted and seem less than before.

In our modern times of immediate gratification and narcissistic agendas, thankfulness sounds somewhat masochistic. It has the connotation of groveling and smiling while forced to swallow a bitter pill. The nonbeliever may come to have an experiential realization of the brevity of life and that our days should be lived to the fullest but rarely associates this with gratitude. *(And to whom would the nonbeliever be grateful?)* There may be a sense of relief and general good fortune that, by the luck of genes or one's family situation or never having been in the wrong place at the wrong time, life is going relatively well. These feelings do not have the emotional power or sense of gratitude that a relationship with God brings. The person of faith *feels* thankful and, as in any relationship that is truly loving and mutual, feels that such thankfulness is appreciated.

This is one difference between having and not having a relationship with God and why nonspiritual people often seem so empty, bitter, or angry to people of faith. The spiritually committed person *loves* God and feels *loved* in return. There's a real bond, which is filling, supportive, dynamic, and plays out in the individual's life. On the other hand, once God becomes an actual presence and relationship, there is a Higher Authority to answer to. Life becomes a more serious and disciplined endeavor with responsibilities. In faith, there are clear directives as to values and behavior as well as the directive to reflect upon and assess one's own values and behavior. In staying the course and following the directives, the person not only experiences benefits *(i.e., sound guidance)*, but subjective experience overall seems broader, deeper, more meaningful, and authentic.

Thankfulness is one such directive. Through thankfulness, we show devotion and appreciation to God. In doing so, the spiritual bond is strengthened. As in any relationship, in *giving*, we also *receive*. How do we give thanks to God? We do so when we feel or show gratitude for people, circumstances, opportunities, or a general sense of blessing. We also give thanks when we delight in the gifts of life *(such as a natural setting, a musical piece, good humor, or good food)*. We also show thanks when we honor and nurture the specific gifts we have been given *(such as talents or loved ones or special opportunities)*.

In return, thankfulness is a rewarding state of mind. Like many spiritual values, there is a positive feeling attached. True thankfulness is actually a condition and expression of joy. When we acknowledge gifts and offer thanks, there is the sense of a fortifying exchange of energy or love, which is uplifting and feels good. This occurs in everyday life when two people make a positive exchange, even as minor as just sharing a genuine smile. Even nonspiritual people have probably had the experience, at least in childhood, of being so thrilled because something so wonderful happened that they reached up and said "Thank you!" to the universe. This spontaneous, overbrimming, childlike expression of joy is the spiritual feeling of thankfulness.

In the feeling of thankfulness, there is a sense of connection and almost compulsive sharing with others. When something incredible has occurred, there is an urge to spread the joy around. The joy feels as if it's exploding inside of us. We start smiling and talking to people we don't know. We call up everyone we do know with this gift of screaming euphoria… our cup runneth over. We also share in the thankfulness of others from afar. Even in our cynical times, if a car goes by with streamers and rattling cans, a Just Married sign, and young couple scrunched together on the front seat, we give thumbs up in congratulations amidst happy honking and waving from the passing cars.

In modern life, we tend to reserve true thankfulness for the biggest events. The spiritual person tries to apply thankfulness, perhaps in a more serene manner, to every element of living. Like faith, this is hard to maintain on a regular basis. But spiritual people try to maintain an outlook of thankfulness as much as they can. Like so much of spiritual practice, this is a discipline that becomes a habit. We might not continually have the joyful *feeling* of thankfulness, but we can attempt to maintain an *attitude* of thankfulness as much as possible. It is something you have to develop, to drill, to work on. The result is not only a positive mindset *(as being thankful is clearly seeing the glass as half full)* but also testifies to and reinforces the loving relationship with God within an individual's life.

This is why people of faith try to remain positive and optimistic. To turn lemons into lemonade. To find opportunity in crisis. To find blessings in every aspect of their existence… from another sunset… to food on the table… to how delicious it feels to be stuck on the freeway on your way back to work after being out sick for a week. It's about the ins and outs of mundane existence as well as the turning points and major events. The day-to-day and moment to moment. That's what life is, moment to moment. Even very devout people don't always succeed in maintaining such a positive attitude. Human life can be so challenging. Yet they try, knowing that every moment is an opportunity and gift from God that is then gone forever.

Nonspiritual people often characterize people of faith as cloying in their cheeriness and accuse them of being in unreasonable denial about the realities of human existence. Spiritual people counter that it's not denial but the love of life. They fully recognize the stress and difficulties that are involved, but they choose to hold the conviction that, in the long run and the wholeness of existence, there is great joy, beauty, meaning, and potential in what life has to offer. Conversely, spiritual people often feel that those who are nonspiritual are missing out, existentially cutting off their nose to spite their face, by such a negative approach.

The spiritual *joy of living* is similar to what most human beings express at the birth of a child, which is celebrated as a great miracle by people the world over, whether spiritually oriented or not. Most parents, gazing in awe at their newborn, are overcome with feelings of amazement and jubilation as to what a gift this is. They also realize what a responsibility they now have for bringing this child into the world, for giving the gift of life. They're rarely pessimistic or derogatory about it nor cautious in their elation.

There are people who choose not to have children because of their hopeless feelings about the state of the world or human existence. Yet most, upon seeing any infant and especially their own, fall in love, at least momentarily. They become flush with the magnificent possibilities, the future thrills and joys, the delights and discoveries that are automatically assumed to lie in store. The human heart fills with hope in the presence of babies and young children. It's not just their gentle and playful naiveté or vulnerability. We project our memories and see in their faces the wondrous future experiences that they have ahead… the birthday cake… the glorious movement of one's runty legs in a game of Hide-and-seek… the first solo bicycle ride… a firefly. We rarely think about the negative eventualities, which is a lesson. If people held out the same protective and optimistic attitude about their own lives, as they do about their children's, there might be a lot less unhappiness.

What is the substance of living? The modern approach is to compartmentalize the various aspects of our lives. Work. Play. Family. Children. Faith. This helps us to organize in a way that may be necessary and more efficient. It may also be fun and more fulfilling or just part of the broad range of human experience to express one's self in changeable ways, playing varied roles for different people. What also tends to occur is that at some point the individual may have difficulty balancing the multiple departments. There may also be a feeling that life or one's self is being taken over by one department at the expense of others, leading to burnout and frustration.

It is also natural to judge our experience on a scale of *positive* to *negative*, depending on how much pleasure versus effort is involved. This ends up with the division of life activities into categories of *work* and *play* with *work (or school)* being the *negative* state and *play* the *positive* one. Since most of our objectives and certainly resources are obtained through work, this creates an unfortunate situation. We begin to associate the bulk of our existence with a negative state of being. So often today, work is viewed as mandatory drudgery with the idealization, *not* of having a more meaningful life, but a more playful and irresponsible one. We glorify the image of doing nothing, other than sitting on the beach or being pampered.

Sadly, many today seem to be ignorant of or want to deny that reality is about the experience along the way of life, most of it pretty ordinary and run-of-the-mill. The tendency is to eternally be looking towards something else and something big in an attempt to elevate our day-to-day existence. "If only… I didn't have to work… won the lottery… got the promotion… fell in love… had a child… sold a painting…" Many people spend a lot of their time fantasizing about being somewhere and doing something else.

Obviously, the problem with this mindset is that we are spending our time *yearning* for what we think we want *(but don't have)* instead of enjoying and maximizing those things that we do have. Then it all passes so quickly, and the gifts of life seem scattered and inevitably lost. Furthermore, if and when we do attain the desired objective, it is rarely as abundant or wonderful as we think it is going to be in the wishing for it. This can only add to a sense of life as futile, stagnant, and unfulfilling.

We are told not to sweat the small stuff. Good advice, when it comes to a sense of crisis or emotional reactions. There are other types of small stuff that make up the fabric of our existence, and this we need to honor. Most of us are subliminally aware of certain moments and habits throughout the daily routine that are special but fleeting… the first waking up morning coffee… the interchange with the bighearted, motherly receptionist or wisecracking joker in the office… the crimson cardinal who visits outside your window… the tree-lined route as you turn off the freeway on your last leg home. How often do we stop to savor and fully appreciate such moments, let alone feel thankful?

So much of what we do, particularly the toil of life, is looked upon as aversive. A lot of it is, but we need to remind ourselves that this is part of the wholeness of human existence, a most cherished gift. And what's the alternative? The spiritually committed person tries to hold an attitude of appreciation as to the complicated miracle of life while in the midst of it. If we focus too much on the uncomfortable or burdensome aspects, we may end up wallowing in anger and stress and the wish to escape, essentially putting off any happiness until a future time. We can so easily get fixated or trapped in the negatives. By doing so, we then run the risk of missing a fuller experience of the positive elements in the immediate experience or situation. When this attitude becomes a chronic habit, life becomes oppressive; the individual, gloomy and resentful.

There is richness in the most ordinary activities of living, which we tend to downplay or ignore or take for granted. At one point, I worked in a nursing home with frail elderly patients and learned how precious the humdrum workings of routine existence can be, particularly when you can no longer participate. Many elderly people remain in the swing of life, even some in nursing homes, but most of the patients I worked with were extremely frail, physically or mentally. They were no longer afforded the option of living a normal life. That was over.

At the extreme, the deterioration was frightening as to its effects and what the person must be struggling with. There were stroke victims who were mentally sharp but couldn't speak or even communicate through writing because of paralysis. Wheelchair bound patients were totally dependent on the staff, not only for minimal mobility, but for bathing, feeding, washing, getting their diapers changed. Alzheimer's patients, who couldn't remember where they were or if they had eaten dinner five minutes earlier, seemed sentenced to endlessly roam the halls and their own memories in total confusion.

The subtle losses were also cautionary. Sometimes when the residents were having lunch, I would sit in the common room of the home and pay bills, an activity I always detested *(both for the time it took and that so much of my hard-earned money had to go for such things)*. As the higher-functioning residents would wander in after their meal, it was striking how many of them would focus on my checkbook or bills and comment, "I used to do that!" Often this would provoke a wistful reminiscence of personal habits or chores they used to perform, such as paying bills, doing errands, or organizing grocery shopping.

Sometimes they would begin to recount memories of their former daily working lives. It was never about the positions they held or what they had accomplished but the trivial details of the day-to-day… taking the subway… using a typewriter… going for a ham and cheese sandwich and a soda pop at the corner drugstore… the turning of the autumn leaves. There was always a sadness, nostalgia, and longing beneath this, although the person seemed excited by talking about it, as though in the swing of life once again in fantasy.

The irony was staggering. As children, we cannot wait to grow up and engage in the most tiresome activities of the adult world. In our desire to be just like Mommy and Daddy, we spend hours *playing*… at cooking, having to shave, going to work, cleaning, even getting into an argument with the auto repairman. Once grown, we then spend an appreciable amount of time wishing and imagining about getting away from these same monotonous and irksome responsibilities we so idealized during childhood. Now, in the nursing home, it was this same type of childlike glorification of commonplace, often annoying aspects of human experience that seemed evident among my frail elderly patients, especially because, like children, they were once again excluded from them. Many even commented upon the absurdity that they would long for those tasks they so resented at the time, such as having to work and pay bills.

The spiritual directive of gratitude and seeing the glass as half full is a very important one, both in the bigger picture and in the banal moments of our lives. We also need to focus more on the immediate moments. Each and every one is a gift of time. Today we endorse *living in the moment* as a desirable mindset, but the connotation is that of gratifying relaxation or lack of responsibility. There is an associated idea of pushing the envelope or excess, a kind of frantic doing it all now or maximum personal freedom... because tomorrow is not guaranteed.

In the popular attitude, *living in the moment* has also become glamorized, similar to the appeal of the road movies and long car trips, such as leisurely traveling across country without schedule or destination. The frame of mind is that of a dream and the youthful vantage point of an endless expanse with mortality a lifetime away. Everyday reality has been suspended in lieu of an intoxicating edge of adventure with anticipation of countless virgin roads to explore and potentialities around the next bend. This is not true *living in the moment* but *living in no moment* although it can definitely be thrilling or restorative to take off from time to time.

True *living in the moment* is about fullness and richness in our experience and the opportunity for learning and creating in the immediate focus of our lives, no matter in what situation we find ourselves *(whether pain or pleasure, a massage or a root canal)*. It is a mindfulness of what is going on around us as well as the feelings and sensations within ourselves. The song of a bird, the look of a stranger, a memory erupting from the distant past.

Spiritually committed individuals try to maintain an attitude of thankfulness, in at least the *opportunity* of every moment, if not the *actuality*. Paying bills may be irritating, but thankfully we are finding the money to do so. We may hate the monotony of cooking and doing dishes day after day, yet fortunately we are able to feed ourselves and our families. Having a root canal may promise a period of marked discomfort, even agony, but we are healthier and lucky to have dental care in the long run.

The tedium and tribulation of so much of what we do is part of the gift of living. This is not to say that we put on rose-colored glasses and stoically deny suffering and pain. What it means is the experience of any moment in time is the sum total of many factors, psychological feelings, and physical sensations. We may be in pain... but have love. We may *not* be in pain... and also *not* have love.

How we view the world affects how we experience the world. What this means is that our expectations and preconceptions create a filter for our experience, but that filter can always change. In every moment, there is the opportunity to look at things from an alternative perspective and to create a new reality from this point forward, no matter where we find ourselves. The spiritual instruction is that we learn to value all our experience. We may not like it, but we recognize there is value in it. If nothing else, this is because we are living and have another chance for a *new* moment and opportunity.

Learning to value experience is not blithe or vacuous denial. Rather, we recognize that all aspects of our experience serve a purpose. Even the most painful events or situations have value in what they teach us about ourselves and what is meaningful. They force us to grow and to expand our horizons and behavior. The dreary and onerous elements of life may also have value in what they provide in terms of steppingstones to other things, such as enhancing the quality of living for ourselves and our loved ones. Whether it's doing homework or laundry or grunt jobs in trying to move ahead in the corporate world, we should honor and take pride in such endeavors.

A grateful and appreciative focus on the mundane glories of living is the traditional reason for giving thanks before a meal. It focuses us on the simple blessings of having another day and our needs provided for. In doing so, we not only give thanks to God, but indirectly show

HOLE OR WHOLE?

appreciation to God's stewards and the effort and cooperation that went into the preparation of the dinner *(from the growing of the food to the setting of the table)*. The message is that these unassuming activities have value and, for those who did contribute, should be a source of dignity and pride. Even more indirectly, by giving thanks, we also are thanking God for the connectedness in *spirit* of us all.

When life is viewed as a gift and having value, this has certain psychological effects. First, is the realization that we have the choice and responsibility to make the most out of what our existence has to offer. That part is up to us. From a spiritual perspective, we are given resources and opportunities that, if pursued, tend to lead us in the direction of our greatest good, at the same time contributing to others or the world at large. Sometimes embedded in these opportunities are life lessons, which can be challenging. Some might say that the lessons and opportunities are one and the same. To live up to such gifts and blessings may require effort and stamina, even courage. Unfortunately, this may take more than some people are willing to give, generally to their emotional detriment.

Second, if life is viewed as a gift, then the individual begins to look for opportunities and blessings in the crevices of everyday living. Through an attitude of thankfulness, the plain, even monotonous, activities can be recast as sources of potential richness. It is a human tendency that, if we assign value to something, we then experience it as more valuable. So, if we determine that the incidental aspects of our lives have meaning, we will step back and look for ways to find them meaningful. This can have a cumulative, uplifting effect over time and may positively ripple out into other aspects of our lives.

Lastly, if life is viewed as a gift, there is the mandate to truly seize the day. The spiritually committed person honors the gifts of God by staying in touch with, not only how precious, but time-limited they really are. We connect, in the heart, with the ephemeral majesty of life. This means, not just taking advantage of obvious gifts that we have been given, but actively seeking to make the most out of every moment, even if it's just passively enjoying the experience of being in that moment in time.

Of course, nonbelievers also feel existential pressure and may just as passionately seek to make the most of time and opportunities that are available in life. The difference is that faith provides a spiritual as well as an existential mandate and introduces an emotional component because of the relationship with God. There is a sense of personal gratitude and responsibility, again similar to enjoying a special gift from a loved figure, perhaps in the manner of a child who is given something by a favorite grandmother. The gift is cherished, not solely for its intrinsic worth, whatever that may be, but because of the great love and meaning within the relationship. There is a desire to fully honor the gift and, by doing so, to show the strength and dedication of one's love in return.

For the person of faith, the motivation is clear. While we are in the midst of it – we are thankful to God for the gift and the privilege we have in living life.

10 How Barbie Got Fixed

In the therapy room, Katherine, pigtailed and seven years old, surveyed the bookcase full of worn and overused toys. Picking up a make-believe telephone, plastic stethoscope, and one-armed, naked Barbie doll, she climbed up on the desk to arrange her game. It looked like she was going to play "doctor." Katherine had been referred to the outpatient children's hospital because of problems at her most recent foster home. The victim of extreme sexual abuse, she had been prostituted between the ages of 3 and 5 by her crack addicted mother in exchange for drugs. There had been several foster placements since that time. Her behavior either could become wild and disruptive, so she would kick and throw, even bite, if she felt too contained, or she was provocatively sexual with the male family members.

After a month or so of therapy, we had the beginning of a trusting bond. Most sessions had been spent getting to know each other and taking walks all over the hospital campus, which helped to dissipate her anxiety. For Katherine, being alone with an adult, even a female therapist, was no doubt fraught with danger at some level. She loved to go to the empty hospital auditorium and perform dances and songs on the dark stage. This seemed to help her gain some control over her shattered world and traumatic bodily memories. Artistic expression is almost always a positive strategy for channeling negative emotions, but this seemed a bit too much like a torch singer. I wanted to get her to the point that she was able to play like a 7-year-old child. Choosing the Barbie in the therapy room was a step in the right direction.

Children's play can be so transparent *(this is exactly what play therapy is all about)*. Wearing the stethoscope like a necklace, Katherine began jabbing and poking the one-armed Barbie in several places, a look of grave concern on her young face. Shaking her head, she sighed and rolled her eyes in my direction. *(Barbie clearly was in bad shape.)* Then her eyes lit up, "I know." She pretended to dial the telephone, "7… 3… 4… 2… *(pause)* … 9… 1… 1…"

She shot me a masterful, reassuring look, as though to signal she had the situation handled, then spoke into the plastic phone, "Hello, God?" *(Pause.)* "Yes, this is Dr. Katherine. Yes… yes… God, it's nice to speak to you, too." Katherine cleared her throat as if to indicate there were serious matters to discuss. The plastic receiver to her ear, she plopped Barbie squarely down on her lap and sighed heartily.

"We need you down here, God." *(Pause.)* "Not today?… um-hum… um-hum… I see… Okay…" She began patting and fiddling with the Barbie, while testing its remaining arm, as though taking instructions in some advanced medical technique. "Um-hum… okay… um-hum… I see… Now, let me see if I got this right…" Squinting, she held the worn out doll up to the light and spoke into the phone, "Yep, all better. Thank you. Talk to ya' later, God."

Putting the plastic receiver down, Katherine hugged the broken doll and announced definitively, "Me and God fixed Barbie."

For the next month, Katherine began therapy sessions with the God game although the reasons she was calling varied as to her mood. Sometimes she would call on behalf of a doll or other toy. Sometimes it would be more direct with a problem or question or even to express anger at "that woman." *(Her teacher? Or foster mother? Or me? Perhaps, even her abusive real mother?)* The God game seemed to provide a net of safety, a way to express her feelings through play. Sometimes she became quite emotional and explicit, communicating *(to both God and me)* exactly what she was dealing with and feeling and how she needed to be helped.

How do we have a relationship with God? Katherine's therapy game actually gives a lot of information about how we can seek and relate to God in adult life. First, God was immediately available, but she was the one who initiated the direct contact. Second, she approached from a position of innocent and childlike respect for God's caring and greater wisdom. Third, although she understandably had a hard time trusting anyone in the human realm, she trusted God entirely. Fourth, God worked with her to heal Barbie, obviously believing in her ability to learn, and didn't just come down here to take care of everything. Fifth, there developed an ongoing relationship, in which Katherine sought counsel with God for many types of problems and used their relationship in the way she needed, sometimes for guidance and sometimes for her own emotional well-being. Finally, even though she still had only one arm, Barbie was fixed.

Different belief systems conceptualize a personal relationship with God in various ways. Sometimes a relationship is referenced directly; sometimes not. For me, the important psychological dynamic is that there is a real emotional attachment. This is what is powerful and meaningful. Spiritually committed people speak of experiencing and being sustained by feelings of actual *connection* and *trust*. They may describe an intimate one-on-one bond, which is structured in whatever way the person wants or needs to structure it. It is said that God, always wiser than we and the source of unconditional love, accepts us gladly, wherever we're at and in whatever way we want or need to communicate.

For some, this is very personal. They talk to God. For others, the relationship is nonverbal, indirect, or may be expressed through formal worship, but this doesn't mean it is any less intimate or strong. Spiritual knowledge and connection are always enhanced through contemplation, meditation, and prayer. Many also intimately connect through private devotion that is not formal, such as communing with nature in some way or through activities like long-distance driving or gardening or painting. All these allow the person to spend time in contemplation and pull towards internal reflection at the deepest levels. The important point is that, for the truly spiritually committed individual, faith is experiential. God is not just an idea but a presence in the person's life. There is a *living* relationship.

A sense of connection and approaching a relationship with God is a lot simpler than many people assume. I have repeatedly been asked: How does one begin? What does it feel like? It is difficult to explain as the feelings are deeper than words and likely unique to the individual's experience. Many probably already have an awareness of God without knowing it. I recall trying to communicate to a friend that, for me, the relationship is felt in the heart and there is a sense of presence that is always there.

"Oh, I have that," she said in a matter-of-fact manner although she still seemed perplexed as to what to do with it. If God's presence is felt, all the individual really has to do is listen, open up the heart, and emotionally engage. Perhaps, this is too vague or undefined. Maybe people just expect more, such as an immediate and astounding insight or transformation, obvious miracle, or front row seat in an altered reality. In the legacy of Hollywood, we look for our personal version of the voice booming from on high, the Big Experience! *(with orchestra and in Technicolor)*, the earth-shattering awareness in our own life, making it clear what is going on. But what we need to do is follow Katherine's example and just pick up the metaphorical phone.

Unless someone comes from a solid religious background, to seek contact with God seems difficult for so many to comprehend or even begin to conceive. There may also be surrounding anxiety. Within the secular context of our culture, this is a huge step to take. Believing in God is seen as a lack of intelligence, and communicating with God is associated with blatant psychosis. When people are truly interested in opening to such a relationship, this is also very intimidating. In this case, they generally are respectful of God as all-powerful, so it is a daunting prospect to approach God directly.

There may also be a sense of guilt or regret for not having believed in or attended to God for so long. I know when I started that first prayer, after rejecting faith for all my adult life, I felt ashamed on one level. It felt embarrassing as though I should deserve to beg or could be told to beg. Suddenly opening up my heart and assuming that God would listen seemed impertinent and demanding, as though I was asking to move into a house of a friend scorned twenty years ago and never called back, despite numerous voicemail messages left over the years to get together. Of course, I didn't have to beg. The sense of reception I felt was welcoming and joyful.

Initiating the relationship really has to do with the willingness of the individual to engage, to seek God. It is the willingness that is the essential and crucial step, the opening of one's heart. Many people would be surprised by how present, available, and loving God already is in their hearts and lives or consciousness, even if unacknowledged. As *spiritual beings*, all of us are inherently spiritually connected, whether we recognize and honor this or not.

God is already there for us *(and always there for us)*, but the commitment to a living relationship has to come from the individual. This means, first, give it a try. Second, hang in there. As we have discussed, there are so many ways that people can seek connection and communication. Again, this can be from formal prayer to becoming quiet within one's self to contemplation in the background of consciousness while going through the routine activities of daily existence. There are also religious services and education and many types of programs and spiritual practice. Sometimes group endeavors that are not specifically spiritual but have a higher purpose or involve altruistic activity can be where the person feels a profound sense of connection to God. Every person is unique and needs to find his or her own way. If the willingness is there, the promise is that way will be found.

As described previously, people who find God after a period of not having had such a relationship or even basic faith often report an immense divide in their experience. A river of demarcation, which signifies a period of transition and healing between the time they did not and did have God in their lives. This shift is generally one of tremendous power and also identified with an overwhelming feeling of gratitude. Usually there is a sense of being healed or saved or reborn, even if the belief system, to which the individual subscribes, does not specifically use such terms to describe what has occurred.

It feels like a miracle. God gets us right. For some, the change is externally apparent. They noticeably turn their lives around. A person may be able to get control over addiction for the first time. There may be a striking change in behavior or attitude or a sudden desire to take seriously responsibilities that were shunned in the past. For others, a positive transformation is felt more internally although almost always there is some observable change over time. I'm sure many of the people I had known for years wondered when I began painting and spending so much time alone.

The internal metamorphosis may not happen overnight or as a result of one incident although it can. Sometimes it is more gradual until at some point the person has the astounding realization of how much and how totally everything has seemed to change. It's a qualitative, not a quantitative difference. There is a sense of personal reorganization, an altered perspective, a different world. Often there is the startling impression that the negative cycle, whatever that means for the individual, has been broken, and life can now be whole.

Perhaps, this is why the hymn "Amazing Grace" *(John Newton, 1779)* has been so immensely popular for so many years. "I once was lost but now am found. Was blind, but now, I see…" This so clearly describes the feeling and the power. I know it sounds corny, but I have become emotionally overwhelmed, even broken down in tears of gratitude, on hearing these simple words. This hymn speaks so succinctly to how faith has affected me. I know I am not alone.

Still, while the individual may feel fundamentally transformed in the newfound spiritual relationship, it is not a magic wand. It's a *relationship*. It's not that everything-is-now-healed-good-as-new and everything-will-be-perfect-in-the-future type of change. This is not to say that miracles don't occur. They do everyday, and there is also the power of prayer, to which people of faith strongly attest.

The miracle of the newfound relationship with God *is* the newfound relationship with God. It's that simple. For the individual, there is the experience of a wondrous internal transition that occurs with faith, but this can be subtle. The person feels whole because God is now present, a companion and ally, a force in the individual's life. The new relationship becomes a potent source and resource of love, comfort, support, and guidance. The presence of God can be so powerful that everything seems changed. In the spirit of Katherine's God game,

Barbie gets fixed, *not* by being given a new arm, but rather through a new way of being.

The relationship with God is like no other. Psychologically, on the most basic level, there is the experience of another ever present and encouraging alliance within the individual's psyche. There may also be a sense of great, enveloping love. On the one hand, this relationship is limitless and unchanging in the sense of being permanent and eternal. This loving spiritual bond can never be broken although we may choose not to see it. On the other hand, the relationship is malleable and ideal in that it can be structured in the way the person needs. The presence of God may serve as a companion to stave off loneliness, a comfort or friend during hard times, a soothing and nurturing source, a guide, a protector, or all of the above.

People of committed faith may say they rarely or never feel alone. The awareness of God can be quite strong and present at the forefront of consciousness *(most often during prayer or meditation)* or recedes into the background because the individual is so immersed in the flow of life. Sometimes the connection is only felt *(or most keenly)* during times of trouble, but the potential to access and connect with God is always there when you need it. Emotionally, this can provide a comforting backdrop, a sense of sustenance, supportive love, and encouraging pride as though from a glowing parent or friend, an enthusiastic coach or cheerleader in one's corner. This spiritual bond is immensely healing and nurturing for everyone but particularly for those who feel isolated, alienated, or unloved in their human lives.

There is the popular expression of "being there" for someone. This means that one person is willing to put his or her own concerns aside to support another who is going through a difficult time. This is one of the most precious gifts that one individual can give to another. It is this type of feeling, only more so, that spiritual people speak of when the relationship with God is solid and a dynamic presence. The support and love are complete and unwavering. This relationship can provide an atmosphere of emotional bedrock and safety net, a sense of *spiritual* womb, in which the person feels not only sustained and bolstered during the rough times but may be nurtured and encouraged, such as to take constructive risks and try new things.

In other words, God becomes and remains our *primary caretaker* once we allow this to occur. What does this mean? From a practical point of view, the caretaking bond can be an unbroken and unlimited resource of emotional anchor, guidance, and unconditional love for the individual in a very real way. We allow God to take care of us. God is not a remote, intellectual assumption that there is someone up there who's in charge. A spiritual caretaking relationship means there is an intimate and vital connection, a constant, harmonious, and loving presence in our experience. At the same time, this doesn't mean that the relationship with God exists for our personal need fulfillment or to provide an endless supply of whatever our version is of happy lollipops, protection from human pain, or blanket absolution from guilt and responsibility.

From a psychological perspective, our relationship with God, as primary caretaker, is again similar to that of a child to a loving and protective parent. We may finally feel filled up in the sense of limitless love and support as though from the ideal mother or father we never had or *could* have. Our parents may have loved and wanted to protect us and provide the best for us *(as much as any parents on the planet)*. Or not. Parents are human beings. God is Divine, all-knowing, our Creator, and can provide the ideal bond or fulfill the specific need. Some might even say that the bond with God is the only possible relationship of complete and sustained unconditional love, which most of us crave, even as adults. It is here, in faith, that we can have it. This caretaking relationship can be such a thankful haven, again creating a sense of *spiritual* womb.

But parenting is *not* just about love and support. The ideal caretaking parent is one who also guides and protects us, including in ways that we do not always understand from our childlike position. A truly caretaking relationship is a loving but inherently unequal one. As children, we not only are loved but entirely dependent upon the greater authority and knowledge of the caretaker. This is also true in the relationship with God. A spiritual caretaking relationship requires that the individual accept that the existence of a Higher Power means just that. God *is* the Higher Power. We can be receptive but not equal in that relationship.

At the same time, while the spiritual bond is unlike any other, there is also the sense of reciprocity and exchange that is critical in most relationships. Like any relationship, developing and maintaining intimate spiritual connection takes trust and devotion. If we commit and attend to the relationship with God, we strengthen the source of ultimate good in our consciousness and lives. This is similar to what occurs in an attitude of thankfulness. To *give* is to *receive*. People of faith often have a clear sense that, whenever they give to or serve God in some way, they receive great benefit in return. Like a good parent, God is always potentially there for us, but it is by our giving that we appreciate this more fully and strengthen the bond between us.

One example of giving is regular spiritual practice, however this is engaged in by the individual. This not only allows the presence of God directly into a person's life, but practice shows devotion and is an expression of love. By spending a piece of one's time and attention in activities of worship, contemplation, meditation, or prayer, the individual tends to, nurtures, and reinforces the caretaking spiritual bond. As in any relationship, there is bound to be some work or discipline involved. Again, to *give* is to *receive*. Taking time for spiritual devotion generally results in an enhancement and uplifting of internal feelings that last far beyond the devotional practice.

This is why so many religions advocate taking time out each day to engage in prayerful or meditative devotion. On a day-to-day basis, most of us spend most of our time and attention in the psychological and social world. This is as it should be. We are *human* beings living on the *physical* plane. There are those who have committed to a life of contemplation and worship, which is their calling in life. For most of us, it is not. We are supposed to be engaged in and supporting the unity of *spirit* in the mainstream world... raising and teaching children... developing knowledge and expertise... providing support for our fellow human beings... interacting and sharing with others. To have that daily space of quality devotional time is anchoring and healing. It celebrates and reinforces the spiritual bond in our lives and honors our Creator, who has given us life and makes it all possible.

Optimally, the *connection* with God is present and directs us like a guiding and loving parent in the background most of the time. There are also periods when the connection may seem more remote than others, even when the relationship is strong. In general, the stronger the spiritual caretaking relationship becomes, the more the individual perceives and seeks to serve God through the activities of living in the physical world. Typically, once spiritually awakened, a person will begin to look for greater purpose beyond the *self* and may feel the presence and guidance of God in activities that are associated with that purpose. As the individual goes through daily life, there may also develop a feeling of greater connection and desire for service in interactions with others. People of faith *feel* the presence of God through these interactions. As I discovered, the feeling of spiritual connection seems to expand out and begins to manifest and be experienced in various aspects of life beyond formal worship or private contemplation.

On one level, the relationship with God can give extraordinary comfort, connection, and guidance on a day-to-day basis. On another, it unleashes a host of complications. Like any relationship, once we agree to depend on the reality of another, we lose some control over our own grasp of reality and ourselves. When a person commits to a relationship with God, there is duty and accountability implied. Like being in a family, it's not only about you any longer. And, if we are all *connected* and spiritual brothers and sisters, this raises the question as to what degree am I my brother's or sister's keeper? To what extent, do I have to follow Higher guidance and accept limits to my behavior (*i.e., stay within the God rails*)?

Because of all these issues, a caretaking spiritual relationship is a difficult premise for many people to accept in the contemporary era, even if they are interested in spirituality. This may be one of the reasons why God as an actual Higher Power is sometimes left out of the modern spiritual equation. First, a sense of intimate connection, a true relationship, is simply incomprehensible, even threatening, to many. The idea of truly feeling an internal presence arising beyond one's self is just too out there or spacey, if not spooky, to most in our physically oriented world. Yet I have been told by numerous people that, as occurred with my friend, they do feel a presence although hadn't necessarily associated this with God.

Second, even for people who might be spiritually inclined, a greater resistance may come from the fact that the relationship with God is not interdependent or equal, which is 180 degrees from what we are taught to value and seek in contemporary life. The bond with God is *not* based on compatibility or respect for boundaries. It is *not* about making everyone feel good above all else. It is *not* the mutual fulfillment of the partners' individual needs. It is *not* reciprocal in the sense of two entities that "click" in a big way but also "do their own thing." The relationship is submissive and receptive on the part of the individual. There is a major imbalance of power. At best, such power differential tends to bring some measure of ambivalence or is regarded as unhealthy in this day and age. For many, it would be frightening to invite this type of unbalanced relationship into one's mind or heart or consciousness, even though it is presumed to offer great rewards.

Modern people especially find dependent, unequal relationships difficult and unappealing. We are taught, above anything else, to be independent and autonomous. To be receptive, even too reliant on another, evokes the identity and position of a child, which most of us shed long ago. The idea of someone else in charge provokes feelings that we are no longer our own person but rather smothered or controlled, meek, and lacking in value. There is the image of being forced to live by another's rules, consumed by another's needs, and rewarded or punished by the judgments or expectations of a more powerful other. Most of us in adult life do find ourselves in some relationships that are unequal, such as with a boss or spouse or even a parent. We generally don't like it.

As adults, we usually do have the sense, no matter how much we may *not* feel in control of ourselves and our lives, that we do have some degree of independence and freedom that we did not have as children. We also tend to feel, as adults, that we have the capacity to make the best choices for ourselves if given the chance. Even if it turns out *not* to be the best choice, at least it's *our* choice. We feel this, even if others think we actually do depend on others too much or can't make the best decisions for ourselves. It is simply a human tendency to feel that we do have control, at least over our own hearts and minds *(even when we don't)*. It is easy to see why there might be resistance to the idea of a dependent, caretaking relationship with God.

Plus, it gets even more unnerving. The relationship with God occurs at the deepest levels of our being. There is, not only a sense of unconditional love, but God accepts us wherever we're at and in complete honesty. To enter into such a relationship exposes us in an intimate place that we are not used to sharing. It pushes past a boundary of privacy that most people never go beyond. To enter into a dependent relationship makes us feel vulnerable anyway, and we have learned this is to be avoided at all costs in modern living. We tend to be afraid of vulnerability, weakness, and tenderness. We also fear showing too much of ourselves.

This is one of the things that seems so wrong and unbalanced today. Most people do have a deep and often very delicate, emotional side but tend to suppress this so much of the time. As a therapist, I have been privy to so many painful, trusting, tearful moments. The sharing of fragile, heartfelt dreams. Humiliating secrets and petty fantasies. Ravages of love and loss… scorn and disappointments… remorse and pride. Feelings of penetrating guilt and regret. Underneath, we're mostly the same. There is a more meaningful, softer dimension to life and ourselves. Underlying, what seems longed for by most people are loving and loyal relationships, kind treatment from others, a world where goodness means something and in which we, as individuals, are accepted and appreciated for what we do and who we really are.

It is this vulnerable and often confused part within that we begin to share with God and, surprisingly, it's okay. We find that God does accept us and love us unconditionally, wanting to take us by the hand

and invest in each and every one of us. As human beings, as children of God, we are loved and embraced, should we allow ourselves to be so, no matter how flawed or vulnerable we may feel. God knows our flaws and vulnerabilities and loves us anyway.

In a spiritual caretaking relationship, vulnerability goes with the territory although this is such an uncomfortable place for most of us to be. Yet, as a result of honestly sharing at this level, the relationship also leads to feelings of wholeness and acceptance that the individual has never experienced before. We are sharing who we really are and opening up a path of truth, authenticity, and potential, going forward. Especially for those who struggle with major holes or dysfunction in their human lives, this can feel life-saving.

It is also at our emotional depths and in a context of honesty that such acceptance actually means something. We may fool most of the people most of the time, but we don't fool God, who sees beyond our surface persona and the mask we project to the outside world. It is the totality of who we are that is accepted, which makes us feel whole. It is also within the spiritual relationship that we can have that sense of specialness that we all yearn for and tends to be so lacking in modern life. Like the mother who cherishes the distinctive attributes and essence of each of her children, God loves all the children, but each is also loved and enjoyed for that special something that makes us different and who we uniquely are.

This is why a caretaking relationship with God can be such a thankful haven, creating a sense of a *spiritual* womb. In so many ways, we feel truly loved.

11 Refuge In The Up Escalator

For the person of faith, the spiritual caretaking bond holds out a *lifeline*. It offers a refuge, a source of solace and reinforcement during difficult times.

There is a famous Christian poem of unknown authorship "Footprints (in the Sand)." This captures the idea that there is another support and resource through a spiritual commitment. The poem tells the story of someone who dreams of having died and, with God, is reviewing the course and journey of this person's life. It becomes evident that during most of the journey there are two sets of footprints in the sand, signifying that God was walking alongside.

Yet, during the most challenging periods, there is only one set of footprints. Surprised and feeling abandoned, the individual questions God as to why there is only one set of footprints in the sand. God explains there was no abandonment. The person was being carried during the roughest times. This is exactly the impression that people of faith describe once they open up to God and allow faith into their lives. God carries us if we allow it.

How do we react to life's minefields and losses? How do we deal with emotional pain? Human suffering is universal, which doesn't diminish it. There are moments and periods for all of us when the world seems too big or too cruel and painfully disappointing. We can face life-altering bereavement and tragedy, crisis and upheaval over the course of our lives. It is just at these junctures and in the midst of psychological storms that people of faith turn to God. Faith may become stronger, and a person might even be drawn to faith for the very first time. On the other hand, sometimes it is in response to stress or turmoil that the strength of faith is tested, to the point that the individual becomes angry with God.

It is said that "Everybody gets the blues." People who are distressed may actually hurt. The world tends to look dark, foreboding, distant, or fraught with terror. Human contact becomes aversive. The future appears bleak. A bout of depression or anxiety, even if brief or temporary and quickly snapped out of, for the duration can seem to weaken or destroy our *life force* and self-esteem. At the extreme, an episode of serious depression can lead to such despair and immobilization that an individual is unable to get out of bed or take a shower, and it becomes physically dangerous if the person stops eating or because of the potential for suicide.

I know about the black hole of depression. In the months following my father's and sister's deaths, I crashed, splintering in bizarre and previously unimaginable ways. It seemed that I had become encapsulated in a heavy, sticky deadness that made the slightest task an insurmountable effort. Anything other than smoking cigarettes seemed to require energy and initiative I simply did not have. A previously exemplary student, I rarely attended class. Books and cigarette butts next to me on my unmade bed, I would stay up all night in a numbed state, with the intent to complete the entire semester's reading. The pages blurred, at times too heavy to turn.

It was as though I had fallen into an endless black hole that was empty and cold, perforated by incredible longing just to see my father and sister again. Hovering above was a claustrophobic blanket of apprehension. Sometimes my fragile psyche appeared to tip, and the anxiety would become unbearable. For a few minutes, which seemed like an eternity, my heart raced uncontrollably until I was certain that at eighteen I was suffering cardiac arrest and going to die. My hands would become clammy. Cold sweat emanated throughout my body; at some point, the terror culminating in exhaustion.

This is the negative side of the human condition. Either on a chronic basis or for a relatively brief space of time, emotional pain is an excruciating inner journey, whether or not we have faith. I was lucky as my depression and panic attacks resolved in about six months and never returned. In the years since, I have heard so many similar stories of black holes and sat with people who were in the midst of their own or struggling to psychologically tread water amid terrifying, crippling anxiety. I have also seen people traumatized and trying to extricate from the rabid grasp of PTSD symptoms, which can turn daily existence into a hair shirt of fear for a period of time.

Sometimes it's not the big stuff but just dealing with life that is so emotionally formidable. We can be overwhelmed with negative feelings or get twisted up through bad coping mechanisms, such as addiction *(usually arising in the first place in an attempt to short-circuit the emotional pain)*. In my own life since adolescence, both before and after my episode of serious depression, my sensitive nature could have me bouncing all over the place. In reaction to some discomforting exchange or sense of my own inadequacy, I could end up spiraling down in a frantic tailspin to a place of self-deprecation and low depths from time to time, a kind of mini-depression or black hole, lasting a few hours to a few days.

As I became spiritually awakened, I began to notice that I was able to handle things better as I reacted to those nuances of life that had formerly been so challenging. This wasn't intentional nor did I even think about it, even though I tend towards the obsessively self-analytical side. Yet somehow I had let that go. Then I did begin to notice. Over a relatively short space of time, maybe a year, it seemed that I wasn't getting depressed anymore.

Oh, I could still get sad or discouraged, which is never welcome nor fun, but the dips into that dark, self-deprecating hole became fewer and farther between and then dissipated altogether. I never really submerged that far again. I might become worried, sometimes rationally and sometimes irrationally so. *(Who doesn't?)* I've been overcome with choking and visceral grief when someone I loved has died. There are times when I've felt simply too worn down and beleaguered and just not up to handling the ways of the world, at least until tomorrow. But I stopped beating myself up about it.

Was life becoming more manageable? In the day-to-day, I could still feel vulnerable and apprehensive, demoralized or wee, but all this was tolerable and would pass, particularly if I could just let the feelings play out. I could still react strongly to some external situation or disturbing interaction from time to time, but the rough passage, however tumultuous, felt more superficial. I learned that, with my new coping strategies that appeared to be part of faith, my negative feelings did seem to sputter and run out of gas, and I was back up and running on the positive track in a relatively short span of time.

Of course, it wasn't *(and isn't)* all rose-colored glasses, but there had been a monumental shift. For the first time, I seemed to be able to accept my negative reactions as just that, nasty but understandable emotions precipitated by the challenges and realities of living. In doing so, they seemed less severe. There was also less involvement with my ego and self-worth during low moments or periods. In the black hole, everything merges and feels sucked in by the negativity, but now I was able to say, "This is life," instead of, "This is me, a loser." I just wasn't getting sucked in anymore. It was ironic. All those years

I had wanted equanimity and had unsuccessfully tried to achieve it. Now that it was happening, I was barely aware of it.

It even seemed this shift took it one step further. To some degree, I began to embrace, even prize, my sensitive swings. Now that the lows were not so devastating, I learned that I could feel deeply, even poignantly, and there was richness in the intensity of my feelings, as though experientially true to the colors on the canvas of living. For instance, discouragement might lead to a period of melancholy but not depression, and I was able to ride its various tones, which spoke to a depth and mystery in life and were even plaintively exquisite in a bittersweet way. In the past, in anticipation of tumbling into the black hole, I would have been scrambling to get back on top above life's messiness far too quickly. Again, my mood didn't have the self-esteem involvement that I had struggled with in the past. Emotions were now my feelings but not the entirety of who I was.

Why was this happening? The obvious answer was that this was an unanticipated consequence of turning to God. Why? Through prayer and extended periods of meditative reflection, particularly through my painting, there did seem to be a resource of emotional sustenance and consolation that I had never experienced previously. Looking back, I can now see that sense of subtle *connection*, so soothing and embracing, became the sanctuary to which I would retreat with my wounded or weary psyche. Without realizing it, I was beginning to depend on that *spiritual* womb of love and renewal, in which I could wait out or go through whatever I needed to in the psychological realm. *(Was I being carried by God?)*

During periods of upset, sometimes the need for emotional refuge was great. Yet my relationship with God had become such a part of my day-to-day reality that there also seemed to be an inoculation of replenishment, a kind of cushion against stress, through my spiritual practice alone. With this new infusion of support, it seemed that I just couldn't fall as far as I had in the past. There had also developed a purposeful focus in my life that hadn't been there previously. Instead of obsessing so much about myself and reacting to others around me, I was able to remain centered on the immediate task and activity, whether painting or working or interacting in a social setting. Part of this seemed to result from a feeling of greater spiritual direction, based on the increasing insight that every moment is an opportunity to explore and share in God's gifts. My life had become so full with just too much to do to obsess about myself too much.

It was also at this time that I began to notice and understand the impact of faith on the people that I worked with. In one aspect of my practice, I performed psychological evaluations of people from all over the globe. Many would not ordinarily have sought therapy but were being evaluated because something distressing or traumatic had occurred which resulted in a lawsuit. Sometimes what was alleged to have occurred was life-changing. Sometimes it was petty. Whatever had happened, what was striking was that the reaction seemed overall less severe in those with faith, no matter what their religious background. It became apparent that people of genuine faith tended to relate a sense of sustenance and positive mindset that was extremely beneficial. Ironically, this wasn't good for their case *(since they weren't that "damaged" in a legal sense)*, but it was great for their lives.

That didn't mean that there wasn't torment. There was plenty. Yet, as I evaluated people struggling with inner turmoil or depression, there was something positive and something more. At times it would seem as though both the negative *(depressive)* and positive *(spiritual)* states were present together, almost like two different levels of consciousness, simulcast on a split screen. At other times, there was the feeling of conflict, like the cartoon of the shoulder devil and angel in consciousness. It was as though the angst or bleakness of the moment was battling the detachment of the broader and wiser perspective. As long as the wiser perspective was there, it seemed the bleakness could never really fully or permanently take hold.

I also noticed similar patterns in working with frail elderly people, for whom despairing feelings are common. People with strong faith, on the whole, seemed to do better. They still got depressed or felt lonely and suffered with mental and physical pain like everyone else, but there was also a sense of another dimension, an anchor. As long as they could maintain their commitment and connection to God, they seemed to bounce back relatively quickly and to remain as vital, interactive, and involved in life as their limitations would allow. Since many of my clients were from a generation that unabashedly embraced old timey religion, they were often quite verbal about the impact of their spiritual beliefs on how they were coping. Sometimes during sessions, it seemed as though there were three of us in the room (*myself, the client, and Jesus*). This always got an affirmative chuckle when I shared such impressions with my clients.

By its nature, faith is an antidote to depression, anxiety, and other negative emotions, at least to some degree. The perspective of faith is inherently hopeful and optimistic. The glass is definitely half full. The spiritual worldview teaches how to maximize the positive and offers, not only a broader view, but a fresh start, no matter what the issue or situation. There is also a clear directive to be staunchly resolute in faith, to remain strong in bad times as well as good, and to focus on the lesson, opportunity, and higher spiritual values as much as possible, rather than getting caught up in the emotional rapids than can so easily pull us down into crisis and despair.

Even for the person of committed faith, this can be a struggle. In the midst of depression or any negative feeling, it generally seems to overtake us. Even in a fleeting case of the blues, we can find ourselves in a painfully catastrophic and dark place. We not only lose sight of reason, but we become identified with the undermining emotion. For years, therapists have described how people regress to childlike states during anger outbursts or episodes of demoralization. We are no longer our adult selves but become like wounded, abused, or vulnerable children. The nasty emotions also become the totality of our experience. The depression, anger, or fear seems to run through our veins *(and brains)*, poisoning every cell. We feel out of control, cannot see beyond the immediacy of the moment, and are drowning in the negative feelings.

As a psychologist and in my own life, I've noticed that it is when discouragement turns to pessimism and despair that the individual is in real trouble emotionally. People can tolerate pain if they know there is an end in sight. Once the hopelessness creeps in, there is a spiraling down psychologically. Again, there is the perception of a black hole or tunnel with no way out, and then they become trapped by their own hopelessness. It's a vicious and self-devastating cycle. Even with less acute problems, such as chronic low self-esteem, there tends to be deadening sense of futility. On some level, the individual has absolutely become convinced that nothing can ever change. This isn't the black hole of despair, but the hole is still there *(less deep perhaps)* in an attitude of bitter and stoic complacency, which can be exceptionally damaging. The person is stuck... with the expectation of never-ending rejection, self-loathing, lack of success, hopes dashed, and slavish hypersensitivity to the reactions of others.

So it follows, since a perspective of faith is an inherently hopeful one, that the more an individual is able to hold onto this mindset, the more reinforced he or she will be against the poisonous bleakness of negative emotional experience. As long as the light of God is present in one's consciousness, it can never become quite as dark again. The person may suffer other symptoms associated with the depression or anxiety and even go in and out of the despairing state because the negative feelings can be so strong. At least with faith, there is a sense that a *lifeline* is available, whether the individual is able to grab onto it or not.

This, in itself, is very powerful. Just knowing the *lifeline* is there. The really devastating part of negative emotion is that it overtakes us and tends to start a downward and dangerous spiral into disconsolate depression, paralyzing fear, or destructive action. We get so caught up in the self-sabotaging illusion that begins contaminating our consciousness, which is that the negative feelings are the entirety of who we are and can be. Having a *lifeline* of spiritual Truth and connection, however thin, *(again, just knowing that it's available)* can help the person hold on and stops the spiraling out of control.

During distressed or agonizing passages, there may also be an active attempt to reconnect, to find a way to catapult off the *psychological* level and return more quickly to a sense of being once again strongly aligned with God. The most obvious way to do so is through prayer, meditation, or solitary reflection, all of which tend to take us to a different internal place. As with so many aspects of faith, it is not just the optimistic assumptions that are so powerful but the *experience* of the spiritual caretaking bond. That internal sense of anchor and love tends to be accompanied by calming feelings and bodily sensations *(such as tranquility and warmth)*. These may counteract and disrupt the lower psychological experience of anxiety or depression to some degree, including on the bodily level. It is also interesting that during prayer or meditation or however an individual finds spiritual connection, there tends to be the perception of going deep within *beyond* emotion or to an elevated level *above* emotion.

For people of faith, all these factors are important in dealing with turmoil and suffering. The *spiritual* level, which is the place of sanctuary with God, doesn't fix or take away the pain. It holds out a *lifeline* that at least allows us to hang on or to see the light. From a spiritual perspective, depression, anxiety, and other negative emotions reflect a *psychological* state that is part of the human condition. This is something we go through, a rough spot on our journey. It is never part of our basic identity as a *spiritual being*, as a child of God. Even if someone has a genetic, recurrent depressive disorder, this is viewed as a specific, *psychological* challenge that the individual is facing in life. It is never a reflection of that person's real worth, adequacy, or purpose. Within a spiritual viewpoint, our true essence and potential is our *spiritual being*. Depression and anxiety or loss of emotional control can never be part of this but occur only in the *psychological* and *physical* realms.

For people of faith, as I observed with my clients and myself, there is the impression of operating on two levels at once *(the spiritual and psychological)*. This is always true in our existence as human beings. We do hold dual citizenship in two different universes. Yet the separation between these two kingdoms, so to speak, and the qualitative distance between them can be particularly magnified in times of emotional turbulence when the psychological realm feels so devastating and unmanageable.

So, on the surface, the *psychological* reaction may be overriding depression or anxiety, which hurts, and the individual feels out of control. The *spiritual* perspective deep within is wiser, comforting and seems to speak the reassuring Truth that… "It's okay. The painful feelings exist on the surface. This is part of being a human being. You need to feel these emotions at the surface, psychological level, and when it is time, they will pass. You will move to a new place and begin a new phase of the journey." The spiritually oriented person tries to hold onto this Truth while experiencing the negative emotions.

In my own life as my faith has deepened, I have certainly noticed a change in how I deal with emotional upheaval. There really is a sense of living on two levels at once: the *spiritual* level of my connection with God and the *psychological* level of emotional experience. The spiritual tends to feel more underlying or in the background, except during prayer or meditation or intense creative activity. I know this is as it should be. We are *spiritual beings* living a *human* life. Most of the time, the two levels feel in sync, even enhance each other, at least when life is going smoothly.

It is during periods of emotional pain or crisis that the *psychological* level negatively takes over and can be quite strong, even though I never dip as low as I used to. Still, it's not always easy getting back to the *spiritual* level, including through prayer or meditation, which is always the first line of defense. Sometimes I can't get there… for awhile. The emotion is just too much, too agitating or distracting, but at least I have the knowledge that the *spiritual* level is there and that God is available. This holds out hope and the all-important *lifeline*, even if the emotion is out of control and seems to be winning in the immediate moment.

This hope or *lifeline* is the stopgap and prevents the negativity from going further. This is probably why my dark bouts of mini-depression seemed to eventually disappear once I opened to a relationship with God. I just wasn't being dragged down into the emotional depths as I had previously. I now had that *lifeline* to elevate above or beyond emotion, at some point to reconnect to the higher level. Until that time, at least I could just hold on. In the midst of distress, I could tell myself, "I've been there before and I will find it again, maybe not now although I'd like to, but sometime." With this understanding, I could reassure myself that I am simply on a painful detour, but I know I *will* be returning at some point to my *spiritual* home.

In other words, spiritually I know better, no matter how distraught or upset I become. There will be a way to get *above* or *beyond* it, to return to the sanctuary, at least eventually, even if I can't at that specific moment. Sometimes there is a sense of being held by God while I work through the emotional rapids on the physical plane. Sometimes I become so overcome amidst those rapids that I have to struggle back to that sense of sanctuary. At other times I feel I am knowingly choosing to stay in the psychological fray, to feel sorry for myself, to wallow. It never feels good, and clearly I am prolonging the pain by being self-pitying. I even know this at the time but still persist. Sometimes the psychological urge can be that strong.

It is important to point out, while the *higher* spiritual bond does provide a place of sanctuary, love, and support that is so essential during upsetting times, it is not solely about emotional comfort. Within the caretaking relationship, God leads us. What this means is that, within the emotional ordeal, there is information that we can use for guidance as to the broader trajectory of our lives. So it is essential that the person of faith reflect upon the meaning of the depression, anxiety, or negative reaction although this analysis is very different from what goes on in traditional counseling or psychotherapy.

From a spiritual perspective, since life is viewed as a journey and we learn from all experiences, emotional distress serves to focus, teach lessons, or provide a discernible signal that it is time for adjustment or change. The spiritually oriented person wants to know what the depression or anxiety or tumult means beyond the psychological or precipitating factors. What am I learning here? Or supposed to learn? Is this an indication it's time for redirection? What role does this period of crisis or upset play in my spiritual growth?

This spiritual analysis is entirely different from the traditional psychological approach, which tries to understand the root cause, often going back to childhood. The spiritual perspective is always present and future-oriented. What am I learning *now*? Where do I need to go *from here*? The spiritual view is also the journey. So the objective is not to put the person back together because the *spiritual being* was never affected by the depression, anxiety or turmoil to begin with. The goal is to get the person headed in the right direction *spiritually* and on his or her way. Once the lesson of the depression or anxiety or crisis is apprehended, the individual can then move on. There is no need to dwell in the negative feelings, to try to understand them, or to work them through. Just move beyond when it is time to do so *(i.e., once the spiritual growth or guidance has occurred).*

The spiritual concepts of *journey* and *lesson* and *purpose* also help counteract distressing feelings when we are in the midst of them. *(We will be talking about these at length in a future chapter.)* First, as long as one believes in spiritual *purpose*, at least a mandate to serve God, there is always a reason, a light at the end of the tunnel, even if we cannot see it. We have a *purpose* beyond ourselves, which is always more powerful than our individual needs and frustrations if we allow it to be so and blossom in our lives.

Second, the idea of *purpose* reframes the episode of emotional pain. There's a reason for this misery, which could actually prove to be worthwhile. We learn something from such experiences, perhaps a very painful lesson, but there is always opportunity in learning *(although maybe we would prefer to be ignorant)*. Lastly, since *purpose* is a lifelong endeavor and God works in ways incomprehensible to human beings, a spiritual perspective fosters patience. It takes the long view and addresses the larger picture. How things play out are at least partially beyond our control and can eventuate in entirely unexpected outcomes. The person of faith learns to accept this reality and may even become used to it to some degree.

So the positive part here is that the spiritually committed individual tries to withhold judgment before exploding into a full-blown emotional reaction. On the deeper level, one's inner voice may be saying, "Hold on. This may not be the entire story. Maybe I should wait a bit and see." This strategy of patience does put the emotional brakes on to an extent. The person may react, even strongly, but is more likely to remain somewhat open and resist the tendency to get trapped in the immediate, encroaching darkness or rage or fear or crisis of the moment with only bleak prospects of more of the same. Again, there's a kind of *lifeline*.

All that being said, in dealing with negative emotions *(i.e., depression, anger, anxiety)*, there is a complication for people of faith that nonbelievers do not have to deal with. Depression and other types of emotional pain may be seen as a crisis or test of faith. For a spiritual individual, depression, fear, or negativity of any kind may be quite threatening *spiritually*. Why would this be? What seems to happen is that the more the negative emotion takes over, the farther away the person feels from God and faith.

To use a cliché image, the spiritual level of experience is the *Up* escalator. Depression or other negative emotion is the *Down*. You can't be on both escalators at once although you can wear yourself out by jumping back and forth. At some point, you may also find yourself trapped firmly on the *Down* escalator, essentially traveling in the wrong direction and further from God.

Depression, in particular, endorses a negative mindset *(i.e., seeing the glass as half empty)*. This outlook more than any other makes us harshly question the benevolence and wisdom of God. If depression gets to the point of despair, this may feel like a repudiation of hope and God's love, in fact, a lapse of faith. Similarly, too much anxiety contradicts the stance of yielding control to God as primary caretaker. So, although the person of faith may have an easier time handling the *psychological* aspects of depression or anxiety, the crisis in faith that occurs is of major *spiritual* concern.

It is also not uncommon for spiritual people to become angry at God when they feel depressed or distraught. In the throes of depression, rage, or fear, we can also cause immense hurt and pain for ourselves and others. In the wreckage of emotional turmoil, people can feel even more demoralized, rageful, despairing, or self-rebuking. This may get to a point that the spiritual person feels abandoned by God. Sometimes there is even a feeling of being punished by God, which can uptick the anger, ambivalence, and questioning even further. All this is very distressing for the person of faith. Just as when disruption occurs in any close relationship, this can cause guilt, fear, avoidance, and additional emotional anguish. As in any relationship, denial of the problem only makes the situation worse.

When a person of faith becomes angry or upset, even dissatisfied, in the relationship with God, it is important to examine and explore that relationship and why and from where these feelings arise. Like any relationship in trouble, outside guidance, perhaps counseling with a spiritual mentor, may be helpful. Direct confrontation of the issues between the two parties is also likely necessary and could involve getting into areas not previously traveled. If someone is angry or depressed and feels there is a problem in the relationship with God, this needs to be dealt with, with God, in whatever way the individual chooses to do that. Naturally, for a person of faith, this can be quite an intimidating prospect.

On the other hand, the relationship with God is unbreakable. It can handle whatever it needs to.

12 Light Thy Fire

Among my earliest memories, there was one incident at three years old that I held onto for many years. This seemed to reflect a major conflict in my identity. Artistically sensitive, even as a toddler, I was attracted to the brightest, most vibrant of colors. Once discovered, my crayons became a magic bag o' tricks to create breathtaking trees, flowers, people, and fairies out of the lifeless forms in my coloring books. All the reds, purples, and blues were so pretty. The hard part was just staying in the lines. It was with this sense of wonderment about the transformative power of crayons that I hatched the plan to light up the family living room by coloring in the beige flowers on our plain brown couch. I was going to make it so beautiful.

The opportunity came when my parents went out for the evening. Once I explained to the babysitter that it would be fine with my mother to smear crayons all over the cloth sofa, the coast was clear for my creativity. She had seemed perplexed but oddly didn't question the truth of the 3-year-old *(I don't think she ever babysat again)*. Diligently and carefully *(these lines were also hard)*, I filled in the bland flowers with the most brilliant hues I could find. All the colors of the rainbow. With swelling pride and thrilled anticipation *(as I surveyed my masterpiece)*, I awaited my parents' return. This was bound to be an exciting surprise.

Needless to say, the reaction was not what I expected. During my punishment *(I either had to spend extra time in my room or go without dessert)*, I remember a sense of stunned and hurtful confusion. I had wanted to please them. Plus, it didn't make sense. Just a few weeks earlier I had gloriously surprised my parents with another crayon project by meticulously copying the block letters of my name from a birthday card into my coloring book. When my intellectual parents saw that their daughter had written her name at age three, they were ecstatic *(I think I got extra dessert that night for my potential genius)*.

For the next week, the grand event of my precociously writing my name was glowingly talked about around the house and trumpeted to the neighbors. Their 3-year-old daughter had written her name! This was why, from my young perspective, after the couch fiasco I was hard-pressed to understand how writing my name had garnered such attention and applause while magnificently redecorating the couch *(a much larger and more difficult project, from my perspective)* had caused the opposite reaction.

The couch incident became symbolic of a dichotomy that persisted into my adult life between art and academics. In my family, academic accomplishment *(whether it was precociously learning to write one's name or getting a Ph.D.)* was unquestionably what was valued and the direction I was led. It wasn't that art was looked down upon, but to succeed in an intellectual profession was considered optimal. It meant that you were a winner in the world in which I grew up. Like many university brats, I spent much of my adolescence alternately complying with and acting out against the strong pressure to excel in school. Any artistic interest seemed to fall by the wayside.

I also couldn't draw or thought I couldn't. When I see those crayoned pictures from my early years, it does seem there was a potential beyond a child's random scribbling that could have been developed. It wasn't. It also had been communicated early on that the smart path was to only go after that at which you could really excel. As time went on and I worked through the adolescent rebellion around the academics and eventually became a psychologist, I wasn't dissatisfied.

I loved psychology, but there was this other nagging voice within that sought expression. I danced around it for years by getting involved in crafts and creative writing or endlessly painting and redecorating whatever apartment I was living in. Sometimes this last was looked upon as slightly obsessive by others, but the reality was that I just loved spending time working with color and design, just like some people love playing among the dirt and leaves and foliage while gardening.

To be sure, this art thing did seem to reflect some subtle inner need that I found strange. As a psychologist, I knew all the theories about what is supposed to drive human beings, but I just couldn't fit my art/design compulsion into any of them. Occasionally I would broach the subject in therapy, but the exploration seemed to veer into interpretations of longstanding issues or dysfunction. Maybe this represented some undiscovered conflict deep within? Possibly I was using such playful interests as a way to avoid growing up? Perhaps, the constant redecorating was symbolic of trying to redo my emotional world? In retrospect, it does seem strange that only one person, a friend, ever suggested that I take an art course in over twenty years *(and he had such interests, himself)*. By the time this occurred, I had so programmed myself that I shut down the suggestion quickly, immediately announcing, "I can't draw."

It was when I opened to faith that I owned the artistic need and part of myself, full force. Why? What did faith have to do with it? Was it going off the social grid and allowing myself to spend time in more meditative and meaningful activities? Was it purely coincidental and I was bored? Was it a direct act of Divine intervention, and I was walked into the art store, had my credit card plopped down for a bunch of paints and canvas, and a paintbrush placed in my hand? That's how led and beyond me it all seemed. Who knows? It was a transformational time.

The important thing is that I felt whole, whatever that means. And it wasn't that I wanted to renounce everything academic and become a Bohemian painter. Nor did I think I was that good at art. What seemed to have occurred was that I finally realized that both the art and the academic were important parts of who I was. The conflict between the two, which I had tried to deal with in therapy and also projected to some degree onto the outside world, was no longer an issue. Each of us has our own path. Again, it just felt so whole. Predictably, the commitment to art also opened up my life to different social outlets where I seemed to fit in well and felt very much at home. It's all connected. Everything we do ripples out.

In addition to helping us cope with emotional pain, the relationship with God can lead to a more authentic sense of personal identity. How does this happen? Once God becomes a reality and, more important, a presence in one's heart and consciousness, individual experience appears to change in several respects. Faith creates a new vision, both within and outside one's self. Part of this new vision is an altered way to think about who we are and what's important in life experience. Over time this leads to a transformed manner of being in the world. There is a feeling of *journey*... of moving towards something... of *higher* purpose and meaning. All these things begin to define and reorient the personality in a completely new way.

Who are we really? The way we experience who we are *(and how we feel about it)* is very complex. Again, one principle that is recognized by most religions is that we are *spiritual beings* within *physical* bodies. Most typically, this spiritual part within is called the *soul* although there seem to be as many conceptualizations about what the *soul* is as there are belief systems. Some presume the *soul* is an enduring entity, manifesting over many lifetimes. Others assume the *soul* survives in *spirit* alone. Even others believe the *soul* is a loose quality of energy, dissolving into the unity at its return or after achieving a certain level of knowledge. There has also been proposed a hierarchy of *soul* levels with numerous discarnate states. In summary, there are multiple explanations and theories about what the *soul* is, each having a different implication as to what that might mean for us personally.

How do we recognize and know our *soul*? It does seem that we all have a sense of individual identity or *self* although some people are too immersed in living to think about this too much. This sense of *self* (*i.e., who we feel we are as a unique individual*) begins to develop from the time we are very young. There are some cultures in which identity as part of the group is more important than being an individual, but even so, all human beings experience themselves as separate and, to some degree, unique. Where does such uniqueness come from? What makes us who and how we are? Is this entirely explainable by genetics and/or the treatment within the family in which we grew up?

In our narcissistically obsessed society, we hear so much about the *self* and asserting one's *self* and personal needs. On the one hand, we are told it's not what we do but who we are that's important. It would appear this basic and entitled *self* could do no wrong. On the other, we hear of the need of finding one's *self*, obtaining *self-knowledge*, pursuing a journey of *self-discovery*, and *self-actualization*. This is the idea that there exists a "new and improved version of me" awaiting within although exactly what this involves may be unclear. Typically, in our secular age, this seems to have to do with clarifying what one wants out of life.

For some, self-discovery occurs in terms of defining concrete goals (*i.e., "I want the white picket fence… three children… to make my first million by the age of 30"… etc.*). For others, it has more to do with a deeper quest for personally authentic values and where one finds greater meaning, so it's more internal and vague. Sometimes it seems as though the person is searching for a truer identity independent of societal and parental expectations.

In modern approaches to spirituality, the idea of *soul* is popular, definitely more so than God. We hear today a lot about finding *soul* purpose and undertaking a spiritual journey or quest, which may be seen as involving God but often does not. As previously discussed, many modern spiritual approaches seem to reflect and emphasize psychological agendas more than traditional spiritual concerns. The search for *soul* or spiritual quest has been reframed to mean a journey of *self*-discovery and personal empowerment.

In any event, there's a lot of searching going on. Why? Is this essentially hunger for something more fulfilling in our materialistic world? Perhaps. Yet so many people speak of specific longings, a sense of unique passions or yearnings within that lie unattended and undeveloped. It's very idiosyncratic. This is not some feeling of general dissatisfaction or emptiness *(although we see that too in modern life)*. Rather, the craving is individualized, something the person has always been drawn to or had fantasies of doing but has not pursued.

For me, the undeveloped passion was art, and my case seems fairly typical. The passion just lay fallow or was minimally toyed with for years and years. It was always on the periphery and didn't really get in the way of anything but nagged, at times slightly annoyingly, like a drippy faucet you can almost but not quite turn off. Similarly, so many people have some proclivity or singular urging in the direction of a certain type of activity or challenge, group of people, social cause, historical era, even geographical place. It may seem odd and trivial but is personally captivating and persistent although inexplicable in terms of the individual's background and the practical demands of living. Some people feel foolish for having such dreams and may go out of their way to suppress them or, at least, keep them private.

Several years ago I was at a workshop on creativity, and during one of the lectures, there arose an impassioned discussion among the participants *(many of whom were therapists)* about how their creative appetites had been squelched by their parents and modern society. This turned into a lengthy gripe session, the sentiment being that cultural standards were keeping us imprisoned in our colorless, conventional lives. I was astounded at the depth of feeling and sense of void. While there was a general outcry, participants weighed in about specific things they had wanted to do or develop but had not followed through. I felt so fortunate that I had been able to pursue my passion, but this made me reflect again at how, from my perspective, this seemed so connected to and given by God.

It wasn't that I had simply had the luck or personal drive to go after and develop my long held dream although this can be gratifying and results in a sense of accomplishment for the person who does so. By uncovering the artistic part that had been latent for so long, I seemed to get in touch with an essential personal core, a unique template of authenticity for me. This felt like it had always existed within. I just had to find it. It also wasn't just about the art although that seemed to have been the missing piece. Once that was in place, there was such a sense of wholeness and integration. All the pieces of the final puzzle seemed to have come together. Because this had occurred within the context of my burgeoning spiritual awareness, there was the impression of having been led to this destination or connecting with some dynamic internal energy. My *spiritual being*? My *soul*? It was like I had opened the door onto a personal identity that felt very familiar and had always been there... and who I really was.

This gets back to the question: Is there a deeper sense of personal identity within? A directing force that has the potential to guide us in making the right and fulfilling choices? An authentic foundation of who we truly are? When we look within, we do have that cohesive sense of awareness that seems to be in the driver's seat as we travel through life. Is this the *self (again, that sense of who we are as a unique individual)*? Or is it something more? Our sense of *self* does seem closest to our essential being and presumably should know best what we want and need. Yet our *self* doesn't always do such a good job in making the smartest choices in the long run. Within our *self*, we often feel pulled apart or chasing our own tails, so to speak, and we can feel held down by and trip over our *self* as much as not.

This awareness of *self* also seems to include numerous parts or mini-selves within, so it isn't surprising that there can be a feeling of conflict. Our *work self* may be entirely different from and at odds with our *family self* or our *private self*. We also have the accumulation of historical *selves* as we go through life. Most of us have memories of our *teenage self*, who is completely different from our *self* at 30, 40, or 50. Looking back or upon meeting actual teenagers similar to our *teenage self*, we may cringe and think how misled and obnoxious we were, not the same person at all. At the same time, there does seem to be a *core self*, a stable and continuous dimension to our experience and who we are. Most of us would agree that internally there is a part or energy that never seems to change. This sense of *core self* was there and feels the same when we are 5 and 25, 50 or 90.

This feeling of sameness is illustrated by the stark discrepancy that many feel between their biological age and how old they feel within. Often as we age, from the inside looking out, it is unfathomable that we could be as old as we really are. The wrinkles may deepen, the hair turns gray, but in some ways we feel just like a kid inside. When I worked at the nursing home, so many times I witnessed a very elderly man or woman amble by the hallway mirror and catch a glimpse of the passing reflection. Sometimes there was no recognition, at least initially. More typically the reaction would be shock or disbelief *(at times horror or denial)*. The protestation was always to the effect, "How could this have happened? No! That isn't... *me*? It's a really old person!" This doesn't only occur when people are struggling with cognitive decline. It is just incomprehensible, given what is felt internally. For all of us, there is this fundamental part of who we are that never changes, no matter how much we are impacted by biology or the outside world.

Nonbelievers might argue that it is this subjective sense of cohesive being or *core self* that is mistaken for *soul*. People of faith disagree, pointing out that the *soul* goes even deeper and feels stronger than the sense of *core self*. The *soul* has a feeling of dynamic energy, force, power, and vitality. It tends to be equated with an inner light. With *soul*, there is also a clear feeling of *connection* beyond the individual, particularly with God, but also with one's spiritual brothers and sisters and other living creatures. As we have discussed, this sense of connection is real and tangible. As a *soul*, the person feels part of, actually connected to, and affected by a greater force or unity of *spirit*, which is beyond the *self*.

For those who believe in God, the *soul* is who we really are. What does this mean? Whenever we talk about *soul (or self, for that matter)*, it's always subjective. We can't see or measure such things. Spiritual and nonspiritual individuals alike may describe a unique quality or vibe or aura about a person. For some, this is just a sense of personality. Others maintain this is a real energy or *life force* or *spirit*. In any case, this presence or essence is impossible to capture objectively. We may feel or sense it, but it's never in the manner of observing as we do a mountain or human face or even a cloud or mist. It's more about recognizing an entity that is surreally distinct and definable but imperceptible through the normal senses alone.

They say the *soul* is expressed through the eyes. Certainly, there does appear to be an exchange of some kind of vital essence when our eyes meet those of another human being. There also seems to be a feeling of individual energy, again a presence, *beyond* the physical body. We feel this within ourselves and perceive it in others. In fact, it is this essence or presence or individual energy that seems to disappear, as though going elsewhere, in death. People who have seen others die sometimes speak of a distinct moment of passing, even accompanied by a flash of light or quick gust of wind. The perception is that the essence or *soul* has left, not simply become depleted or wound down or extinguished, but actually left and gone someplace else. In open casket services, it tends to be confusing but sometimes comforting for loved ones as to how absent the body seems to be of the person they knew, indeed lifeless and empty. There is the distinct impression that the *spirit* has moved on.

The reality of individual energy or essence became so clear to me in working with the frail elderly. I witnessed firsthand how everyone has a distinctive vitality, a cohesive *spirit* or *soul*, no matter how physically or mentally deteriorated the person might be. Sometimes it seemed that the individual energy or *soul* was all that was left as though the younger personality and physical robustness had just fallen away. Many of the residents sat in wheelchairs or remained in their beds, doing nothing, but there was always a unique *spirit* or presence about them, especially in interaction. This was specific and identifiable and generally agreed upon by everyone from the nurses to the cooks to the other residents. No matter how incapacitated the individual might become physically or mentally, that definable essence or personhood remained strong as ever, and there was always a feeling of void or loss after the individual had died.

I also learned that even people afflicted with Alzheimer's have moods and lives. In our biologically-focused society, we are so quick to assume that, once the brain declines, the personhood goes as well. Yet I found that even those who could remember nothing, either about their long lives or what had happened two minutes previously, had an active, experiencing inner being and vitality just as we all do. They might not be able to communicate in the usual way, but there was an exchange that occurred between us. Sometimes they actively used any time we spent together by discussing feelings, which were immediately forgotten, as was everything we talked about. That didn't seem to matter. It was the sharing that was important. Often we seemed to share by just being together, *soul* to *soul*, which did appear to be remembered on some level.

Mysteriously, over time it also became apparent that I was building relationships with patients who had Alzheimer's. Our interactions were unusual and disjointed perhaps, but we had a relationship all the same. How could this be? Victims of Alzheimer's are not supposed to be able to remember or learn anything new, but the emotional bond between us was clear. Sometimes these patients just wanted to hold my hand. Not any hand would do. It had to be mine. And they would become jealous if I was spending more time with the other residents. Sometimes they would verbalize if I had been there the day before or missed a day, or they might remember if I had been sick. Quite unexpectedly, it appeared that they were becoming aware of my personhood as well.

There was one woman with Alzheimer's in her late 90s with whom I worked for several years. She could never recall she was no longer living in New York and would wander the halls, asking endlessly, "Why are we here?" *(It was never clear if she meant California or the human condition in general.)* As our relationship grew, very defined things about me seemed to become familiar to her. This was odd as she really could not recall almost anything about her life for the past fifteen years.

For instance, she would comment on a bracelet I always wore, remembering that I had told her it was a gift from my mother. She also began to incessantly scold me for a habit I had of drinking water from a liter bottle that I carried in my briefcase. "I hate when you do that," she would reprimand in disgust. "It's unladylike. You look like a beer-swigging trollop. And I *know* you were brought up better than that!" At one point, she even learned my name although she didn't remember it consistently. Over the several years that we worked together, I had become an entity to her. A friend?

At one point, she became so deteriorated that she withdrew to her room, resisting my efforts and those of others to interact and become more engaged. Over the next year, I continued to try, but she would snap a cantankerous comment to create distance or stared blankly. She seemed to have become almost mute. I often felt she no longer recognized me. Then one day she perked up and asked when her niece was due back from her yearly trip to New York. Everyone was thrilled. Indeed, her niece was on her annual trip to New York. *(And how had she known this?)* During the past year, her niece had dutifully visited every week and been rejected with irascible remarks or cold silence like the rest of us. Over the next two weeks, the staff counted down the days until the niece's arrival. The woman's former "Why are we here?" was replaced with "When is she coming?" She suddenly appeared to be returning to her old self.

Upon her much anticipated return, the niece was overjoyed with her aunt's change in demeanor and commented that she seemed to be coming alive once again. It was so good to have her back. They went out to lunch, just like old times, and the niece promised to return the following week. The woman with Alzheimer's seemed contented, happy to finally be reunited with her niece once again. As though moved by the visit and filled with gratitude, after her niece had left, she called each of us who had worked closely with her into her room and thanked us individually for being so kind to her. Later that night, she passed away in her sleep.

While it is not unusual for people to appear to make an effort to say good-bye prior to death, this is not what would be expected *(or even thought possible)* with someone who has Alzheimer's. This woman could not recall where she was from one minute to the next or even something as physically memorable as that she had just eaten lunch or been given a bath. But here she was, showing clear intention, will, and sustained effort *(with great elegance and grace, I might add)* to properly thank and bid farewell to, not only her niece, but the newer staff relationships from her nursing home years. This was particularly puzzling as she had rarely seemed aware that she was even living at the home most of the time.

It was all so baffling to me, both the manner in which she had seemed to plan or put off her death until she could see her niece one more time, as well as the bond that had developed between us during the years of working together. Whatever her former life and personality had been, I never knew them. Yet I felt, on some level, I knew her well and experienced a real sense of loss after her passing. From her niece, I had learned a lot about her ninety plus years, and so I would ask about certain circumstances or people in sessions, but this was minimal in our interaction. Like most people with Alzheimer's, she more clearly remembered people and events from long ago although these too ultimately faded. What was even more incongruous was the person I knew compared with what her niece had told me about her former life. This woman had apparently been extremely accomplished, a female power player in the New York business world, hobnobbing with some of the most famous names of the twentieth century, during an era when women didn't usually have careers.

So all this made me ponder. Exactly who was it that I had been relating to? Was it her *soul*? Her personality or basic *self (or at least the self that she had been for most of her long life)* seemed to have entirely disintegrated before I even met her. The woman I knew, wry and peppery at times, valiantly struggled day after day to make some sense of the sievelike reality she now inhabited *(and to remain as elegant as dementia would allow)*. The externals didn't matter. I liked and admired her, and we had developed a special bond, which she specifically acknowledged when she called me into her room the day before she died. I felt I knew her as well as you get to know anyone with whom you work closely for several years. At least on the outside, this had nothing to do with the over ninety years of living and who she had been before I ever met her.

If we are both *self* and *soul* with two ways of being or parts to our identity, how do they relate? Are they really separate? Or are they more like dimensions or energies that may influence how we feel and behave at any point in time? We have talked about how, as human beings, we seem to coexist on two different levels of experience *(the spiritual and psychological)*. Sometimes we feel a sense of conflict between them. Sometimes they work together just fine. At other times, they seem to come together to truly enhance our experience in extraordinary and unexpected ways.

What goes on inside our minds is confusing enough. The human psyche can be full of surprises and rather unwieldy. The idea of a *spiritual being* or *soul* within complicates things even more. This is especially so as it is assumed that, on the spiritual level, we connect with a higher reality beyond our *self*. So, whenever we think of ourselves as *souls* or *spiritual beings*, this is always bigger than we are. When people open to faith, they begin to recognize and experience this other spiritual part or level within, which does connect them to others and to God. They tend to feel this operating in their existence although perhaps only subliminally. It begins to feel that part of the journey of faith is to discover or uncover this inner essence, to bring the *spiritual being* more into the sense of personal identity and how they live their lives.

What does this mean? And how does one do so? Many belief systems describe that God exists *within* each and every one of us. It is our *spiritual being* or *soul* that connects us to God... and, by extension, to our spiritual brothers and sisters. We exist in a manner similar to a family bonded through *spirit*. Yet, among contemporary spiritual approaches, sometimes this idea that God or *spirit* exists within each of us has been reframed to imply that each of us *is* God. This is not only self-serving, but would be antithetical to traditional teachings. It suggests that each of us has ultimate power and control, that individually we are the Higher Authority, at least over ourselves, and there is no God as Supreme Being and Creator. Some modern interpretations also miss the idea that we are connected in *spirit* to God and each other.

Admittedly, these are confusing concepts. In traditional theories, the fundamental principle is that God *is* the Higher Power or Supreme Being and Creator of us all. From a purely theoretical point of view, the traditional premise is *not* that we are God but some variant of the idea that *spirit* or god *(with a lowercase "g")* exists within each of us while God *(with an upper case "G")* is the Supreme Being and Higher Power, having created and now embracing us all. This means that we derive our *spiritual being* and some degree of spiritual power from God but are dependent on God as Supreme Being for everything.

While all this is mind-numbing, there are a number of concrete metaphors that illustrate this traditional connection of God to the individual and other human beings. One image is that God is similar to an all-encompassing ocean of *spirit* while we, as individual *souls*, are like pools within that ocean. The pools are contained within the entire ocean *(i.e., God)* but hold ocean *(i.e., God or spirit)* within. For the computer wonks among us, God is the mainframe computer and we, as individual *souls*, are the various workstations, connected to and sourced by the central processing unit. For the entertainers, God is the production and show while the *souls* are the players or performers.

In all these examples, what becomes apparent is that the individual *soul* does not and cannot exist as a separate, independent unit without God or does so only in a limited way. An ocean pool needs ocean in order to exist at all. A computer workstation can gather dust, but without the power and communication transfer of the mainframe, it is not serving its purpose. It's a dense piece of furniture. An actor can write and perform a one-person show, which may be brilliant, but the range and impact are not the same as that of a fully interactive, scripted, scored, and choreographed production *(which also includes a live orchestra and the necessary support of the backstage or off camera personnel)*. It's all connected.

Spiritually committed people instinctively understand this essential connection to God *(in spirit)* as well as the interdependent nature of human beings *(also in spirit)*. In one sense, this connection is very simple. We *feel* it. In another, how this plays out and is manifest in our lives appears complicated because it occurs on multiple levels and in numerous, often unexpected ways. Whether they are consciously aware of it or not, people of committed faith tend to increasingly express their *soul* or *spiritual being* in their personalities although it's not all or nothing. Getting in touch with and developing the *soul* does not erase or obscure the *self (i.e., all those unique personal traits, preferences, dreams, talents, and history)*. Usually most people don't think of the *self* and *soul* as separate entities within. That's not the typical experience.

Rather, there is the sense of two types of influences, values, and ways of being. For example, your *soul* may feel warmly connected in *spirit* with others on an elevated level, while your *self* may harshly compete with your office mates for the promotion, including getting into backhanded and nasty behavior. We often have contradictory feelings, sometimes about the same person, over the course of a day. We tend to experience different parts within our identity all the time, but they don't seem entirely separate from each other or in conflict although they sure can be. As human beings, we always have a *self*. As *spiritual beings*, we always have a *soul*, whether we are aware of this or not. One way of looking at this is that the *self* and *soul* are merely different parts or facets to who we are as well as how we experience our lives and behave in the outside world.

At the same time, these are not only personality traits or types of feelings within. The *self* and *soul* represent two distinct ways of being in the world *(each with specific motivations, perceptions, reactions, and urges)*. Some religions do strive to minimize the *self* and human individuality. The goal is, by reducing the influence of psychological needs or desires, this facilitates getting in touch with the *spiritual being* within. Yet the *soul* and the *self* are not necessarily incompatible. For people who are spiritually committed, the *self* can become the vehicle or worker bee or "front" for the *soul*. In other words, it is through the attributes and activities of the *self* that we can fulfill spiritual purpose and serve God in the *human* world on the *physical* plane. At the same time, from a spiritual perspective, the *soul* is the foundation, the cornerstone, and blueprint of one's authentic identity. This means that the more the *soul* is expressed in our human lives, the more fulfilling and whole our individual experience will seem to be.

One metaphor that illustrates the expression of *soul* is that of a photographic negative. The *soul* derives from God, so the image embedded in the negative has already been determined, at least to some degree. This image is God's plan for us but has to be developed *(in the manner of a print or photo)* over the course of a person's life. Perhaps, there are a number of ways in which the "negative" or *soul* can optimally be developed in an individual's personality or life or final "print," but how cleanly or clearly or beautifully the individual seeks to do so *(or not)* is a matter of choice and motivation.

What this means is that we always choose to what degree the *soul* is actualized in our earthly lives. We are all whole before God, whose love is unconditional. It is the spiritual assumption that we have all been given a unique and perfect photographic negative of what our lives can be. Still, it is the choice and commitment of the individual that determines how the *spiritual* negative gets developed into its *human* image.

13 Riding the God Rails

In the nursing home, there was a woman we'll call Kate, who was as ornery as they come. Despite herself, everyone liked her. Underneath the crankiness, you could sense a vulnerable but wounded heart. She had lived a hard life, including homelessness, addiction, and suffering severe physical abuse although she never disclosed any of this *(yet a three volume chart had tracked her institutional odyssey over the years)*. She had a quick wit, and her stubborn facade was transparent, a frank reminder of what we all do to shield the pain within.

An incident that captures Kate's essence occurred when she almost died because of a respiratory condition. For several minutes that were truly frightening, she lay on the floor, blue in the face, silently staring up in helpless terror, as paramedics attended to her. When the crisis had passed, one of the paramedics tried to reassure her, gently saying something to the effect that it was so nice to have her back, she had turned "real blue there for awhile."

Snorting, Kate barked, "I can turn blue, if I want to."

Towards me, Kate loved to hurl salty abuse about "that stupid therapy of yours." She refused to officially participate in the current events group that I held everyday in the common room. What she would do is place a chair exactly half in and half out of the room and then proceed to voice her opinions, reminding us from time to time she was *not* a member of the group. Often she was amazingly insightful about the human condition in an acerbic but poignant way. What also became apparent was that she held bitterly racist views, which were expressed, not only in the group, but throughout the day despite attempts to set limits or change her opinions. This was a true ugliness in her that seemed to go beyond the surface crankiness as though she so desperately needed to project the depth of her self-hatred onto someone else.

As "lousy luck" would have it, from Kate's point of view, she was assigned an African-American nurse we'll call Jackie, an extremely open, loving, and religious woman, who took her work to tend to these patients as a spiritual calling. She announced to Kate that she was going to love her, no matter what. And she did so, in good-humored fashion, simply turning the other cheek to the barrage of vicious racist statements coming from Kate's mouth, almost as a mother does with an oppositional, taunting child but in a loving and guiding way.

"Ah, Kate, my Katie. You can call me whatever you like… that's *not* going to stop the love," she would say.

And she was right. Over time it became apparent to all that Kate was bonding with Jackie. The nasty onslaughts became interspersed with calls for Jackie and wanting to get to know her as a person, even concern for her family. In group, a softer side of Kate began to emerge. In speaking to the other members, she began replacing the racist comments with inquisitive philosophical questions, such as asking if anyone knew why God had created different races. It was as though *within* she was struggling to come to terms with this basic issue.

Finally, there did come a time when Kate acknowledged how much she had grown to love Jackie, her "best friend," and how important she was to her. Sometimes she communicated this directly, more typically in her usual prickly manner. But the racist comments were entirely gone. Much to everyone's astonishment, in group one day, she proclaimed, "Everybody is the same, no matter what the color of their skin." Thereafter, sharing this new belief, this *learning*, became extremely important to her. At every opportunity in group, still with one foot inside the door and one without, she would grunt something to the effect: "Only an idiot would judge someone by of the color of their skin!"

Most spiritual systems describe the importance of *learning*... about ourselves, about what is meaningful and true, about *higher* spiritual values and existing on a physical plane. Opportunities for learning, big and small, occur for all of us all the time. Of course, it is human nature to resist them. We tend to obstinately cling to our defensive or self-oriented perspective, our own little window on the world. It can be truly frightening to let in other information or allow ourselves to be self-reflective. So often the scariest things are within ourselves.

Within the relationship with God, through *learning*, we are always guided in the direction of optimal spiritual growth. What does this mean? Like a nurturing parent, God pushes and leads us along a path of development towards the understanding and actualization of higher *spiritual* values in *human* existence as well as our unique gifts. With God as the guide and ultimate authority, all of us are capable of learning what we need to and leading a productive and fulfilling life of purpose. Spiritually, it is assumed that every human being has important contributions to make.

This brings up another aspect of our experience. We don't remain still. While it is tempting to think of the *self* or *soul* as an entity, there is also the idea that we are constantly evolving on our journey over life's course. We travel a trajectory of experience as we go through it, a progression of personal discovery and growth. This is bound to change our perspective over time. From a spiritual point of view, the individual *journey* of each of us is about *learning* and *purpose*.

Certainly, in evaluating so many people throughout my career, I have seen *learning* in action and been impressed by how wise and insightful human beings can be. No matter how simple or uneducated, most of us acquire wisdom relative to our life experience. All of us have the capacity and opportunity to find some degree of personal truth. For those who don't have formal education or exposure to intellectual theories, their truth tends to be more directly related to real world living and can be startlingly incisive and profound.

Unfortunately, the idea of journey today seems to have been overshadowed by the consumerism of mainstream culture. Journey implies movement, traveling from one place to another. As we make the trip through the years chronologically *(from infancy to old age)*, the traditional assumption is that *within* we are also moving in the direction of deeper meaning and ever greater understanding. That's what spiritual *learning* is, greater understanding. But now it seems the idea of journey has become more about accumulating things along the way. It's no longer about spiritual or even deeper psychological meaning or values; it's about things… stuff… the collection of toys, accomplishments, social networks, and cool experiences. All these things may fill us up, at least temporarily, or serve as tokens of our worth and appeal. They have little to do with a meaningful truth.

The modern existential journey seems akin to costumed young children headed out for a night of trick-or-treating on Halloween. It's a thrilling adventure when you're five or seven. Otherwise, it's a fairly one-dimensional pursuit. It's about gathering candy. It doesn't even matter if it's good candy. You can only eat so much anyway before getting sick, and most children end up throwing a lot of it away eventually. The trick-or-treaters may stay in their neighborhood or expand their journey in ever widening circles, but each stop at each house is pretty much like the last. Just more and more candy.

A couple of tenacious kids could even canvas the city *(with Mom following right behind in the SUV to carry home all the chock-full bags)*. It's a wider, more ambitious expedition but still yields nothing but candy. This seems similar to what many people today appear to be doing in their quest for an authentic, personal truth. It's not about growth *(or even movement or change)* but chasing and hoarding candy, pushing the search perimeter beyond formerly respected limits perhaps, but it's gathering candy all the same.

Sometimes the person does strive to go deeper. Yet, even when the modern quest does involve a clarification of values, in a morally relativistic society, what does this mean? The primary societal value is about amassing candy. Other than that, you're on your own. Values are seen as simply an extension of the individual and may have little meaning beyond the *self*. If the quest for existential truth can mean whatever the person wants it to mean, does it really mean anything at all without some greater frame of reference? Or connection to a *higher* truth beyond the individual? Otherwise, the establishment of personal values becomes like a list of "likes" or "interests" on a social networking page.

There's a haphazard psychological alienation among members of a society where such adamant self-determination rules. There may be a lot of individual journeys going on, each with clear focus and destination, but nothing's connected. This self-absorbed wandering may be gratifying and worthwhile up to a point, but it automatically limits the potential scope and fruits of the journey overall. Again, there is the impression that everyone *(so intent on pursuing his or her own thing)* is existing in a narcissistic bubble, with society now a swarm of narcissistic bubbles, all randomly moving around and occasionally colliding, merging, or crashing into each other, like bumper cars at a 1960s amusement park.

In contrast, the traditional spiritual journey moves the individual *beyond* the discovery of only a personal truth. It's about finding Absolute Truth and God and, once found, then living our lives accordingly. There is a sense of ongoing *learning*, particularly about and through the higher absolute values, the *God rails*. There is also the quest to find and actualize a higher *spiritual* purpose in *human* existence beyond ego agendas and solely the determination of what one wants out of life. What this means is that, once we connect with our *soul* and begin to develop our photographic negative, we open up to God's plan for us. There is also the assumption that this plan fits into a larger meaning and design.

From a spiritual perspective, this thread of *learning*, as well as the lessons we learn, are not vague abstractions. It is through our real world experience and the uniqueness of who we are that we learn spiritually and actualize individual purpose. The story of Kate and Jackie illustrates the multilayered nature of spiritual *learning*. On one level, there was a true shift in Kate's perspective *(internally)* and a desire to share what she had learned *(externally)*, which reflected higher spiritual values. It was almost as though she wanted to teach so others could benefit, and there may have been underlying remorse for learning so late, for the hurt she had caused in the past. Yet there was another piece of the *learning* that was playing out in Kate's journey as well. The catalyst and effect of this spiritual lesson was that Kate was involved in a loving, caring relationship with another human being, probably for the first time in at least forty years. So the teaching, the learning, and a sense of reward all occurred on the emotional, very human level of experience.

This is the nature of *spiritual* growth. It occurs through the prism of our *psychological* experience. We are *spiritual beings* but within *physical* bodies, which does include our psychology, that is, our mind and emotions. The teaching and learning also never occur in a vacuum but are interrelated. For instance, Jackie was rewarded, not for changing Kate's mind, as she had never seemed to be too focused on the racism although this likely was hurtful on some level. She had opened Kate's heart. Because of her spiritual commitment, Jackie had chosen to focus on the heart, not the words. She had deliberately decided to see Kate as wounded and suffering and that, beyond the surface viciousness, there was a lost and struggling *soul*, a spiritual sister, a special child of God. Plus, Kate wasn't just a completed project, a successful student, or a notch in Jackie's belt of Good Works. Jackie truly loved Kate, and the bond between them was a source of tremendous emotional reward for both of them.

Jackie not only did the teaching and experienced love as a reward, but there was also *learning* for her in the relationship with Kate. What she learned *(or, in her case, affirmed)* was the power of higher spiritual values by seeing what change had been wrought in Kate, who was such a troubled *soul*. Unquestionably, Jackie was someone who was committed to a God-centered life, but the depth of her spiritual understanding was increased, given Kate's transformation. Kate had taught Jackie how wretchedly bitter and shut off a human being can become, and her metamorphosis so strongly exemplified the healing power of love. Jackie also learned *(or confirmed)* that taking the high road was the "right" choice, although difficult at times, and she probably discovered some things about herself in the process as well.

Some belief systems assume every *soul* learns specific lessons. This is the idea that there is special, individualized *learning* that each *soul* needs during his or her *human* lifetime. In this view, *learning* is similar to courses taken in school as though each *soul* is supposed to be mastering a customized curriculum of independent study. There are higher absolute spiritual values that we all are supposed to learn, but it is also assumed that each of us additionally has unique lessons to pursue and accomplish.

Again, such individualized *spiritual* lessons are seen as playing out through a person's *psychological* experience. One *soul* might have to learn about betrayal or loss. Another may be confronted with lessons around compassion or situations that challenge the individual to overcome self-doubt. Sometimes there seems to be one central lesson, and this may be presented repeatedly in various ways throughout a person's life. Sometimes there are two or more major lessons that may be presented sequentially or in a progressive manner. One lesson needs to be understood and mastered before another is begun. Whatever the lessons, it is assumed that the necessary opportunities for *learning* will be found and presented through external events and personal circumstances *(e.g, interactions with the outside world... genetics... particular strengths... human weaknesses)*. On the other hand, how one learns, how well one learns, and how consciously a spiritual quest is undertaken depends on the individual. Each of us makes the choice as to how fully we want to develop our photographic negative into its God-given image.

There is also the question, illustrated by the story of Kate and Jackie, as to whether spiritual learning is *passive* or *active*. In other words, is it something we have to seek *(active)*? Or is it something that just happens *(passive)*? Unmistakable, even glaring, invitations for growth and learning are not always pursued by human beings. Most of us probably can recall at least one instance when we did not follow through with some amazing opportunity and even walked away when it was practically handed to us. There may also be times when we appear to have no choice in the matter. Lessons can seem forced upon us, ready or not. Sometimes we have the sense that, if we are supposed to pursue a certain lesson but do not, this lesson is then presented in another way *(and another way... and another way...)* until hopefully at some point we finally "get" whatever it is we are supposed to learn.

The story of Kate and Jackie would appear to illustrate both *passive* and *active* learning. The essentially *passive* and resistant Kate learned a major spiritual lesson because of the choice and determination of the willfully *active* Jackie, who persevered in upholding the higher values and vision. This took some doing. Kate was a tough one, old and set in her ways. Her abuse towards Jackie was brutal, especially as it was so pointed in her racism. It is likely that Kate had been embittered for so long *(and had been able to hide behind her impenetrable wall of nastiness)* that she had kept others at a distance for most of her lengthy life. No doubt there had been overtures from others in the past or opportunities for *learning* that had been successfully resisted by Kate. Perhaps, it was only when she was in such a frail and needy state, brought about by old age, and she encountered the persevering, overbrimming, and giving nature of Jackie that the first small flicker of love was able to penetrate her insulated heart.

Actually Kate was lucky. After Jackie entered her world, Kate had a new lease on life, and Jackie took care of her for a number of years. There was a lot of love between them, and it was a happy ending. This isn't always the case. It is unfortunate yet too often true that human beings learn too late what is really important. Theoretically, this seems so harsh and cruel. But are human beings forced to learn in this manner because they were unable or refused to learn in any other way? Sometimes it appears we are given second chances; sometimes not. Or is it the thirty-second chance we weren't given after blithely ignoring *(or wasting)* the first thirty-one?

I worked with one elderly gentleman who was extremely frail and confined to his bed. His was a tragic situation. He was tortured by the death of his wife, whom he had taken for granted throughout the entirety of their long marriage. While he had provided for her financially, since he had been quite successful in business, there had been nonstop mistresses, and he had spent most nights out of the home "playing the Big Shot." Overall he had treated his wife shabbily in terms of time spent together and her emotional needs. He knew that she had known what was going on, but she had remained loyal, committed to being the devoted wife and mother of his children. He also knew she had loved him.

About ten years before I began working with him, his wife had died quite unexpectedly after fifty years of marriage. It was only then that he realized what he had lost. It was also after he began feeling the emotional pain of her loss and was not being attended to as "the Big Shot" for the first time *(as he became older and frail)* that he realized what it had been like for her to be an "underdog." He began to appreciate how much he loved her. Maybe not at the time, but he did now. In the ten years since her loss, he wanted so much to have the opportunity to just once tell her what she meant to him, to openly share his heart, because he now knew she was the love of his life.

This man had developed true empathy for his wife through his new *learning*, and he realized, from the existential position of being dependent and frail, what her life had been like and what he had put her through. What was remarkable was that there seemed to have been a genuine transformation to a higher spiritual attitude. He never wallowed in what could have been. It wasn't regret or his wanting to feel better about himself. He wasn't self-pitying, and he fully acknowledged his culpability. He even felt he deserved such pain, but he underscored that it wasn't about him or his pain. He knew he would always have that for what he had done. It was about his wife, but not even that he was seeking forgiveness. What he wanted was to be able to look at her, *soul* to *soul*, and give her what she had always wanted, his love. Just once, he wanted to let her know that she had his heart, which he knew was what she had wanted throughout their entire married life. He endlessly obsessed and was wracked with guilt and remorse, but it was too late, at least on the human plane.

The nature of spiritual *learning* tends to be multileveled and may be conceptualized differently from one belief system to another. Without a doubt, the human body, mind, and lifespan offer a smorgasbord of opportunities for lessons about all sorts of challenges *(e.g., love and hate, scarcity and abundance, loneliness and sacrifice, betrayal, illness, loss through death and our own aging)*. Some theories suggest that, as *spiritual beings*, we have chosen to have a *human* experience with all the sticky, bumpy twists and turns that are involved. During the course of our *human* lifetime, we are exposing our *soul* to the ups and downs of emotions, passions, and obsessions. We are *learning* about having a body as well as the perspective of a finite existence.

In some views, it is felt that, as *spiritual beings* having a *physical* and *psychological* life, we learn more deeply and fully about the human condition through experiencing its *negative* and *positive* polarities over life's course. Each polarity enhances the other by contrast. What this means is that we appreciate and understand something more if we know its opposite. We appreciate *pleasure* more if we have felt *pain*. We savor and enjoy *food* more when we have been *hungry*. We suffer *poverty* more keenly once we have had *wealth*. We become clearer about what constitutes *evil* when we have a true understanding of *good*. We learn more thoroughly how challenging a physical *handicap* or even normal *aging* can be if we have experienced optimal physical *fitness* or remember what if feels like to have the boundless *energy* of an eight-year-old child. We utterly understand the glory of *requited* love when we have been romantically *abandoned*.

Yet, even if the emphasis is on learning *about* human experience, we also learn *through* human experience. This is why the traditional view of *learning* is that, over the course of a lifetime, our understanding of basic *spiritual* values is deepened and affirmed because of what we are confronted with on the *physical* plane. Over our life's journey through the experiences we have, we learn what really matters and is truly important *(on any level of being)* are love and the *God rails*, those higher spiritual values.

Human experience is the ultimate teacher because of the finite and physical nature of life. As we saw with Jackie and Kate, human experience makes higher values concrete, specific, and personally meaningful. The higher *spiritual* values are given emotional form through the substance of our *human* lives. For instance, we learn what it feels like to treat someone cruelly and also what it feels like to be treated cruelly by someone else. Through sensations, perceptions, emotions, pain and joy, we learn in specific ways about ourselves and what is fundamentally important.

By the very nature of what is required to survive and thrive in a human world, we also necessarily learn about commitment, choice, and responsibility. Because of the finite nature of *physical* existence, we have to make choices all the time. These can be seemingly major choices, such as who we marry or what career to pursue. But they can also seem rather minor or inconsequential, such as whether to take time out of one's busy schedule to call a sick friend… to return the five-dollar bill the grocery store checker mistakenly gave out as change… or to smile or glare at another human being in passing.

Hopefully, over time we learn that it is the *God rails* that offer the best guidance in living. Definitely, as we go through our lives, there is the sense of accumulated wisdom, which is hard won. With faith, usually we are able to achieve some transcendence and perspective of wholeness over time. For the person of faith, the love of God and the Truth of the *God rails* are confirmed over and over again. This is what works although many people don't seem to get that far. Instead, they appear paralyzed by life's disappointments and may devolve into bitterness or frustration. After setbacks and losses, they seem to abandon hope and vision and then distract themselves through frenetic activity and addiction or spiral down into chronic depression and crisis. They are no longer interested in truly *learning* because *self-protection* has become so important. Generally, without being aware that they are doing so, they shut themselves off from a broader perspective, remaining trapped by a mindset of either brittle defensiveness or negative expectations.

Most spiritual systems assume that *learning* continues as long as we are alive. Some assume that, by learning about human life, we are also preparing for the world beyond. There is also the general impression that spiritual *learning* intensifies in the middle years and old age. This urge may be most noticeable among those who are frail as sometimes there is nothing else they can do but think about and process the material of their lives. Frailty and decline are some of the most difficult challenges that human beings have to face. Still, similar to people of all ages, many of the elderly do not take this opportunity and are too enmeshed in their physical or psychological problems to focus on greater meaning.

But many do heed the call. In working with frail elderly people from many different backgrounds, I was always taken aback by their wisdom, often from unexpected sources. There were those who spoke of living most of their lives focused on materialistic success, sometimes to the point of exploiting others. Now, with the end approaching, they painfully regretted their former choices. In group sessions, individuals who had never been reflective previously were contemplating profound questions and would offer incisive insights into the human condition. Even those in the early or middle stages of dementia would speak of psychological truths that reflected higher spiritual values. They might not be able to remember details *(and sometimes repeated the same truths day after day)*, but the wisdom was there all the same.

I was often struck by how giving the frail elderly were *(or wanted to be)*. Many of the residents seemed so anxious to impart their wisdom to me, a younger person, and to share what they had learned in the hope that I could avoid similar mistakes. It also never seemed so much about the insight and wisdom of *learning* but putting it into action. What was conspicuous was that often it was just love they so wanted to share. The power of love appeared to be a major part of the *learning* during this period. The reality of frailty and old age includes the most basic lessons, not only about accepting one's limits and inevitable deterioration, but the importance of kindness and compassion. For many, not all, there was a selfless love that emanated beyond the neediness brought on by their physical condition and the desolate loneliness that many of them faced day after day. I would feel uplifted and so cared for after I left a shift at the home. Initially, this was perplexing since the environment of physical and mental decline is very difficult to deal with psychologically.

The fact that my elderly patients so wanted to share their love goes to another aspect of spiritual *learning*. It's not only that the lessons of life are geared towards the appreciation of higher values. The goal is then for the individual to manifest these *higher* spiritual values on the *lower* physical plane. Human life has *purpose*. That is why we are here. Each of us has a *purpose* or multiple purposes as we travel our journey. It is believed that we will be given the gifts and support and opportunities to fulfill such *purpose*, which is always in the direction of *spiritual* growth although it may appear at times to be out-of-sync with our *psychological* needs.

What does this mean? What is spiritual *purpose*? How does it operate? How do we find it? As spiritual concepts have made their way into the mainstream, more than anything else I have people ask, "How do I find my purpose?" This is typically believed to be some grand task or assignment with prominent do-gooder intent, such as devotion to a humanitarian cause. Another common sentiment is that one's unique *purpose* should then be all-consuming, making other areas or elements of living secondary, if not abandoned altogether. From a psychological perspective, there seems to be a wish to uncover that one thing that will totally fill or absolutely define the individual's life.

As people awaken spiritually, a sense of *purpose* does increasingly appear to be a motivating force. Sometimes it is the spiritual *learning* that prepares the person to find and actualize *purpose* or stimulates the individual to more actively seek this in the first place. Also, it seems the more the *soul* develops through learning and being led, the more the person gets in touch with a need to serve God and the unity of spiritual brothers and sisters. Perhaps, this is the other meaning of the *God rails*. These not only guide and protect us in the manner of spiritual guardrails. They are also like a Divine system of railroad tracks and the spiritually-powered trains that run on them. By riding the *God rails*, we travel on the track of our greatest good. We are led to what is ultimately meaningful for us and how we can contribute by allowing God to transport us and work in our lives.

So spiritual *purpose* basically revolves around the questions: Where can I celebrate or serve God? Where is the place that God can work in and through my life? As we are led and become more in touch with our *soul*, we discover we have been given unique, individualized gifts and opportunities. Usually when people awaken to faith and begin to apply higher spiritual values in living in general, they also begin to examine where and how they can individually celebrate God and contribute to others in specific ways. It is assumed that each of us has the resources to do so. These human resources may be through special talents, skills, earthly passions, and even the mundane learning we have acquired on the physical plane and psychological level of experience. The task then becomes to determine how and where these personal assets can be mobilized towards the creation of *spiritual* good through our *human* lives.

That being said, how we are led, what the important lessons are, and our *purpose* at any given time are not always clear from our human perspective. For instance, if someone is born with a chemical predisposition for depression or into an abusive family or situation, there is a lot of *learning* involved in dealing with such challenges. Yet what appears so burdensome and negative may eventually turn out to be a steppingstone to wisdom, opportunity, accomplishment, service, or reward down-the-line. It is assumed that our *purpose* and the path to fulfilling this will be revealed over time. We will be led, but how is never logically apparent or expectable.

For some people, consistent with the stereotype, there may be a sense of calling, which does become such a driving force that other aspects of normal human existence are forfeited. For others, finding *purpose* and the correct spiritual path can require an extensive process of self-exploration and soul-searching, which may or may not be understood by others. For most, it is within the unique circumstances of an individual's life that *purpose* is found. Some have an inherently complicated or dangerous road *(with real life burdens and responsibilities)* from which a sense of *purpose* arises. It may also be out of unplanned or unwelcome events, such as finding one's self living in the midst of a war or with illness or taking care of a disabled family member. There are also people who seem to be going along a fairly routine path and then, confronted by a seeming twist of fate, may feel called to step up to the plate and serve God or their fellow human beings in some extraordinary or self-sacrificing way.

For most people, actualization of spiritual *purpose* is not necessarily as confusing or difficult as it sounds, nor is it always as grand and self-sacrificing as the stereotype proclaims. Finding and actualizing *purpose* can occur in the course of normal living, particularly once the person has opened to faith. Sometimes the spiritual *purpose* is simply about living more *purposefully*. If one follows the higher values as the *God rails*, there is a moral compass and a roadmap to consult on one's journey. If one has a relationship with God as primary caretaker, there is a loving, guiding force in the person's corner. The trick is just doing what we know we need to do.

More often than not, the manifestation of *soul purpose* does not mean doing something different but doing what we are already doing different-*ly*. In the course and substance of our lives *(in dealing with other people, raising children, completing projects, or meeting responsibilities in the human world)*, we may already be doing what we are supposed to do. We may just need to do it more in accordance with *higher* spiritual values and attitudes. Instead of feeling overwhelmed by the stress or burdens in caretaking, working, and daily living, we may need to focus on and appreciate what is truly important in life. We need to be thankful and prioritize our living with regard to the gifts and opportunities that we do have, whether this means spending more time with those we love, moving forward with a heartfelt dream or passion, or reaching out to our fellow human beings.

Like *learning*, spiritual *purpose* is not just looking inward but acting outward. Through commitment alone, we may be led to a sense of *purpose* in our lives. We again can look to the example of Jackie, who chose to act out of faith with regards to Kate and actualized higher *spiritual* values in the *physical* world through her intention and will. This wasn't easy and called for stalwart persistence and the withstanding of surly rejection and harsh insult for awhile. Yet she chose to stand firm. She hadn't been looking for it, but she had been handed an opportunity in the situation with Kate, and she decided to step up and was determined to see it through. Whatever hurt feelings or discouragement Jackie may have felt, she chose to endure and continue on her path. This is what gave her *purpose* – by steadfastly giving power to the *God rails*, which she believed in, instead of her personal feelings.

This is why it is so important to have a spiritual compass and to be open to the love and guidance of God. Always the most powerful tool for finding and actualizing *purpose* is listening to God. Through the caretaking relationship, we are nurtured and guided in an ever increasing feedback cycle that affects how we feel and what we do. When we commit to faith, God strengthens the manifestation of *soul* and the actualization of spiritual *purpose* in our lives. At the same time, it is through the actualization of *purpose* that we celebrate and serve God, only drawing us closer.

14 Soul Schmoozing

When the word "hospice" was used, it took everyone by surprise. He had seemed to be doing so well. I had met this man six months earlier a little before the diagnosis, but we had been working on a project and spending a lot of time together. Plus, he was a stoic type. Really old school. On dinner breaks, he washed down the meal with beer or martinis *(which he wasn't supposed to have)* and would reminisce about an earlier era… the summer he worked as a lumberjack… hopping freight trains as a kid… the Korean war… his job as a foreign correspondent. Noticeably, he had been losing weight.

During the Christmas holidays, we had taken a breather, and he had gone off to his family celebrations as his daughter and grandchildren had come over from Europe for an extended stay. He called once… we should get together *(we never did)*… they were having a blast. The treatment was over, and he was all revved up about what the New Year would bring. He then lapsed into a story of taking his young granddaughter *(with her Parisian airs)* to Disneyland. It was hysterical. This guy was such a mix of doting granddad and Hollywood Cool. In retrospect, maybe it was his granddaughter who made him seem to be doing so well.

Shortly after his family left, there was the hospital and then the "hospice" word. "A month, they said," he said while asking me over to watch a movie. He had decided he would spend his time at home. Not knowing what to say as we sat there, I developed an excruciating crick in my neck, giving me something on which to focus, rather than his situation or the sinking pit I felt in trying to deal with it. Wanting to do the best by him, I feebly turned on the shrink routine, but he wanted no part. He was sorry that we wouldn't finish the project and would find one of his associates to fill his shoes *(no way)*. Other than that, he was adamant. He didn't care to talk about his feelings.

There are some people who explode onto your scene and you immediately connect with. For me, he was one of those people. No one knows why bonds form with some human beings who come into our lives and not others. Perhaps, from the outside looking in, he was the father I hadn't had for many years, and I was the daughter who had lived thousand of miles away for almost as long. I so wanted to tell him how I felt, but he wanted me to come over to keep him company as though it was a study date after school. I made up some excuse and promised I'd be by later *(after all, we had a month)*. I spent the next few hours writing and rewriting a letter about how much he meant in my life.

When I finally arrived at his apartment, the nurse said he had just been given a sedative and was falling off to sleep. He seemed to perk one eye half-open, so I went over to the hospital bed, which had appeared in the living room in the past few days, and explained that I had a letter for him, placing it prominently on the table next to his pillow. Grabbing my hand and smiling happily, he closed his eyes. Maneuvering awkwardly so as not to disturb his grasp, I sat down on the chair, which the nurse had brought over and positioned beneath me. His head turned away, with eyes closed, my friend clutched my hand for the next forty minutes, the grip strong although lessening with time, until he fully dozed off.

"You don't have to stay here," the nurse said at one point. "He's medicated and resting comfortably." But I knew that he wanted this, and we felt so connected. It was such a tranquil and quiet space after the news of the week. One unanticipated consequence of being a therapist is that I'm not uncomfortable with long silences. Plus, from my work at the nursing home, I know the power of hands. I've held so many. Politicians have nothing on me. Handholding can be a conduit of affirming *spirit*, like an electrical current going round and round, sealing the people together for a few moments in time. To me, the handholding energy always seems to flow directly from the heart.

"I'm sorry. He never got to read your letter," the nurse said, giving it back to me the next morning when she informed me he had passed. As I looked beyond her to where his form was lying, so still on the hospital bed, I knew it was true. He had completely gone.

What is this vitality among human beings? Traditional religious systems describe a spiritual unity and *higher* plane of being. We are seen to exist... as pools within a greater sea of *spirit*? *Souls* within a spiritual family? Swimmers within an ethereal soup? If individuals have a vibe or essential energy about them, they also share it. The energy of sharing always seems greater than the sum of its parts.

Is love the energy that connects us all? The hallmark of spiritual experience is that transcendent sense of *connection* and presence beyond one's *self*. As people awaken to faith, they tend to equate this with the love of God, an enveloping warmth and light, a feeling of *spiritual* womb and embrace. Emanating from the heart area, the bond feels at times profound and direct, but it also seems that we experience the energy and love of God through our interactions with other people. God is everywhere. It is our awareness of God that waxes and wanes.

When people open to faith, they begin to notice this other type of connectedness and energy among human beings. A light or *spirit* that seems to be exchanged beyond or in addition to our actions in the physical world. As *spiritual* beings, we *feel* it. We give it. We receive it. Sometimes there are warm and softly pleasant or peaceful sensations, which are suggestive of a positive emotion *(such as love)* or an altered state. Sometimes there is no particular feeling attached, but the energy and force are felt and electric as though a magnetic attraction is operating at a *higher* level between the two people. For the spiritually committed person, there is the impression that behind it all we seem to be moving in cycles and bonds of *spirit* as we travel the course of our lives.

Just as people begin to see themselves differently when they awaken to faith, they also begin to see other people and relationships in an entirely new way. First, is the awareness that we are all children of God. In some ways, this makes us more special because God loves each of us unconditionally and individually. We *feel* this love. In other ways, we are less special in the sense that we are no longer primarily the center of our own little universe. We are now part of a spiritual collective. A member of a family. A player on a team. One planet in an infinite cosmos, no longer the sun in the center of an ego-driven solar system. From this point on, as part of a unity of *spirit*, our individual life and unique path are interconnected with others.

Each of us has a *soul* within. This means that within everyone there is the potential to live a life of *higher* meaning and purpose. We are always more than we seem, and so is everyone else we meet. In faith, as we learn about ourselves, we begin to understand how all human experience, not just what happens in our minds, reflects two levels of being, two spheres of influence, so to speak – that of the *spiritual* and *physical* domains. We also appreciate that, just as we struggle at times with this duality and have to make the choice moment by moment as to whether we go with God or not, others are in this same situation.

How do we understand the interaction between two people from a spiritual perspective? As one *soul* to another, we can and do relate on a *higher* spiritual level, even if we may not always be aware that we are doing so. And, as it is for the journey of one *soul*, when two *souls* come together, the interaction or relationship is also assumed to have a higher spiritual *purpose*. On the spiritual level, as *souls*, we come together to *create*... to *teach*... to *learn*... to *support*... to *love*... and to *share*. This is true, whether the interaction is a lifelong bond or the briefest of encounters. This means we should try to approach all human interaction from as spiritual a perspective as possible as we go about our daily lives.

In relating to others, we have a choice. Whenever we meet another person, we can interact as *spiritual beings*. By supporting each other and letting the purpose play out, both in individual relationships and collectively, we honor and serve God and enhance the spiritual unity and family to which we belong. We also have the choice *not* to relate on the *higher* spiritual level but solely on the basis of *lower* physical or psychological needs. Of course, we can't choose the behavior of the other person, and the old cliché is true. It takes two to tango although this doesn't make us any less responsible for our own choices and behavior. In every situation and interaction, we can make the decision to come from the *higher* spiritual place or not.

The way spiritual *purpose* plays out in our relationships can be both obvious and not so much. Many of our long-term relationships and commitments involve caretaking, altruism, and teaching. Sometimes this is in a formal capacity, such as being a parent or an educator. Sometimes it is more indirect, but in some manner one individual has assumed responsibility for another. Raising children, taking care of an elderly parent, volunteering by bringing food to shut-ins, working as a nurse, ministering to those in grief, teaching a fourth grade class.

All have a *higher* purpose. These are serious endeavors affecting other people and tend to pull us out of ourselves or cause us to go that extra mile, even in our narcissistic culture.

Relationships that involve *caretaking* and *support* of the weakest among us, such as children or those in current need, almost always have a spiritual purpose. But purpose also plays out in a more subtle fashion whenever we love and support others, even those who are not in obvious need. Loving and supporting others is part of the fabric and network of human life. We do this with family and partners *(romantic and otherwise)* and friends all the time. And they, with us. We also offer support in more casual interactions, often without knowing it or indirectly, even through just a smile.

As members of a spiritual family, everything we do is important. Therefore, whenever we are supporting our spiritual brothers and sisters in some way, even if it seems extremely trivial or mundane, this is important spiritually. There is *purpose* involved. We are stepping up to the plate to do our part. Whether working on a medical cure or working the fields so that others can eat, we are serving God and our spiritual family.

Unfortunately, the support and love exchanged in interactions is so commonplace that too often we tend to take it for granted *(when receiving it)*. Or we don't take the responsibility seriously *(when providing it)*. At least in modern life, we don't seem to honor the interchange or connectedness with others as precious or meaningful. This can happen at all levels of relationship and interaction. Some people wear their duties towards others as a self-congratulatory badge. Some are so caught up in their own narcissism that other people don't exist for them anyway, except for fulfillment of personal needs. Most people just seem complacent about their relationships and how significant they really are. In being so, they miss out on the experience of deeper connection and meaning. There is always a spiritual undercurrent that can enrich the interaction for both parties when the purpose plays out and is appreciated.

Sometimes the higher *purpose* in the relationship or interaction is underlying, indirect, or not what we first thought. We can have short-lived alliances that are quite intense, even as passing ships in the night. What starts out headed in one direction may change course and take on a life all its own or evolve into something else entirely. We may be involved with someone in one way, but the relationship becomes meaningful to us in a completely different area or may have a greater purpose than was initially apparent.

The relationship with my friend who passed away is an example of how the greater purpose may not be what it first seems. The project, on which we had put in a lot of enthusiastic hours, was aborted by his passing. Since it had to do with education and spiritual values, its higher purpose had seemed fairly straightforward when we first began. Yet the friendship that developed between us over that six months before he died was so much more important to me, even after a number of years. And I actually let the project fall by the wayside because it turned out to be a springboard to other things that took me in a different direction. For my friend, was the true purpose that I was supposed to be there in the months or even hours before his death? Did my spiritual leanings or training as a psychologist or the spiritual nature of the project give him solace *(in ways of which I was totally unaware)* as he moved forward on the next phase of his journey beyond the human plane? Do we ever know?

Practically all of us have had the experience of being uplifted by a phone call from someone we care about. Even a smile or positive remark from a seemingly random stranger can turn a "down" day around although why is often unclear. We say that others "pick us up" or "bring us down." Human exchange is dynamic and full of energy and impact. Spiritually oriented people have the sense that it's all connected like a web of *spirit* or energy or love. There is the impression that even the most insignificant encounter or exchange may ripple out to affect others or pick up strength, resulting in much greater influence down-the-line. We begin to appreciate that, on the spiritual level, our thoughts and actions reverberate throughout the unity and may come back to haunt or reward us several times over or from unexpected sources.

From a spiritual perspective, all actions, thoughts, and interactions are important. Since we are part of a greater family in *spirit*, each interaction we have with a brother or sister is significant and has the potential to contribute to the greater harmony and love of the unity as long as we choose to interact on the *higher* spiritual level. We can also cause hurt and suffering, although often unintentionally, if we act solely out of *lower* personal needs or desires, and this can also ripple out beyond ourselves but in a negative way.

How we relate with any member of the greater spiritual family, no matter how briefly, is assumed to affect us all. It is from this principle that arise the appeals for harmony, compassion, and forgiveness. The idea is that anything that solidifies or enhances the spiritual unity is positive or "right," essentially honoring and serving God. Anything that causes separation or discord is negative or "wrong." It is also this principle that is so difficult to reconcile with the realities of human existence. While it is obvious that inflicting suffering, injury, or death is a transgression *(although even here it is not always a clear-cut, all-or-nothing situation)*, there are many things that humans do, think, and say in ordinary interaction that also cause separation, discord, and pain. Whenever we judge, speak harshly, scam, blame, or manipulate, we are also potentially violating this principle.

Many people seem so unaware of the effect they have on others. Again, this may be the result of narcissism. They just don't care or are too self-absorbed to notice. More often, people just assume that what they do, at least in the small details of life, doesn't matter *(or at least they want to think that)*. What difference does it make if they don't return a phone call... or treat someone badly whom they will never see again... or even cheat on a spouse if it didn't really mean anything anyway? From a spiritual perspective, it does.

The truly spiritually oriented person has to accept responsibility as a member of the spiritual family. Beyond the obvious spiritual *purpose* of providing *love, support* or *caretaking* of others, there is another higher purpose that plays out in the cycle of *teaching* and *learning*. The spiritually committed person knows that, just as we are always *learning* throughout life, we are also *teaching*. At the very least, we teach by the example of our lives, whether we want to or not. This underscores how our responsibility to others isn't something we can turn on and off. Even when we are unaware of it, the example of our actions and demeanor may eventually come to have great meaning for another person. Teaching by example can change another's life course and often does.

This is another illustration of how the web of *spirit* and the interconnectedness of all of us play out. Every time we interact with another, there is the opportunity for us to learn something... about ourselves, about the world we live in, about giving and the power of love and higher values. In every interaction, there is also, not only the opportunity to teach someone else, but the likelihood is that we will teach someone else, whether we want to or not. We sometimes hear that celebrities don't want to be role models. From a spiritual perspective, they don't have a choice. None of us do. Each of us is a potential role model each and every moment of our lives.

Our demeanor and behavior always carry a message that is communicated to others, both those with whom we directly interact and those who observe us. We may be inspirational in ways we could never imagine by demonstrating a positive effect or outcome or attitude. We may also communicate a message that our attitude or behavior created a very negative result. What this means is that we also teach and learn through the negative circumstance. We see or demonstrate what *not* to do. Sometimes our greatest teachers are those relationships, interactions, or events that are exceptionally painful. Such indirect *teaching* and *learning* go on all the time although most of the time we may not even be aware of it.

The potential impact on others of our actions or lack of action is quite intimidating when you really think about it. It's an immense responsibility. Every time we act or interact, we are communicating a message. Plus, once we do behave in a certain way, it's done for all to see. You can't unring a bell. Yet, again, the repercussions of what we do are rarely considered in the modern world, at least in the everyday little things, although it is probably in the details and smaller interactions of life that we have the greatest cumulative impact on others. Long after the messenger may be forgotten, the message may live on in someone's mind or heart.

Sometimes the higher purpose in human interaction is simply about *sharing*. As *souls* within a web of connectedness and *spirit*, we are sharing this experience called human life, ideally in the richest way possible for everyone. What do we mean by *sharing*? How is that spiritual? This is best illustrated by first looking at the most striking cases where being together with another person or group of people seems to create a solid bond at a *higher* spiritual level.

Many of us have had what appear like unusual, chance episodes of joyful connection with others that seem to occur out of nowhere. It just feels so special, even perfect, to be with this other person or group of people although we may not be able to pinpoint how or why. These episodes can be associated with recreational interludes, even a wacky sense of adventure, but are atypical in that the people just feel so connected, even merged, in being together, which happens so rarely in life. Perhaps, it was hanging out with a group of friends one lazy spring afternoon. On a lengthy car trip. An unplanned get-together after work. Meeting a stranger on a train. During a relatively brief space of time, we seem to *connect* in this exceptional and more meaningful way. There may be a sense of great fun or humor although most recreational or even playful get-togethers do not have this feeling of pure and joyous sharing.

Sometimes there can be a similar sense of profound *sharing* in very serious endeavors and projects that consume our energy and that of the other people involved, usually for a limited space of time. Again, the interaction seems to be on a merged and *higher* spiritual level with total dedication of focus and energy to the project at hand. Participation in this team effort towards a goal can be intense but so is the sense of connection, and the learning and memories last long afterwards. We see this with artistic and work projects, rescue missions, political campaigns, volunteer drives, support groups and during periods of natural disasters and crisis, even a sports season or class or seminar. The focus and energy of all the individuals who are participating in this greater effort beyond themselves is just so centered around the common goal. This is consuming but equally fulfilling, even if exhausting.

After the goal has been attained or the project completed, the people drift apart because they no longer have the common focus, the *sharing of life*. This can be a frustration. They may have felt so bonded with the other team members during that period of time when they were involved in the collective effort. Now they want to continue the relationships in the same intense manner *(and may even expect to be able to do so)*, but it doesn't work. It's just not the same. They may still have the bonds coming out of the experience, sometimes significantly so, but now being together just *feels* different.

A very meaningful example is of those who have served in war together, particularly in the life-and-death situation of combat. They may feel deeply connected to one another although the sharing is in the life changing memory, thankfully no longer the immediate moment. But it can be disappointing and demoralizing when people try to reconnect with the intensity they had before, even though they are enormously relieved and grateful to be out of the dangerous and traumatic situation. What was shared was life-altering, maybe even life-saving. They are bonded forever, but after the fact the two people may find that they have nothing in common *(and frankly may not even like each other)*. It's a mystery and a dilemma.

It is the *sharing* of life, whether spontaneous or purposeful, that connects us and has so much impact, both in the moment and across time. Still, there seems to be less appreciation today for the value of connectedness and sharing among individuals, other than in the big events. When people lived in villages and depended on each other for the flourishing of crops for survival, their lives were much more intertwined. As a result of such material interdependence, they were tied together in other ways. There was a real sharing of the ins and outs, the nonessential backdrop of daily life.

Even when I was a child in the 1950s in a suburban milieu, I can remember how there was more incidental sharing among people in the ordinary aspects of living. This seemed to subtly consolidate some kind of underlying connectedness between human beings that was recognized and seen as worthwhile. There were weekly visits from the milkman, the egg man, the bread man, and they would attend to us children and linger in conversations with my mother about their children and families, illnesses, interests, and recreational pursuits. There was also more personable interaction with physicians, the pharmacist, shopkeepers, salespeople, conductors on trains, as well as neighbors and people on the street. In fact, to *not* engage was interpreted as rude or unkind. It was a slower and simpler era with time to share.

Now, in the wake of advanced communication technology, I teach over the internet to classes I can't see. I have developed long-term professional relationships via email and telephone with people I wouldn't recognize if I saw them on the street, face to face. Some of these have evolved into friendships, in which we share a bond of experience and provide support in dealing with the trials and tribulations of the day-to-day. In many ways, this is no different than it's always been, and there is something exciting about extending our human reach in communication throughout the globe. Yet it does feel like there are new challenges and limits in the sharing department that weren't there previously.

We are more connected than ever before in the *physical* world, but what about that web of *spirit* and real human connectedness? The interaction with the milkman may have been brief and nonessential, but there was heart in it on both sides. In today's world, there seems to be such a rote and cursory quality to so much of social interaction, including some friendships. In so much of contemporary relating, we appear to assume a mask of superficiality, offering lip service and glibly going through the motions. The words and narrow smiles are there, the perfunctory European hugs of greeting and departure and Hollywood air kisses, but no deeper human contact seems to have been made. How many of us have driven by a couple, sitting together at a sidewalk café, both people talking in an animated fashion on cell phones but seemingly oblivious to the person across the table?

Beyond narcissism, there are many aspects of the contemporary lifestyle that would appear to lead to a sense of alienation and depersonalization, such as lack of community, fractured families, the likelihood of serial, not lasting relationships, and that everyone and everything seems to be in a chronic state of flux. Many feel devalued as though only a statistic, an impersonal demographic, unctuously courted for the vote or potential sale, merely one unit among many. We're all part of a faceless numbers game. The message becomes, "No one thinks I'm important."

"But neither are you." As we feel depersonalized, so may we depersonalize others. So much of the time, people seem to move through the constant stream of strangers and incidental associates in their lives as though they are shadow images projected onto a screen and don't really exist. These shadow figures are seen as serving the individual *(e.g., in the grocery story, post office, to perform plumbing repairs)*, but do they even exist as human beings? One example is how people cram into taxicabs and start outpouring intensely private matters that they wouldn't tell their therapist but are totally heedless to the presence of the driver. With the ubiquity of cell phones, we are all subjected to the self-involved minutiae of other people's lives, at the same time being relegated to background anonymity and non-importance in the manner of a potted plant or piece of furniture.

SOUL SCHMOOZING

In contemporary life, there is the impression that people are barely relating at all beyond the fulfillment of narcissistic needs, let alone on the spiritual level. For people of faith, a prominent directive is to commit to honor those they encounter in daily living, whether major relationships or minor interactions. Spiritually oriented people try to remain *open*, that is, to fully notice and respect other people as fellow *souls* and spiritual travelers... and to reach out and attempt to introduce another *positive* dimension into relating, no matter how insignificant the exchange may seem.

This doesn't mean there aren't nonspiritual people who do this too and are *open*, ethically motivated, and involved with others and social concerns. Yet, as we have discussed, this seems to be more of a choice in terms of what values the individual has deemed are meaningful as well as who should be the recipient of the ethical behavior. Secular morality is relative and discretionary. It is not necessarily across the board. Within a relativistic framework, nonspiritual people may feel entirely justified *(and may even assume they are doing the "ethical" thing)* in treating one person with disdain or disrespect and another with compassion. *(Of course, some religious and superficially spiritual people do this, too.)* For the truly spiritual person, being *open* is not a choice but goes with the commitment to honor and serve God and *(by extension)* to honor and serve one's spiritual brothers and sisters. *All* of them. The person of faith may not always live up to this directive, which should prompt some self-examination, but it's not a personal option as to whether this is an important value or not. It's a spiritual familial responsibility.

That being said, even when a person is *open*, the attempt to share or elevate the interaction to a *higher* level is rewarding when it works and falls flat when it doesn't. Sometimes the attempt to relate on the *higher* level is ignored or rebuffed, which doesn't mean the spiritually committed person should respond in kind. The person of faith knows that deep within the other person is a *spiritual being*, another *soul*, even when the surface behavior does not reflect higher values and there appears to be no interest in interacting on the higher spiritual level. The directive is to reach out and try to connect anyway.

It is also true that sometimes the *soul's* light seems too covered over. We live in a human world where psychological reactions, good and bad, tend to prevail. We need to protect ourselves and our loved ones, emotionally and physically. The reality is that not everyone is coming from a spiritual place. There are also people who do not have good intentions or are defensive, mean-spirited, even sadistic or evil in their objectives. Being *open* does not mean that we suspend commonsense or fail to protect ourselves from negative acts or dangerous situations. Being *open* also doesn't always get a positive response, but it does give the person who remains *open* a sense of integrity and the subtle, positive feelings that go along with coming from a *higher* spiritual level within. For genuinely spiritually motivated people, the fact that others may not respond in kind tends to lead to a sense of sadness. The feeling is that they are selling themselves short by not being able to look beyond to a *higher* way of being. It's a lost opportunity for everyone involved.

There is a certain harmony of feeling that occurs just by connecting on the *higher* spiritual level. It feels good to engage in the *sharing* of life with another human being. Sometimes the spiritual purpose of a relationship, interaction, or get-together is simply to celebrate and share in the wondrous gifts of life and God. Watching the seagulls. Listening to music. Sitting down to a spread of good food. Hanging out to pass the time and fill the boredom. Enjoying a joke or laugh. Listening to an enchanting story or a fine piece of music. Doing nothing... but doing it together. Sometimes the sharing even involves surface conflict or competition, such as in the manner of a sports game or friendly rivalry, but it is sharing nonetheless and therefore meaningful. Spiritually we are always bonded by sharing our lives.

I learned a lot about the power and pleasure of *sharing* when I worked at the nursing home. From the first time I walked through the front door, I came to the realization that the usual ways of interacting and doing therapy were not going to work, given the mental and physical impediments with which so many of the residents were struggling. I saw that I had to come up with some other way to relate and communicate if anything meaningful was going to occur. Much to my surprise, I soon learned that all I had to do was share. Sometimes, for residents who had all the normal capabilities stripped away *(i.e., the ability to speak... or any memory of what had happened five minutes previously)*, all there seemed left to do was to spend time together, *soul to soul*. Then I realized this is what most of us are doing most of the time anyway in daily existence. We are just hanging out spiritually or *soul schmoozing*, in other words, sharing life.

Soul schmoozing... spiritually hanging out... *together.* This seemed to have an extremely positive effect, especially for those patients who were so impaired. This wasn't therapy in the true sense of the term but a type of support, which resulted in improvement in mood, more cooperation with staff, and less problematic behaviors. Yet this wasn't just a palliative measure to calm the jitters. Through *soul schmoozing*, real bonds were being formed that were emotionally significant and even remembered by people who couldn't remember my name.

Soul schmoozing. The power of *sharing.* I had a telling experience as a result of the current events group that I ran before lunch with an initially small group of residents. Since about half the participants couldn't remember, I would have to repeatedly explain the same news events *(often stories which we had spoken about many times before)* in a manner that was encouraging and respectful but at the same time not too boring for the others. It was a challenge. Sometimes the topic for the day would begin with a news item, which would then lead to discussion of more personally meaningful subjects. At times the discussion veered into historical events *(e.g., where the group members were when they learned about Pearl Harbor)* or questions of philosophy, religion, social justice, or raising children.

I tried to make everyone feel welcome in participating, and over time there arose a sense of group cohesiveness. Not only among the original group members, but soon most of the residents in the home began coming to lunch early and standing around the periphery of our session. I increasingly tried to include as many people as possible, even if just to smile and speak their names.

Eventually the group became a before meal ritual or happening in the home with residents showing up over half an hour early so they could indirectly participate. Wheelchairs were brought in and lined up, bearing residents who were typically confined to their rooms but just eager to share in the collective experience. Frail men and woman were propped up on walkers for forty-five minutes or longer because there were no seats available. They didn't seem to care.

Like an auditorium before a concert, everything seemed to become more chaotic and disjointed as more people meant more noise and movement back and forth. There was a buzz in the air of excitement, group bonding, and anticipation. Trying to include so many people became quite a juggling act and meant less thorough and meaningful discussion since everyone was seeking to weigh in. For me, it was becoming less manageable and more unwieldy, almost uncomfortably so. From the perspective of the residents, they loved it.

Residents and staff alike would comment that our group created a sense of belonging and connection, even "family," for everyone. It was enjoyable and uplifting, making the mealtime go more smoothly *(not a small feat, given there were many who resisted eating and had to be fed)*. Everyone was happier and calmer and therefore more cooperative, and a few close one-on-one relationships were formed as a result of the group interaction. Some of the clinically depressed and withdrawn residents even began coming out of their rooms outside of meals and group sessions. Again, it wasn't that anything specific was being accomplished nor could many of the members even remember what had been discussed.

But they remembered the *soul schmoozing*, the *sharing*. I was amazed when I returned for a visit to the home a year or so after I no longer worked there. Many of the residents did remember me but most particularly "those groups before lunch." There was one woman with Alzheimer's *(and the associated severe memory impairment)*, who had literally spent the majority of her time during all the years that I worked at the home, searching for her room. Staff members and other residents would repeatedly walk her to her room, but within ten minutes she would be frantic and lost and searching once again.

Upon seeing me, her face lit up, and she ran over, engulfing me in a grandmotherly hug. "Oh… you're the nice lady who came for a long time… and then didn't come for a long time," she said. She paused, as though struggling, but then her face brightened further as a dim recognition appeared to crystallize. She clasped her hands together with a small shriek of delight, "We used to talk. All of us. That was so much fun… for *all* of us."

15   House of Souls

"What is your personal fantasy of Heaven?" The question was first asked in a course that I took in college, which led to a lot of joking among the undergrads.

"Party, hearty!"

"Don't forget world peace."

"If everyone partied, man... we'd have world peace, man."

Once the class settled down, I don't remember any consensus. People offered various higher social values or personal needs, which the professor then listed on the blackboard until the bell rang. I think if anything came out of it, it was an illustration of age-old questions *(and perhaps that was the point)*. What do we mean by bliss? If bliss is subjective, how do we define it? To what degree is our own happiness dependent on others?

Afterwards I occasionally thought about this personal Heaven question, particularly when I started teaching. It's a good starter for class discussion. One day it came to me. My personal Heaven would be like a house of many rooms. In each would be a favorite period of time or relationship with a loved person. In other words, it was a house filled with happy memories of one's own choosing. But it wasn't just the memories. The individual could then revisit and reconnect with, actually relive and re-engage, all the people and places and moments of life that had been so special. It was kind of like a museum of personal positive experiences but interactive.

Admittedly, there were a lot of technical problems. Since the house would represent "the Best of" my entire life and hopefully a long period of time, how old would I be? Did I enter the room of "My Second Grade Class and the Teacher I Loved" as an adult or a 7-year-old? I have minimal memories of my great-grandparents but have pictures of them holding me as a baby with great love. I'd like to reconnect with them, too. Would I be an infant?

Also, what about relationships that had started out so wonderfully but later turned sour and caused a lot of pain? Should these be represented? If so, would I still be able to revisit the heartwarming feelings and happy times, knowing what eventually occurred down-the-line? Could I change the outcome? That might throw off the rest of my life history, and some of the other people I loved I might never have met. This was becoming far too complicated.

More important, what about the people I had chosen? Some of my rooms would be filled with relatives and inspirational role models or mentors, many of whom *(like my great-grandparents)* were already well along in years when our paths crossed. I may have remembered the summer I spent at age six at the lake with my grandmother as idyllic, but she was in her late fifties at the time and suffering from severe arthritis. Just maybe she would prefer to be immortalized in Heaven by a younger, healthier version of herself *(from long before I had even been born)*. What if there were people, whether I was aware of it or not, whom I would like to put in my personal Heaven, but they would totally reject the role I had assigned to them or didn't want to be there?

This was logically spinning out of control. Of course, if this was Heaven, it didn't matter. We could each have our own. Heaven doesn't have to follow natural laws. The fact that there might be an infinite number of Heavens also didn't matter nor that one person might be represented differently from one version to another. Anyway, that person would have his or her own Heaven where it really counted. Then it occurred to me. Forget about Heaven. Isn't this what happens anyway in consciousness? We all have our own, and it's chock-full, peopled out of our own needs and experiences. Maybe what I was conjecturing wasn't Heaven, after all, but just a psyche from which all the pain and nastiness had been removed and what remained was the perception of a very happy life?

Who are the central players in one's life story? How important are they for our personal happiness? There are people who have major impact and great emotional significance in our journey over life's course. With some, we feel such an overwhelming love and intimate bond, including long after the person has passed or we've parted ways. For people of faith, these profound relationships are some of the greatest gifts from God. For a period, we are real partners in *spirit*, at times almost seeming to merge to form an experiential bond, which feels greater than the shared life between us. From an emotional perspective, the depth of sharing and sense of meaningfulness that such relationships involve tend to lead to the conviction that they are soul-based, fated, or "written" on a higher level. Feelings of love do seem centralized in and emanate from the heart area, which is often associated with the *soul* or hub of spiritual connection.

Spiritual and nonspiritual people alike would probably agree that it is within our closest relationships that a lot of life challenges are played out, yet the bulk of our meaningful opportunities are also provided. Some close relationships are more or less lifelong; others may be relatively brief but intensely influence us far beyond the person's physical presence in our lives. Some relationships are purely by chance or choice. But many of our most intimate bonds, primarily family, are not by choice. We can choose to walk away from them, if we so desire, but we don't get to choose our parents or siblings or children in the same way that we do the other relationships in our lives. *(And we may never be able to emotionally walk away from them.)* There are also some that start out by choice but seem to become complicated and enmeshed beyond choice, such as work associations or when there are problems with your ex-spouse, who is the parent of your children.

The emotional power of close attachments is astounding. The connection between the two people is almost tangible. We physically *feel* the love, the yearning, the link from one individual to another. Family and romantic ties, in particular, are the focus of a level of love and hope and ideals that is truly mysterious, beyond words. They may also be the source of immense ambivalence, disappointment, anger, betrayal, guilt, loathing and self-loathing as well as violent crime. Most people feel intrinsically bonded to family members, whether or not their history together has been positive or negative, even when they have not been engaged in each other's lives.

There are differences in how people who are spiritually oriented and those who are nonspiritual seem to understand and approach close relationships. First and most important, people of faith assume there is a higher *spiritual* dimension that is acknowledged and experienced in their most intimate ties. Just as the *soul* or *spiritual being* is felt to be our true nature and the most important part of who we are, close personal relationships are presumed to be two *souls* together with a foundation and truth on the *spiritual* level. Because this higher dimension derives from God, it is experienced as beneficial, meaningful, ideal, and potentially healing. It is also assumed to be beyond human understanding. We may feel so spiritually bonded to another person although we don't know why or what this means. We just *feel* it throughout our being. It also goes without saying that this idea of a higher *spiritual* dimension in relationships is not acknowledged *(and felt to be foolish fantasy)* in the secular world.

Like so much within a perspective of faith, relationships are about greater meaning and purpose and optimally serving God and the greater unity. The person of faith is always aware of being part of a spiritual family. We interact and connect through cycles and bonds of *spirit* with our brothers and sisters over the course of our lives. Some of those bonds are particularly strong and some of the cycles long-lasting. The relationship in *spirit* always seems greater than the two partners involved but also part of something greater still. Again, there is the image of a web of *spirit* connecting us all, which is paradoxically fluid but binding. In close relationships, it's almost as though the individual is sharing a particular spot on that web with certain other people for a period of time. Once bound in *spirit*, the love or feeling of connection tends to remain, at least in some form.

Within a spiritual view, along with the idea that interactions with people in general are seen as having a *higher* purpose, our closest and most intimate relationships are assumed to as well. They also come into our lives to provide *love* and *support*… to *teach*… to *create*… or to *share* life, but all in a major way. It is often through those closest and most intimate ties that we learn some of our greatest lessons and find individual spiritual purpose. However long they last, people of faith know that our human bonds come from God and that we need to honor and cherish them for the magnificent gifts that they are.

What does all this mean? Practically, there is always presumed to be a higher *soul*-based level of interaction within the intimate bond between two people, whether this is honored as such or not. On the human surface, the two people may be mother and daughter, husband and wife, best friends, or long-time business partners. On the spiritual level, it is assumed that these are also two *souls* who have come together for a reason. Perhaps, for these *souls*, spiritually there is a greater history or future beyond the current human attachment, in which they are so involved, and the present earthly relationship is just one small part of a much larger spiritual picture. We just don't know.

What we do become aware of is that, just as human beings in general seem to exist on two levels at once *(the spiritual and psychological)*, relationships also play out on these levels as well. Again, we grow *spiritually* through the prism of our *psychological* experience. Thus, the spiritual purpose in our relationships will be played out in the individuals sharing in the *human* world on the *physical* plane. Obviously, we don't go around constantly discussing with our spouse about how God is teaching us about love through our union, even if we are strongly spiritually committed. What we do is, first, love each other. Second, we share our lives, which sometimes tests our love and clearly illustrates and calls for a range of loving actions, such as patience, compromise, loyalty through the rough times, or putting one's own desires aside for the other person. What this means is, by fully engaging in our relationships *(through our human actions and emotional reactions, experience, joys, and regrets)*, we learn about love and ultimately honor the higher purpose in the relationship. We fulfill the purpose by *living* it. We learn about *love,* by *loving.*

That being said, the duality of human experience and balancing the *spiritual* and *psychological* parts within ourselves is never easy. This is true in all aspects of life but especially when it comes to personal attachments, where the desires and needs are so strong. This can seem to work in two ways. First, the ups and downs of human relating can impact the very foundation of faith. In the relationship with God, it can be so difficult to maintain faith when we have been betrayed or disappointed by someone we trusted or deeply care about or when a loved one dies. When we lose a close personal bond, for whatever reason, the painful emotions are excruciating and destabilizing. The bottom seems to have dropped out of life. Relationships are that important in our human existence.

When it comes to personal bonds, it can be extremely challenging to defer to God's greater wisdom and to accept what has occurred in a faith oriented way. Sometimes the spiritual purpose of the relationship is not what we want it to be or ends too quickly, which feels so intolerable to have to accept. The purpose of any relationship will play out in its own time although sometimes that "time" means it fizzles out quickly, goes nowhere, or seems to harshly and abruptly be snatched from our lives. Whatever its purpose, while the relationship is ongoing, optimally we need to let it breathe and grow in its own way. As with life in general, we need to have faith that the relationship is being led in the direction of its greatest good. In faith, we know that we can't second-guess God, but this can be especially difficult when it comes to loss or disappointments because the human emotions are just so fierce.

The second challenge in dealing with personal relationships in a faith oriented way is the nature of human interaction. God is a source of comfort, if we allow this, even during the most dispiriting times. Human beings, not so much *(even during the best of times)* or at least not consistently. In our close relationships, things can get messy fairly quickly as the never-ending parade of self-help books, relationship experts, attachment workshops, soul mate seminars, family therapists, and divorce lawyers can attest. Whether in a family or marriage or even successful business partnership, amicable coexistence can be a challenge to maintain, let alone harmony or those warm feelings of joy and love that we all crave.

Why is human relating so difficult? Even with the best intentions, whenever two people relate to each other, this automatically creates two sets of potential complications. Each individual has his or her own self agendas, personal needs, expectations, sore points, defenses, dysfunctional issues, values, and relationship history *(and that's just for a start)*. In families or groups of people, this is compounded many times over. Whenever we are involved with others, not only do we bring our own baggage to the table, but there are also the questions as to the balance between self and others, the roles each person plays, how they communicate, and how dynamics like power and control are handled in the relationship.

Plus, *lower* psychological needs and emotions are part of all relationships, no matter how spiritually committed the two people may be. Not that this is necessarily negative. Human life and emotion can be so beautiful, a magnificent gift. It's what living is all about. Shared life and love can be awesome... raising children... bringing dreams to fruition... support through the rough patches and heartbreaks. People can be so generous in how they will love, support, and sacrifice for each other during difficult times. But even the smoothest relationships and those of great love *(whether family, romantic, or friendship)* can breed disappointment and conflict, big and small. When this happens, it is easy for one or both people to revert to a perspective of self-focus and defensiveness. Up pops the hurt and dejection, the testy frustration and accusatory anger, and the love goes into hiding.

Unhappily, the tendency is for these negative feelings to snowball, so there is always the possibility that the interaction between the two people begins to spiral downward to an even lower depth of disruption, defensiveness, and pain. In interpersonal friction and hostility, the natural pull is for each person to retreat into oversensitivity and negativity, even if he or she does not want to or tries not to. The *soul-*

based, *higher* dimension of the relationship, if even recognized, may become more and more obscured. What's worse is that there can be a cumulative effect over time with people hanging onto and beating each other up with all sorts of ugly feelings and projections. A lot of people would rather be "right" or "on top" than happy.

This is where a genuine spiritual approach can be so valuable. First, just knowing there is a *soul*-based purpose and dimension to the bond creates a higher standard. Second, just as a spiritual perspective holds out a *lifeline* in the midst of personal turmoil, it also does to some degree for relationships when problems and disagreements arise. When the toxic spiraling down dynamic begins, the spiritual directive is to seek the higher ground. So the person of faith tries to remain mindful that the relationship has a *spiritual* purpose and is a gift from God. Not only does this cast the attachment in a positive light of blessing but provides some staying power during the difficult periods. The more we can focus on the relationship as a gift, the greater will be the desire *(as well as a sense of responsibility)* to treat this precious affiliation with honor and care.

Similar to life in general, in relationships, the spiritual directive is to focus on the positive, to see the glass as half full, to appreciate what one has been given, and to give it a chance. This becomes a guiding principle, and when disputes or other issues arise, the individual is motivated towards self-examination and direction within the bond with God just as in other aspects of life. The person of faith will try to get past the hurt and self-oriented emotions enough to be able to step back and examine the bigger picture.

This can be a struggle and doesn't mean to suppress or ignore one's genuine feelings. These should be examined, too. But, in a relationship, it's never only *(or even primarily)* about one person's emotions or needs, although if we are hurt or feel mistreated, it's easy to fall into that position. The perspectives of both people need to be considered, and the higher meaning and purpose of the relationship are also critical elements. Most important is to get the relationship back on track and in sync spiritually with both parties once again recognizing and honoring the immense gift in the bond between them.

Yet, beyond an orientation of blessing and purpose, there are other positives in a spiritual approach. A belief in a higher level of being means just that. There is a *higher* spiritual dimension to our shared experience that involves both inner depth and transcendence and the feelings of connection, harmony, wholeness, and peace that are associated with the *spiritual* level of being. The bond between two people on the *soul* level enhances the quality of the emotional connection because there's more going on and it's being guided from a higher place.

This *higher* spiritual dimension creates a sense of great meaning and value, the uplifting of experience, and a depth of emotion. This holds the potential to enrich the relationship and the feelings between the two people. Spiritually grounded relationships tend to be experienced as more joyful and inspired, which is reinforcing. They just *feel* more fulfilling and open up a sense of ever greater potential, going forward. Also, when people have experienced a higher level of relating, they tend to want more of it and thus are more motivated to do what it takes to remain at this elevated level.

Is love synonymous with *spirit*? Is love the energy of God and the spiritual plane? Spiritually committed people believe in love as a higher emotion and unifying, motivating energy and force. This goes beyond solely sexual or romantic love but is understood as a *spiritual* love, which holds tremendous power, including to make us whole. It is love that binds us to God and to our spiritual family and envelops us in the mutual embrace of all things. It is also this higher love that can heal and transform us and connects us to those special people or *souls* and does so forever. This adds to the sense of wholeness, not only within our current situation or relationship, but over the course of our lives… and beyond.

This was brought home to me with regard to missing my father and sister. Time does dull grief and loss, but there are birthdays, anniversary dates, and holidays that pull for old memories, and the pangs arrive. It is only very occasionally, but there are still periods of outright pain from time to time. During the celebrations, big events, and good times, there is also a wistfulness and a little bit of feeling cheated. There was so much I would have liked to have shared with them… from getting my doctorate… to my art and what I thought about things… to having my father know me as an adult… to knowing my sister, had she become an adult… to some people in my life I really wish they could meet… and who would like to meet them.

As I became spiritually oriented, I began to reframe the pangs and the longing. I continued to have the painful feelings at times, but I began to see them differently. They were proof that the love was still there and strong after all these decades. I began to understand that the hurting and the love were two sides of the same coin. Once I realized this, whenever I started to have the irrevocable missing, I would immediately try to focus on, to feel, and even be enveloped in the love. It was sad, but the sadness meant it still mattered and that the love was still there and very deep-seated. We could no longer share on the physical plane *(and hadn't for a long time)*. Still, the love gave power and meaning to the bond that I know connects us forever. I could feel that intensely. So it felt less sad, in fact, more loving than sad, and ultimately whole.

From a spiritual perspective, love has many facets. It is both an intensely emotional and transcendent *feeling* as well as a higher bond and purpose that gets played out between two people. It is also a binding energy with the power to renew our lives. Love is also a higher absolute value and Truth. It may be viewed as one of the *God rails*, perhaps even one of the most important, and provides the basis for some of the other higher values, such as loyalty, compassion, and forgiveness. In other words, on a practical and human level, love involves responsibility and obligation. We don't only *feel* love. When we genuinely love, there is a moral imperative to behave at a *higher* level beyond the focus and needs of the *self*. We seek to come from a *higher* level of being with respect to the other person.

What this means is that a spiritual orientation places the relationship issues *(as well as the emotional reactions that such issues cause)* in the larger context of greater meaning and Truth and doing what is "right." In faith, the spiritual directives are fairly clear as to certain steps to take and others to avoid. There are "right and wrong" ways to treat other people, particularly within a committed or family relationship. To ride the *God rails* means that we are provided with both a *guide* to move the individual and relationship forward in a positive direction and on the "right" track, as well as a *guard* against loss of control, excess, or destructive action.

Again, we see the importance of the *higher* values as a compass and anchor, in this case, in navigating and nurturing our closest human attachments. In dealing with relationships, the *God rails* offer another benefit in that they provide an agreed upon standard and code of behavior that is outside the subjective and biased perspectives of the two individuals. Even if the two people can't agree and interpret the *God rails* differently, at least there's somewhat of a reference point, a starting place, and more objective "authority."

There isn't in the morally relativistic, secular world. This can be very disorienting. Of course, most people, whether spiritually oriented or not, do see love as a higher, purer emotion, whatever that means for them. In theory, most want to keep it that way. Those who are nonspiritual can be just as disturbed by ambivalence and conflict in their relationships and take their interpersonal responsibilities very seriously. They may also seek guidance when problems arise and can engage in honest examination of feelings with good results.

But, as we have seen in so many areas, without the clear spiritual directives and guidance of God or the higher values, any discipline is self-imposed, which is a tall order, particularly in the midst of negative emotion. For the nonspiritual person, making productive choices is more haphazard and less mandatory, and there can be a lot of confusion as to what those choices are. Without connection to a Higher Power or the experience of one's self and the relationship as part of something larger and meaningful, the tendency is to get sucked into and stay embroiled in the *lower* negative emotions despite an attempt to understand and resolve them.

In our secular world when relationships problems arise, we are advised to analyze both the issues and our feelings about them. We are told to be open and honest about our feelings, to talk things out, to compromise and negotiate. Great advice, when it works. For people, who are reasonable and thoughtful and able to maintain emotional control, this approach can be quite fruitful. It's the ideal. Yet, in order to affect real change *(whether with a therapist or the two people on their own)*, both have to be willing to take responsibility and to be open to the other person's point of view. They both have to be motivated to work on the relationship and amenable to trying new things. Even with well-intentioned insight and understanding, positive change or healing in the relationship is not guaranteed.

More often, when it comes to emotional situations *(and almost nothing is more emotional than close relationships)*, many people just can't maintain the control or perspective that is needed for constructive discussion and analysis. In working as a therapist, I have witnessed *(and been continually amazed by)* how incompatibly people perceive and interpret things. The most innocent remark or the tiniest difference in perception can explode the dialogue into stinging hurt and accusation. The two parties retreat, becoming entrenched in their anger and defensive positions. There is a true clash of realities, intention, or behavior that neither party can get beyond. There is an astute saying among marriage counselors that there are always three versions of truth *(his story... her story... and what really happened)*.

There also seems to be lot of free-floating negativity in contemporary life that can't be helpful. As I noticed when I removed myself from it, a lot of social interaction seems to be around crisis and emotional release, often through venting and especially about relationships. This may be beneficial and restorative up to a point. A friend of mine likes to compare negative feelings to venom from a snakebite… you need to get it out before it poisons the system. Then, once you get it out, it's time to get back to productive living. From a spiritual perspective, the negative feelings are *lower* level so there's always the risk that you can get stuck at that level. On the other hand, from a secular perspective, that's all there is.

So many people today do seem to be lost in a morass of destructive relating and feelings *(negativity, victimization, and self-pity)* with seemingly nowhere else to go. Again, there's the sense that, without clear guidance from external, agreed upon higher standards *(such as the God rails)*, people don't know what to do or where to go and end up spinning their wheels. There's a lot of complaining going on, which is then reinforced by others who are in the same situation.

Unfortunately, negativity begets negativity and tends to increase. At some point all this negativity, particularly the complaining and self-pitying, is guaranteed to seep into and affect the quality of the relationship, even if one of the reasons for venting in the first place was to get rid of the nasty feelings or keep them separate and outside *(e.g., by venting to a girlfriend about a child or husband)*. Negativity is a self-perpetuating, deteriorating cycle.

The narcissistic attitude of modern society also seems to be taking its toll on relationships. At the extreme, when it comes to relating to others, the narcissistic mindset seems to be "What can you do for me?" Or worse, the direct or implied message is "You are only valuable to me because of what you can do for me." A healthy, truly reciprocal relationship between narcissistically oriented people is an oxymoron anyway unless the two partners have perfectly similar or complementary needs. In the quest for romantic love, this seems to be exactly what many are seeking today, a mirror image of themselves. So many people seem to be embracing these narcissistic values without being aware they are doing so.

Even outside romantic attachments, the focus of so much of modern relating seems to be on defining, asserting, and fulfilling personal needs. Understanding what makes you "tick," where your partner *(or parent or child)* is coming from, and how to put it all together can be beneficial. Yet, when self agendas and the fulfillment of individual needs are the primary goal, the interaction runs the risk of becoming calculated and mechanical, sometimes to the point of minimizing the feelings and what is shared. Instead, the two people may become fixated on a formula of what each requires, personal boundaries, where compromise is possible, and exactly what it will take for both to be satisfied *individually...* instead of attending to the *shared* experience and bond between them. If need fulfillment is the goal, what can also happen is a lot of manipulation and control maneuvers with a progressive lack of regard or appreciation for the other person.

At the same time, when individual needs and agendas are the focus, what is expected from the other person or the relationship may be too idealistic or demanding. Sometimes there's little or no tolerance for pain or frailty or mistakes in the other person or the interaction. If needs are not being met or some aspect of the relationship calls for patience or compromise, this may be interpreted as an affront or a failure. Friendships and business associations are even more likely to be geared around personal agendas and immediate results. Even in family situations, there's a lot of hurt or blame and just plain nastiness thrown around, which can then escalate into major conflict, often out of relatively minor frustrations and disappointments.

And what about those bonds that don't involve choice, such as family? Although the attachments and feelings are so profound, it may be unclear why or how these two people would ever get along, at least on the surface. How could they be expected to perfectly complement one another or fulfill the other's needs? Often our family members are not the usual types of people we are drawn to or tend to socialize with because of wide differences in interests, attitudes, or lifestyle. Too often there's nothing in common, other than bonds of blood and tremendous love, and that's the dilemma. There's so much love, but both family members have the experience of coming up against a brick wall in terms of feeling or expressing it.

What's love got to do with it? Everything and nothing, or so it seems. A person can become so focused on the *lower* emotional needs that this gets in the way of feeling, let alone appreciating, the love. Modern people often appear caught in a push-pull ambivalence about what other people can or should mean and provide in their lives. This is particularly played out in their closest bonds. If the individuals could just focus on the tender, loving feelings and experience that sense of *higher* connection binding them in the first place, there tends to be a stabilizing effect... with the potential to cut through the turmoil or pent-up resentment and get the relationship living and breathing again and moving forward.

This is another way that a spiritual approach can be beneficial as it focuses on the tender, loving feelings and smaller moments as meaningful and important, again a gift from God. A spiritual directive is to honor, encourage, and cherish the *sharing* of life... to delight in the *soul schmoozing*... to celebrate the love that is inherent in the *higher* connection. The greater purpose of the relationship is always important. But, as in a spiritual approach in general, it is the small stuff that is the real substance of living and the human bond. Even if just one person in the relationship is able to stop and enjoy the loving feelings, a negative cycle may be halted in its tracks... with eventually both people able to return to and appreciate the blessing and *higher* love between them.

From a spiritual perspective, we also need to allow for healing in our relationships, including beyond our understanding. We have been so programmed to analyze ad nauseam our emotional issues, needs, and relationship dysfunction. Yet, from a spiritual perpsective, resolution or healing tends to occur in unexpected ways. On the *human* level, we easily get stuck in the mechanical ideas of tit for tat... of figuring things out... of fixing things. On the *spiritual* level, it is miraculous how one unintended meeting, an expression of tenderness, a moment shared, heartfelt forgiveness, a sudden insight, or truly being open to beginning a new chapter in the relationship can *(just like that!)* heal and even erase years of anguish, estrangement, or emotional pain.

On the human level, the more we can honor and connect with the *soul* of the other person, the better the relationship will be. We open up the potential for enrichment and unfolding of the bond of *spirit* with another individual in ways that previously seemed impossible. The spiritual is the level of love, redemption, and healing. We give it up to God, and miracles can and do occur.

16 Revving the Spiritual Engine

"I'm in love with you," he said. "Know that you are loved." I had expected something might happen between us, but the intensity of his feeling took me entirely by surprise. We had been friends for a long time, years really. I remember when we first met, there was a clear attraction, but I saw that he was with someone so I let that go *(having learned that lesson)*. Then over the years, there were late night phone conversations that went on for hours, and increasingly we began working together on artistic projects. Once it was business, at least on my end, it was easy to keep boundaries intact *(another lesson learned the hard way)*. Plus, sometimes you just become such good friends, why risk it?

In the six months before he "declared" himself, as we would later joke *(i.e., kind of like a Western beau in a frontier town)*, we had been working together on different locations throughout southern California. I would wander off as he was doing his photography, for hours it seemed. I never understood his fiddling with the lenses, the angles, and the light. I always felt so at peace, surreally so. Underneath the blazing California heat or more often at sunset, I roamed through the desert brushes, the beaches or dunes, always turning back to see him… a man and his camera. Was it the beauty of the natural settings? I wondered. It felt so strangely joyful and full, and I never understood it… there was the familiarity of family… a security of long ago… a feeling of home… Then I'd push aside such feelings as we'd pack up the gear and return to the city.

Within a few short months after the declaration, we had begun the process of dismantling our separate lives. Quite unexpectedly, the circumstance presented itself, and we decided to move away from California. On a whim and a prayer? I know people from our respective circles thought we were crazy. *("What?" "With who?")* One day we climbed into an overfull car, immediately getting stuck in rush hour traffic for three hours… one last time. That didn't matter. We were together. I would say that we drove off into the sunset… except that we were heading East.

How do you step up to your own destiny? How do you grab that personal brass ring? Spiritually oriented people almost always feel they are being led, but that's only part of the story. At some point, it doesn't seem to be about God any longer but the courage of the individual. We are given opportunities, but do we use them? To take action… to have the guts to live an authentic life… to be honest with one's self… to follow one's heart and dreams… to stand up and be counted? To step into the shoes or life that God has provided? All of us have our own path, but do we live it to the fullest? Why are some people immediately able to grasp opportunities… to make the tough but right choices for themselves… to walk the walk… and jump off that existential diving board into the unknown?

I've learned that, if you want to really bond with others, ask how they got to the turning points in their lives. How did you two meet? How did you end up moving to… *(fill in city)*? How did you decide to go into this business or end up with that job? The eyes sparkle but then glaze a bit with heartfelt nostalgia. Sometimes the person may seem to trail off into memories of his or her own special life story with the focus on the unusual, entirely unexpected, and mysteriously coincidental parts.

From the outside looking in, sometimes it sounds so fragile. A whole life built on the smallest of occurrences that, if they hadn't come together just right and the person hadn't made those exact choices, everything would have turned out completely differently, which would have been so wrong. Usually for the author of the saga, there's a mixture of wonderment and pride. Sometimes there is the sense of a larger force, whether God or Fate, involved in these stories but also a point of individual action. "If I hadn't gone to that coffee shop that morning… made the wrong turn… slipped on the curb… indulged the strange, old duffer, spinning his yarn in the hardware store…"

Sometimes there is a sense of sudden, urgent clarity or determined resolution: "I knew this was the woman I was going to marry…" "I sprang into action…" "It was like something deep within was propelling me…" "I said this is 'the One' and I have to do whatever it takes…" "I drove up and down until I found…" "I saw my destiny standing in front of me… and then slipping away…" There may be a feeling of haste or limited time, almost a mandate to act or forever hold your peace, as though life's carousel going round and round is about to pass on by. It may seem it is this moment and this moment alone that will capture the prize. Some people even describe some version of feeling "the chilling hand of Fate on my shoulder" as though warning "Now or never."

There are also those who relate similar experiences but did not act on them. These tend to be presented in the manner of cautionary tales, the message being to listen to that inner voice. Sometimes this is portrayed as what could have been in tones of wistfulness and regret. Others describe a missed opportunity or road not taken as a difficult but pivotal lesson learned the hard way. What is interesting is that such occurrences are given such importance. It's almost as though there was a glow around the opportunity *(however it was presented)* or there was something just so striking and personally riveting about it that seldom occurs in life. Even when people do seize the moment, they may feel so thankful and sometimes mystified that they were able to do so. Always in the background lurks the question: Is the window of opportunity random luck and serendipity or is there the involvement of a greater Power beyond ourselves?

In contemporary society, to act impulsively is frowned upon and advised against, usually equated with emotional loss of control and irresponsibility, even when there's none of either involved. We are taught to be cautious and rational, to do research, weigh options, consider choices, to logically and objectively think things through. All this is good advice but works better in some areas than others. In matters of the heart or morality, making the right decisions and when to take action may reflect an entirely different process. Certainly, the secular mainstream discounts the idea of external "signs" or being led or even intuition *(beyond a socially sanctioned comfort level)*. Those who are more spiritually or metaphysically oriented tend to rely on such things.

Not that they always get it right. I've noticed that spiritual people can focus on the smallest occurrence as holding possible significance *(I do this, myself)*. Sometimes such ruminations are productive; at other times, not at all. Still, it's part of an overall process that does seem productive. People of committed faith assume they are being guided by God although they know that they can never read God's mind, so to speak. But they remain watchful and seek to listen for God in the playing out of their lives. As a result, there does seem to be more openness to the entirety of their experience. They anticipate direction and opportunity, even when not asked for. People of faith assume Absolute Truth is beyond human understanding. So they believe in miracles and look for meaning, even guideposts, in those occurrences, however trivial, which appear so enigmatic or unexplained.

The first part of stepping up to your own destiny would be *believing* in your own destiny. The second would be *recognizing* opportunities when they exist. The third would be *acting* upon them. We can't do the last if we don't know the opportunities are there... or we don't believe in the concept in the first place. How can we grab the brass ring if we don't look for it? Worse, we may not even see it because we're so focused on the carousel twirling by. The secular focus on what is rational and the assumption that everything derives from chance *(the creed of the Coincidence Crowd)* can translate into an individual discounting, even being blind to, potentially meaningful aspects of personal experience.

Too much rational analysis can sometimes get in the way in decision making in general. Human intelligence is one of the greatest gifts that we have, particularly for carrying out effective, goal-oriented effort in the physical world. Yet it is easy for a feeling of intellectual control to become equated with total control, which it isn't at all. We can over-think things and even hide behind endless analytical deliberations (i.e., the pros and cons... alternate hypotheses and possibilities... the what ifs and gray areas). We can also be lulled into complacency by the assumption that, if one opportunity presented itself, especially so easily and unexpectedly, the probability is that there are bound to be others down-the-line, maybe even something better in store. Of course, we never know if there will be another anything.

People who do grab the brass ring may have similar hesitancies. Sometimes there is a backing off, or the psychological defenses come up, flashing "Abort! Abort!" The person may do so for a space before final commitment or charging ahead full steam. There is no escaping the reality that opportunity is potential but never a guarantee and a process fraught with uncertainty. Nevertheless, it is this process that people who do get the prize speak of time after time. Even those who take the plunge but don't get the prize often feel that they learned something important or were led to something else worthwhile. Just the feelings of integrity and authenticity that come from having plunged can be significant in a positive way. There is great pride in stepping up to the plate, even if the final outcome is not what was anticipated or hoped for.

One thing that always frustrated me about psychology is the reliance on formulas. This doesn't mean that all human beings are assumed to be the same, but formulas can give the impression that they are and that life is a lot easier to navigate than it is. Notably, within popular trends and self-help, we are offered a lot of programs and recipes or techniques... to find the key, solve the issue, create the ideal. We may also seek any little snippet of information that might apply to who we are, from newspaper astrological summaries to formal tests like the Myers-Briggs Type Indicator *(i.e., Are you a Extrovert or Introvert? Thinker or Feeler?)* I know I'm a sucker for all those psychological quizzes in women's magazines, which define "What type of... lover... worker... color... season... dessert...or music... is embedded in your personality?" *(i.e., Are you crème brulee or chocolate cake? Country western or classical?)* Sometimes we actually do learn something from these seemingly silly scraps of data, but probably more important is that they provide reassurance that there are others at least somewhat like us, so we don't feel so abnormal or alone.

As a therapist, I've learned we may all fit into some formula to some degree although no one seems to end up that way. Using a formula or program may be helpful and might seem to be a more focused and efficient approach to life. At the same time, by totally investing in a formula, we also run the risk of losing sight of the gift of our individuality or of straitjacketing ourselves into limited expectations or unimaginative plans as to how to move forward. Such formulas create an illusion of predictability, which is rarely found in life, especially when it comes to the important choices. Formulas can become a crutch instead of a springboard. People get lulled into the assumption that the formula or program is supposed to do the work and then unwittingly assume they don't have to.

Nonspiritual people might argue that faith or religion or the *God rails* are nothing more than a formula and provide a program for dealing with life. So why wouldn't this be a crutch and the same caveats apply? After all, faith does provide principles of belief and behavior that have been manifest in some form in societies throughout the globe and recorded time. People of committed faith will acknowledge that faith does represent a program but one of Absolute Truth *(i.e., coming from God, not human beings)* and thus worthy of following. In contrast, those who are secular tend to maintain that truth coming out of scientific endeavor is more accurate and should be relied upon, including fact-based formulas. This gets down to one's basic belief system, and there is no way to reconcile these two perspectives. Do we depend on God or humankind for piloting our lives?

Whatever one decides, it usually requires some measure of courage to take advantage of what life has to offer. Beyond belief in and recognizing your own destiny, you have to be able to go after it when it appears. The common association to courage is *physical,* when an individual willingly risks bodily harm. There is also *psychological* courage, which can manifest in different areas and may be even more difficult for some people. Existential courage *(i.e., being honest and authentic with one's self)* may require social courage *(i.e., to go against the tide of convention)* and moral courage *(i.e., to do what is "right")* in following one's destiny and dreams. There's no way around it. In courage, the cold winds of risk are always nipping at one's neck.

As a therapist, I am quite familiar with how people confront and struggle with emotional danger. Sometimes the risks are very real, or they may be perceived as out of proportion to the true threat involved, a product of the imagination or strong emotion. Often there is a combination of both *(i.e., Yes, you do run the risk of being rejected if you ask the woman out... but it's not the end of your world if she does so).* Sometimes the analysis of costs and benefits is multilayered. Some feel it is almost always better to take the risk, even if there is a high probability of rejection or failure, because at least they'll *know*, which means no regrets later on. This is the idea that "when I'm sitting in my rocking chair at 90 years old, I don't have to wonder what could have been..." The more I saw clients in therapy and how they struggled with inhibition and the stagnation it caused, the more valid this perspective seemed to be.

Sometimes it's not even the emotional risk but the accompanying anxiety that is so toxic. Fear and anxiety are nasty stuff, perniciously creeping in under the radar and doing a number on our lives. Anxiety can be crippling, literally paralyze a person from doing anything or cause a retreat backwards to presumed safety. One of the most common and self-destructive maneuvers that people use to cope with anxiety is *avoidance*, which can become so entrenched that it turns into a way of life. What happens is that, instead of dealing with an issue or person that is causing the anxiety, the individual backs off and does everything in his or her power to avoid the situation *(which only makes it worse)*. Whatever thoughts or fantasies are associated with the anxiety tend to grow bigger and scarier the longer we don't deal with the fear. And, if every time we summon up a modicum of courage to approach the feared situation *(or person)*, we then clutch or run away, there is such overwhelming, even bodily, relief that the *avoidance* gets reinforced as an easy out. *Avoidance* becomes a very difficult pattern to break.

The effect of anxiety and fear is unpredictable. Sometimes such uncomfortable feelings can prove to be motivating because the person is so desperate. At times, this can be productive. It becomes the final push to get the issue resolved, to take the necessary chance, to move the individual forward in the right direction towards a goal. There can also arise an urgent compulsion, a need to do something, *anything*, to rid oneself of the anxious feelings *(i.e., gotta do something, don't care what it is)*. Such precipitous calls to action are usually not productive. Impulsive behavior, just for the sake of doing something, more likely goes nowhere and can be self-sabotaging. Yet there are times when anxiety seems to create an exciting edge that is useful. For example, performers, public speakers, and athletes often speak of needing that edge of fear in order to do their best.

From an emotional perspective, one of the most debilitating fears is of disapproval from others. Lack of social courage is definitely one of the greatest impediments to moving forward on one's optimal path. Sadly, despite the freethinking and tolerant veneer of present-day society, condemnation of outsiders is alive and well. Societal norms are supposed to provide guides as to how to achieve an appropriate and successful life but too often seem to end up being inflexible prescriptions of normality with the intolerant result that those who veer may feel negatively categorized or scorned. This can be an extremely uncomfortable place to be.

What is ironic today is that in fiction, the media, and the culture at large, we glamorize questioning authority and living to the beat of a different drummer. But, when most people meet others who really do make atypical choices, even when they appear relatively successful or admirably together, the reaction tends to range from viewing this unconventional person as benignly eccentric *(but still deserving of the mocking eye-roll)* to unseemly or downright creepy *(although some sinister people certainly are)*. The popular directive seems to be to "Do your own thing," but the hidden message is to make sure you do it within societal norms. It can take a lot of courage to truly go against the tide of conformity. Although this has always been the human condition, it does seem rather convoluted that what is considered irreverent or superficially rebellious has become the agreed upon normal standard. To adhere to traditional values, including faith, is going against convention at the present time. This is especially true with regard to moral courage, rarely a consideration anymore.

If we conceptualize courage *(in any area of life)* as involving working through fear, is it easier for people of faith? In some ways, the fear dynamic and how to deal with it would seem to play out differently since courage would appear to go with the territory of a spiritually committed life. The definition of faith implies *spiritual* courage by looking to God *(not humankind)* for direction and the commitment to try to follow one's correct spiritual path, whatever that calls for. Faith also involves trust without proof, to exercise will and choose to act *(despite uncertainty and without guarantee as to outcome)*, and to do what is "right" *(often going against societal norms)*. This doesn't mean it is easy. We are *psychological* as well as *spiritual beings*. Courage is courage. This means you've got to bite the bullet in some way.

Theoretically, faith should be expected to take away some of the fear because there is the assumption of Truth… of trust in a Higher Power… of ultimately being led towards a positive outcome, at least in the broader picture. Having made that commitment, it is definitely better when you feel that God's got your back and you are doing what you are supposed to do *(such as what is "right"… or to act upon an opportunity to which you have been led)*. There is also the assumption that life is about taking action and *learning*, even if you don't get what you think is going to be the prize. It's all part of the journey and may eventually be a steppingstone to something more important or you learn something important. Faith is inherently a challenging course.

For the spiritually committed person, there is also the loving and supportive relationship with God, and with God, we are never alone. In times of risk or crisis, adversity and hardship, it is always better *not* to have to handle everything by one's self, but to have a friend and companion, a coach and cheerleader in one's corner. Spiritual people may also derive great strength from "giving it up to God." This means taking a mental leap of faith that what will be, will be *(but in accordance with God's plan)* and then resolutely going forward. It is also interesting that the bodily feelings associated with courage seem to involve the heart, also the focal area of love and spiritual *connection*, suggesting a kind of mobilization of energy, a coming together of emotional and transcendent power.

Sometimes it's not taking that leap but sticking with it over the long run that is so elusive. Most of us know people who take the leap… after leap… and leap again… and may even spend the majority of their lives looking for the next cliff from which to jump, but they seem to have no staying power. Beyond courage, there is also the importance of *will*, a quality not much talked about today. *Will* is associated with extraordinary determination and resolve, perseverance and fortitude, strict discipline and self-control, the ability to ardently push towards a goal and see it through. With *will*, individual motivation has become so strong that it seems to take on a force all its own.

In today's instant gratification world, with so many assuming it is their inalienable right to get what they want and to *feel* good, lack of willpower... and the false promises, shortcuts, and quick fixes this engenders... are some of the biggest moneymakers around. Yet, when people do finally quit smoking, lose the weight, or get on top of the addiction, it is often a major turning point that wasn't necessarily precipitated by anything clear-cut or in the outside world. Rather, the crucial piece seems to be an intense decision *within* to finally do what needs to be done. Sometimes the stories of willful motivation are truly astounding. I have had several people tell me that they used to be painfully shy, which is generally a lifelong and self-sabotaging problem that may even have some genetic or biological basis. This means the person may be wired to be shy, so it's very hard to change. At some point, each of them just decided they didn't want to live their lives that way and made the willful decision to overcome it and did.

Where does such willful resolution come from? Sometimes what is described in successful *will* is that there appears to have been accessed an empowering and compelling inner force, arising from an unexpectedly deep place, unlike anything the person has experienced before. There's the perception of a decisive internal shift as though a personally monumental corner has been turned... a kind of feeling that 'This is The Day...'" There may be bodily stirrings of vigor or arousal with an accompanying feeling of desperation or hunger or "fight" that propels the person forward. There may even be a sense of strength or energy coming from beyond one's self, which carries the individual along.

At some point, *will* merges into *intention* and raises the question as to the nature of spiritual Power in our lives. Getting control over an addiction or dysfunctional habit is one thing. While this requires tenacity, it's about stopping a real problem that regrettably has been part of the person's life. There are also people who report a sense of *intention* or *will* with regard to future events or creating something that doesn't yet exist. For example, there are those who describe a specific moment when they decided they would find the person they were going to marry *(or similar life-transforming opportunity)* and within six months did so. Accompanying such points of decision may be that same sense of strong internal shift and bodily feelings that are associated with *will* and unlike anything previously experienced.

How does this happen? Can we really draw something into our lives? Through *will* alone, can we send out messages that are then heard and affect the cosmos and/or our personal existence in some way? Does *intention* create reality? Not necessarily. Often such wish-fulfilling occurrences can rationally be explained as a marked change in attitude, and this resulted in a new psychological readiness to take realistic effort towards a goal. In other words, what happened was not fantastic or metaphysical at all, but something was motivating the person, whether consciously or not, to get serious in an area of life.

An example would be an unmarried woman *(who has always wanted a family)* begins to hear her biological clock ticking louder and louder. She may suddenly come to the panicky realization that "Time's a-wasting." This may impel her to undertake a comprehensive dating search and be more interested in the practical, kid-loving, family-oriented qualities of real men for the first time, rather than waiting for Prince Charming to magically appear and whisk her off to a life of endless champagne brunches on tropical shores. Obviously, such changes in mindset and behavior do increase the probability that she will meet someone and marry as a result of her quest.

But the popular idea of *intention* is that we can affect what happens, actually manifest a result, through our thoughts alone. The individual may not seem to be doing anything differently in terms of behavior but describes an *intention* in consciousness, which then appears in real world events and opportunities. What this means is that the personal *will* in one's mind is assumed to create an energy that has a physical impact on his or her life. In this scenario, the caricature of the marriage-seeking woman above would be that, instead of scouring the dating landscape, she could simply conjure up Prince Charming through consciousness alone *(although she would still have to be able to recognize him when he materializes)*.

More seriously, this notion of *intention* is similar to the ancient Buddhist saying, "When the student is ready, the teacher will appear." The effort may still be there, but it's in consciousness, not through organized planning or goal-oriented behavior. Thoughts are assumed to be things and, if given enough energy, will manifest in the external physical environment. On the other hand, this isn't a fairy tale wand of automatic blessings. There is always the possibility that our true *intention* may be unconscious *(and thus not what we think it is)*. In this case, we may be unaware of what we are projecting, which could be risky if it happens to be negative.

The concept of *intention* is common but interpreted variously in modern metaphysical theories, some of which do not necessarily involve God. This is why *visualization* is talked about so much today. By *visualizing* what you want or need in consciousness, it is assumed that the likelihood is maximized that this will materially appear. *Affirmations* represent another technique, in which verbal statements of *intention* are repeated and sent out *(e.g., I will find the right job)* to presumably load cosmic energy in the direction of a desired result.

While sounding far-fetched to the scientifically oriented mainstream, sometimes such ideas *(or some version thereof)* are accepted and sometimes rejected by more traditional spiritual belief systems. This line of thought does raise the question, which most traditional belief systems do address, as to the Power of God in our lives. What is the interplay between the Power of God and our individual power and effort in the physical world? Is there a way that we can access such

Power? To what degree does our attitude or goal or *intention* mesh with God's plan and creates or influences our own destiny?

Clearly, a relationship with God can provide encouragement and support as the individual navigates through life. Yet spiritually committed people tend to experience faith as going beyond the immense emotional benefits of feeling God in one's corner. The Higher Authority and Power of God are felt to be very real and impact us directly. As people open to faith, it becomes apparent that there is opportunity and power when we invite God into our lives. This seems to be experienced as a cycling dynamic. Through faith, we yield control and power to God, who then gives us power. This cycle is also ever increasing. The greater our faith and thus the power we give to God, the greater it seems that the Power of God will play out in our individual existence.

Prayer is one of the most observable instances of such cycling Power. For people of faith, prayer works. Sometimes we pray by making a direct and specific request. At other times, prayer may be more open-ended or vague as to what is asked, although what we receive may be quite clear, such as an answer to a particular question… a relationship healed… an opportunity appearing… a life saved. There is also prayer, not of any distinct appeal or personal request, but of invoking God's will. This is the idea of "So be it" or "Thy will be done." Sometimes this represents a general openness to be led on our true path; at other times, there is an entreaty for God's will to be manifest in a defined area of our lives or concerning a special issue. We may ask for a sign or a direction or that a certain situation be dealt with. But we leave it up to God as to if, what, when, where, and how this will occur. We also leave open the possibility that the resolution will *not* be in accordance with our human desires.

In dealing with some of the most challenging or devastating life circumstances, sometimes people report coming to a point of utter deference and yielding to God. This tends to be experienced as though hitting an emotional wall, followed by a leap into complete faith. This is then accompanied by feelings of peace, clarity, even acceptance. For instance, when faced with the tragedy of a critically ill child, the individual may reach a place of total surrender with the profound realization that this circumstance is beyond human understanding and can *only* be in God's hands. Perhaps, the person has become so exhausted, internally buffeted, or overwhelmed by the ravages of the emotional upheaval in trying to deal with the situation. In giving it up to God, similar to taking a mental leap of faith before some action, there may be a sense of transcendent release… of acknowledging this horrific situation is outside personal and human control. In doing so, the individual may be able to move beyond the emotional level of clinging and pain to some degree or at least receive some temporary respite from the traumatic situation.

For most people, whether spiritually oriented or not, the tendency is to focus on the miracles and turning points in discussing faith… the obvious gifts received, the reprieves at the last minute, the requests granted, the critical opportunities and lessons learned. More often, the Power of God is indirect and subtle, and it is this larger but less visible picture, which is not as clear-cut, but most significant in the overall life course. In faith, it is believed we are nudged and pushed along in a certain direction, sometimes through ostensibly negative and sometimes positive circumstances, but always towards our greatest good and spiritual growth. Spiritually committed people will feel and see the Power of God all around them, as well as the nudges and blessings, although it always remains a mystery as to the exact nature and full extent of that Power in their lives.

As we have repeatedly seen, one important aspect of faith is a belief that the greater spiritual order is benevolent. It is a higher order often associated with love. *Positive thinking* is one variant of faith. It can be powerful in our lives because it affirms the love of God and implies gratitude. When we maintain a positive attitude towards life in general and see the glass as half full, we are exhibiting our trust in God's love and Power. Like faith, *positive thinking* needs to involve acceptance of possibly going in a different direction or being surprised by a multitude of possibilities, many of which are beyond our understanding *(and perhaps even our capacity to imagine)*. Being positive means remaining open to the hope and potentiality. We don't know what the opportunity or answer will be, but we do know that the opportunity or answer will come.

For people of faith, one of God's great gifts is the potential brightness of the future horizon. *Positive thinking* in any given situation means expecting the best outcome. This is advised in almost everything that we do or hope for, even if what we are hoping is that something negative will *not* occur. This is similar to planting a flower seed. We don't really know what the actual flower will look like although we can hope that it will be somewhat like the picture on the package or better. We can't guarantee the result or even that there will be a result, but *positive thinking* is important because we are planting the *positive* seed. We may not have control, but we do have hope and vision and the willingness and courage to give it a go. By remaining optimistic, we are nurturing the *positive* seed with hope and love but at the same time acknowledging that we don't have control and ultimately giving it up to God.

On the other side of the coin, spiritually oriented people see the expectation of negative outcomes as arising from a lack of faith. *Negative thinking* may be seen as a repudiation of God and God's love and giving in to our limited psychological perspective of fear and anxiety. If we sow the *negative* seed, we run the risk of killing off hope and positive expectations. If it's your worst nightmare, you might just create it. The less faith one has in the benevolence and love of the *higher* spiritual order, the more likely it is that the final outcome will be distorted or influenced by fear and doubt, spawned by *lower* psychological desires, societal values, or an attempt at feeling in control.

In faith, attitude and intention are a commitment to *being* on the *spiritual* level but a commitment to *doing* on the *physical* level. What this means is that we realize, no matter how much *will* or courage we may have, intention or prayer is only powerful when it coincides with the greater spiritual order and God's plan. In general, any intention that supports God and the spiritual unity is *correct*. It is a generation of love. Anything that intends separation or suffering is *incorrect*. It is a rejection of love and may generate harm.

What is *correct* versus *incorrect* isn't always clear or immediately apparent. To use a mundane example, what happens if a man breaks off a romantic relationship because he knows it is going nowhere, but this causes suffering for the woman with whom he was involved? He didn't intend to hurt her. If the relationship was *incorrect* on the spiritual level, the intention to break up would be *correct* although it caused the woman to suffer on the physical level. By going through that pain, theoretically she should be able to move forward, at some point finding the *correct* relationship spiritually.

This is a complicated but important dynamic. God knows the *correct* spiritual order. Human beings do not. In the above example, if the relationship was actually spiritually *correct*, but it was the man's emotional hang-ups that were getting in the way, then the intention to break up would be *incorrect*. So how do we know and make judgments on such things? We don't. We can't know God's plan for us fully and directly although there may be signs and we can be open to being led. Our human perspective has a tendency to convolute even knowledge of ourselves. This is why it is so important to have an ongoing relationship with God, in which the person can undergo honest self-examination and listen, in order to be guided along one's *correct* spiritual path.

In attempting to follow that *correct* path, spiritually committed people may also seek to examine whether they are supported in the actualization of their endeavors in the physical world. They *feel* the power of God directing their lives and over time may begin to apprehend whether what they are pursuing or doing is in the *correct* direction or not. In theory, our intentions are validated and given power when they are in accordance with the *correct* spiritual order. They are given no power when they are *incorrect*. People of faith often have this perception, which is repeatedly validated through their experience. Sometimes the best laid plans or good intentions do seem to just wither away, even when they would appear to be serving God and spiritually sound. No matter what we come up with, it just doesn't work or doesn't seem to attract any support or energy. We are getting the message that the *correct* move is to change course *(which may not be what we wanted to hear)*. At the same time, there may be unexpected avenues that seem to be pulling us in another direction.

It is important to emphasize *correct* does not mean easy. *Correct* intentions often involve obstacles, even extreme tests of will and courage. Yet we feel, in the heart, that this is the *correct* course despite difficulties that may arise. Again, sometimes we are pushed along as though there is no personal choice. *Correct* intentions are rarely just magically fulfilled. Rather, what seem to appear are the external opportunities and resources which eventually can lead to the fulfillment of the intention. Whether or not the intention is fully actualized depends on the spiritual commitment, effort, and courage of the individual.

Although having made that commitment, the opportunities can be fleeting, and we have to seize the moment and act quickly. In fact, to not do so may feel as though the person is not honoring God. If thankfulness is a spiritual directive, it also gives us power by celebrating the love and gifts of God. And, just like those gifts that we have received in terms of specific talents and advantages on the physical plane, when clear and genuine opportunities appear, we need to take hold of, develop, and nurture them. We honor them, not just through gratitude, even though this may be sincere and heartfelt. We thank God most – by making them our own.

17 Soft Heart

It was only a month or so ago that I had my last *soft heart* episode. Ever since I was small, I hated to see what I thought was suffering in another's face. Observing another person obviously disappointed or hurt would produce a smothering, sorrowful anguish for me, always in the heart area. If I had been a perpetrator in any way *(and at times I definitely was)*, the guilt could take days to let up, even when apologies had been made. Driving through the poorer sections of the city or encountering a feeble, downtrodden, or severely handicapped individual could viscerally haunt me. Sometimes I felt a literal bond with other people, even those I did not know. Strangely, even though it felt like I hurt with their pain *(or at least what I imagined it to be)*, this seemed to be a precious thing.

I never talked about these heart pangs with anyone. So it was with great astonishment that it was my youngest sister, seven years my junior, who helped me to understand my feelings. We would be playing with the neighborhood crowd *(there was a brief window when she was entering the group as I was about to matriculate out)*. If someone would tease or say something hurtful or make fun in a cruel way, my sister, the smallest among us, would stop and speak with the compelling conviction that only an honest vulnerability can bring.

"Don't do that," she would inform, matter-of-factly. "You know I have a *soft heart*." Because she was the baby of the brood, we always did stop, and no one ever made fun of her.

Is it the vulnerability of children that we embrace but then reject in ourselves? Is it vulnerability, as children have, that allows us to open our hearts? Even among our neighborhood crowd, the older kids respected the spiritual wisdom of the youngest one among us *(who ultimately did not live beyond childhood)* and allowed her to lead in this one area because of the authenticity of her feelings. It is said, in faith, we come as children to God. Genuine spirituality opens up the heart, but this isn't easy. We also get in touch with our own vulnerability *(the good, the bad, the ugly, and the painful)* and that of others.

So here it was many years later. New Year's Eve at the local grocery store. When the woman smiled at me, I shot a perfunctory half-smile back but was running my credit card and anxious to get home. I always pick the wrong line. This woman had been in front of me and had taken forever. Shakily, she had been fiddling with a million coupons, it seemed, and then her money. Appearing middle-aged to elderly, she probably looked older than she really was as I noticed that she had no teeth, which seemed odd, given her stylish dress and the high-end nature of the store. There was a gaunt, haggard quality that was immediately off-putting. She clearly appeared addled.

While standing behind her in line, I had surveyed the possibility of moving to another checker but had chosen not to. Very peripherally, there seemed to be a tentative sensor coming from her direction as though she was well aware of the backup she was causing and hoped for understanding. To endure the wait, I began to zone out and go on autopilot, something I often do when shopping, especially in that store. Its spacious, designer clean, and pristine nature, in conjunction with the hypnotic, piped-in soft jazz, always reminds me of a sci-fi movie, in which human beings of the future are like floating robots… moving in upright, calibrated fashion on invisible gliders. No *soul*…

"Have a nice day!" The cashier cheerily discharged the woman and turned to my purchases, scanning my key card. "And did you find everything you wanted today?" As I moved to the credit machine, I felt the light of the woman, beaming in on me. She had stationed herself at the end of the counter and was fumbling, repacking several of those reusable cloth grocery bags she had apparently brought to do her part. I had noticed in line that they had been pressed and meticulously folded. Now they, as she, were in total disarray.

This was when she had smiled at me so sweetly, her yearning face melting into warmth and rosy expectation, guileless and ingenuous like a young child. This was when I had managed a half-smile, cursory and even pinched, and then quickly turned away. I could still feel her beaming in on me. It wasn't that I had been mean to her but was distracted although, in retrospect, I wondered if I had passively expressed my frustration at the wait by not returning her light or only barely. I may have sensed a flicker of disappointment but allowed an unseen wall to come down while I signed the credit slip and focused on my purchases. I could still feel her light and the sweetness of her *spirit* pointed in my direction.

I heard a sigh and some rustling commotion as she seemed to be struggling to figure out her bags before quietly scooting away. It was then I had the subliminal image of a retreating, wounded animal. By the time I reached the parking lot, the *soft heart* pangs had begun. I knew she had wanted something. A bigger smile? A word? An interchange with another human being? A sign of acceptance? Of reassurance that her frailty hadn't messed up my busy day? That her toothless grin wasn't off-putting? My help with the bags, but she was afraid to ask? After the fact, the more I thought about her and her expectant demeanor and winning smile that I hadn't fully reciprocated, the more pained my heart became. She had reached out, and I hadn't answered. It was easy to make the excuse that I was simply lost in my own space, but on some level, I had known.

What responsibility do we have for the weaker among us? What do we owe to our fellow human beings? If it's an adorable child who's missing front teeth or a heart-rending commercial for a charitable organization *(usually with children)*, we swoop in and take charge or open the checkbook. This was the ultimate irony as, before going to the store, I had just finished making several end of the year tax-deductible donations to a handful of carefully selected charities *(and was feeling good that I had been able to give more than ever before)*. Yet, with all my charitable intentions, I had rejected an opportunity to give charity to another human being who was seeking it from me, at least in the spirit of love and personable exchange. *(Okay, so I'm fallible... can I handle that about myself?)*

It wasn't only my fallibility. As the evening wore on, I was haunted by the image of the woman, appearing so initially unappealing and struggling so, and her delicacy in seeming so acutely aware of it. As my *soft heart* ran wild, so did my imagination. Was she alone this New Year's Eve? I've been there. True, there have been times when I welcomed my aloneness. I've also known that desolate loneliness... the knifing heart sobs that no one hears. Was the interaction she had attempted with me, so half-baked on my end, the last possibility she had for human contact before going back to the stark anonymity and solitary confinement of a challenging life? Of course, this was fantasy. For all I knew, she could have a passel of loving grandchildren, with whom to celebrate the New Year, or was entertaining friends. Maybe she hadn't been disappointed by our interaction at all or even thought about or remembered it. *(Still, I could have done more.)*

I know for a lot of people this incident would seem inconsequential, made into a mountain out of a molehill in my mind. As I have opened to faith, in some ways, this is typical. My heart seems to have become *softer* and even more like a sponge than ever before. Some protective barrier, always thin in my case *(but that I depended on without even being aware I was doing so)*, seems to have become even thinner although I am more certain than ever that this is a precious thing. It is more painful at times, more blissful and beautiful at others… but always richer, deeper, and more meaningful. Especially when that pure spiritual connection is made.

Truly looking into the eyes of another can be a window to another's *soul* or a mirror to your own. Sometimes briefly connecting with just one other human being on the *soul* level can feel like opening a door into the heart of greater humanity. Perhaps, this is similar to a transcendent mystical experience, in which the individual appears to have fleetingly accessed the collective cosmic mind. Really connecting with the *soul* of another can seem to throw open the floodgates, quickly and momentarily, to the collective cosmic heart, a place of intense joy and love… but also immense agony at the level of human experience.

What do we mean by *compassion*? Formal definitions speak to sympathy or concern for those who are experiencing suffering or misfortune. Also involved is the desire to reach out, to address the adversity or help alleviate the misery in some way. Compassion is generally regarded as the most basic of human ideals and one of the highest of ethical values. This is true, not only in the world's major religions, but also in the traditions of humanism and social activism and has resulted in extensive altruistic activity throughout the world from both spiritually oriented and nonspiritual sources.

Religions instruct that we should be caretaking of those who are the neediest and weakest among us. We also see charitable endeavors, arising out of religious and nonreligious organizations alike, to help the poor and to provide healthcare or research to treat disease. Often the mission is to alleviate *physical* suffering, and again, nothing can draw on our heartstrings like seeing a picture of a sick or starving child. There is also *emotional* suffering, which is sometimes just as agonizing but more subtle. We may see it in the eyes, a look, a nonverbal communication. We also assume that certain groups of people such as those with bona fide mental illness or those who are afflicted physically in some way *(e.g., through illness or poverty)* are also hurting within. In our own lives, we may have the urge to reach out to those who we know are challenged or having a difficult time.

From a perspective of faith, the need for compassion and charity to others is another of those core principles that appear universally *(in addition to the belief in God and the idea that we are spiritual beings)*. In fact, since we are *spiritual beings* and connected within a greater unity, compassion makes sense. We are taking care of the members of our spiritual family and nurturing each other through generous acts and kindly attitudes. We are reaching out in love, and we're all connected through *spirit*, at least on the *soul* level. By caretaking and serving our spiritual brothers and sisters, we serve God, the unity, and ultimately ourselves. By tending to the light of another *soul*, the more our own light is illuminated by the light we are brightening. The light and warmth of the unity, as a whole, only increases.

Where does compassion come from? Scientific explanations look towards evolution and biology. On the one hand, we live in a scrappy, ruthlessly competitive world. Go to any barnyard or cable nature channel, and it becomes apparent how much we have in common with the rest of the animal kingdom. Our evolutionary inheritance is that of a survival of the fittest environment, which can be brutal, replete with clawing struggle for limited resources, combative defensiveness, and fight to the point of death. Territoriality and aggression have always had their place in survival in human existence.

We also see precursors of love, loyalty, and empathy in our animal brothers and sisters. These *higher* qualities are thought to be just as much a part of our evolutionary heritage as the *lower* tendencies. They have allowed animals, including human beings, to mate and form bonds, to nurture their young, and to cooperate in groups or social settings, all of which were basically more adaptive than going it alone. In recent years, scientific observation has suggested that the extent of animal emotional bonds, including a capacity for compassion and grief over the loss of loved ones, is far greater than once thought in some species. Although a city girl with little exposure to animals, I can relate. Once in my twenties, when I was upset over a romantic breakup and having a good cry, my loyal Labrador retriever came over and softly placed his paw in my lap. Looking up, I saw those big brown, soulful eyes staring at me, offering the most wholehearted sympathy and caring.

The neurology underlying the human compassionate response has also been studied with significant findings. Many believe that at some point we will be able to identify the biological mechanisms, including in our genetic code, for the higher qualities *(such as compassion)* and even manipulate these in the human population to evolve further as a species, presumably in a more ethical direction. *(There are also those who assert this is playing God and will only backfire.)* Certainly, this does raise the question as to who among the current *lower* breed of human beings gets to decide what qualities the future *higher* breed should have.

Also, as we have repeatedly discussed, just because the biological processes underlying human experience can be identified doesn't mean that's the entire story. Within a perspective of faith, compassion is assumed to involve a real energy of love as well as an exchange of *spirit*. As we have seen in other areas, just sharing with another individual or *soul schmoozing* creates a sense of connection that truly feels at a higher level. Being compassionate takes this idea one step further. By *sharing* the other person's pain but doing so in love, we are elevated to the *spiritual* level, erasing the cruelty or hardship, at least for a moment in time, of the *human* world and the personal pain the two people may feel. For the individual of faith, this is the experience of a *soft heart*, to share the pain and heal through love... or conversely, to share the love and heal the pain.

This is why, within a spiritual view, compassion is such an important principle. It is about the love of God coming through the human heart. There's the implication of a kind of correction or healing. By reaching out in love, we cut through the harsh reality of the physical plane and return to our *spiritual beingness*. This places the need for, not only charitable acts, but compassionate feelings in the forefront of consciousness with the potential to be a tremendous teacher and driving force. *(After my last soft heart episode, you can bet I am more mindful of others around me.)* When we genuinely interact with another person, another *soul*, in a compassionate manner, it feels good. We know it is the "right" thing to do. When we don't, it hurts.

Too often in modern society, while we admire and even idealize compassion and altruistic acts, these are compartmentalized off from the rest of our lives. Most people do have a sense of themselves as ethical human beings. Yet, for many, whether they ascribe to absolute or relativistic moral values, ethical behavior tends to more likely be expressed in the broad strokes of living. In the smaller interactions of the day-to-day, the tendency is to follow social norms or to act in accordance with emotion and personal needs. Most people will see themselves as honest, giving, or compassionate when it matters. And surely they can be. In times of crisis or in close relationships, when

SOFT HEART

a friend or loved one is going through a difficult time, human beings can be truly inspirational.

In everyday life, there tends to be a divide between the intention and the behavior, often without the individual being aware of it or thinking that it really matters. Many people do give to charitable or humanitarian causes. They may have strong or idealistic opinions about what is fair and unfair and how people should treat each other, whether in intimate relationships or international alliances. But, like myself, in little ways, at work, in the grocery store, on the highway, and even in their close circle of friends and family, they can trample on, exploit, discount, or ignore others all the time.

It seems that the need to be compassionate is often looked at more from an intellectual and remote place. It is viewed as something that we *should* do. We admire those who do embody this ideal and are proud when we, ourselves, rise to the occasion of showing kindness or attending to the welfare of others. Still, there is little emotional connection to how this might relate to daily living. There may even be a resistance to the depth of emotion associated with compassion, at least after a certain point. While it always feels good to act kindly or to help someone out, opening one's heart does blur the boundaries between one's own feelings and those of others. Worse, it allows others, even unwittingly, to tug on the heartstrings, creating a feeling of sorrow or pity or sense of obligation.

For many, the primary emotion that is associated with compassion seems to be anger or outrage, which is directed at the circumstances that are presumed to be causing the affliction or inequality *(i.e., the need for compassion in the first place)*. People become incensed at the way the world is or the way humans are or those specific humans or institutions that are felt to be causing the pain and suffering *(i.e., the rich... the government... the enemy... the uneducated... the profit-hungry corporations)*. The list goes on and on, with the perception of the identified problem differing radically from one person to another.

Righteous anger can be a motivating force, resulting in productive outcomes at times. Anger can impart strength and resolve although there is always the risk that an individual becomes consumed by the anger, which then eats away internally or erupts into out of control or dangerous behavior. Even when anger is constructive, it is very much a *human* emotion on the *psychological* level of experience and the *physical* plane. It does not have the healing and corrective force of love, which is so important spiritually. Rather, in this view, compassion is the sharing of *lower* human pain and *higher* spiritual love, resulting in picking up or elevating the other person, even briefly. This is why genuine compassion always involves *empathy*, which is the ability to understand or share another's feelings. Compassion is not just a far-removed ideal that may provoke justifiable outrage. For a person of committed faith, to be compassionate almost has to involve a *soft heart*.

But to have a *soft heart* or to open one's heart to the feelings of others is necessarily going to involve pain and fosters a sense of vulnerability, which can be very uncomfortable, even threatening. The anger against the sources of suffering and injustice may even be a defensive strategy, a way to escape and distance one's self from the vulnerable feelings. Anger is seductive in that it tends to make people feel strong, even if it's a false strength or pure bluster. In contrast, vulnerability gets us in touch with how weak, tender, and even fragile we really are. This is the opposite of how we are supposed to feel in order to be in control, a together and desirable person, in the modern, secular world. In compassion, there is also an assumption of selflessness, which may feel like a loss or weakening of *self*, another scary scenario for the contemporary individual.

Plus, how much is too much? Within mainstream psychology, there are many who would find my reaction to the woman in the grocery store over the top. A dangerous loss of boundaries? Of beating myself up way too much? Sure, heart is good, but at some point, being too affected by others or being so emotionally sensitive is felt to be indicative of disturbance or problems. This may be true for some people, suggestive of real mental disorder that needs to be treated on the *psychological* level. On the other hand, within the secular point of view, which includes mainstream psychology, there is no consideration of a higher *spiritual* level of being. From a perspective of faith, compassion is a *higher* level response, an extension of love and serving God. Within this perspective, the more we can open our hearts and transcend the boundaries between spiritual brothers and sisters, the better.

So, for the person with a *soft heart* or seeking more of a spiritual approach to living, the potential exists for confusion and conflict. How do we remain *psychologically* balanced and not get emotionally overwhelmed, at the same time *spiritually* opening our hearts as much as possible? There is a tendency in our society to see too much committed compassion and caretaking as problematic. Those who exhibit such tendencies may designate themselves as troubled or weak and overly sensitive and may be warned of being codependent by friends or even therapists.

The issue of codependency is a prime example of this dilemma. *Codependency* is a concept and label that is popular today and associated with excessive caretaking and selflessness. Technically, codependency is a psychological syndrome that revolves around enabling others' addictions and bad behavior. It connotes weakness and passivity and too much empathy to the point of denying one's own feelings and needs. Codependency is truly oppressive for many people and relationships, but at what point does loyalty, caretaking, and compassion become codependency? When does taking care of the needs of others or ascribing to a higher standard beyond self-interest become unhealthy?

In recent years, as cultural values have become more and more narcissistic, the bar of health has seemed to move in the direction of taking care of *self* and away from caretaking, even consideration, of others. Unfortunately, for those who tend to be less self-oriented or enjoy nurturing, the message is that there must be something wrong with you. This is even to the point that many women who are or would prefer to be full-time Moms feel ashamed or scorned or deficient as a result. There's a lot of mixed messages. On the one hand, we are advised that early childhood learning and making sure the child has enough quality time should be top priorities, but when a woman decides to devote her life to her children instead of a career, she runs the risk of feeling or being demeaned. Similarly, we are told that compassionate behavior is the highest ideal but not too much.

This isn't to imply that real codependent behavior is healthy. True codependency isn't at all, but it's not the compassion or selflessness or caretaking or even the *soft heart* that is causing the problem. It's the dysfunctional needs. Truly codependent people are kept in the painful relationship because of self-sabotaging emotional needs *(usually arising out of childhood)* that now somehow are being fulfilled through the enabling. The codependent behavior may originally have been a way for the child to deal with a difficult or abusive or traumatic environment and was self-protective, but in adult life is no longer serving the individual's best interest. There may be a need for passive control... or to be dependent... or for crisis... or to feel valued and needed... or to live vicariously *(and there are undoubtedly others)*. It's not the compassion, which may be genuine and comes from a *higher* spiritual place, that keeps the person in the codependent situation.

Today cultural notions of fulfillment and personal power are almost entirely built around the accomplishment of *self* agendas, so it's no wonder that compassion, while touted as an ideal on one level, gets a bad rap on another. Yet, narcissistic happiness is superficial at best. Narcissism is often a directionless, lonely and empty treadmill with nowhere to go. What is ironic is that, despite the cultural fear of selflessness in our society and the glorification of *self* and materialistic success, spiritually oriented and nonspiritual people alike report a sense of well-being and happiness as a result of making compassion and altruistic behavior a priority in their lives.

From a strictly psychological point of view, a committed focus away from the *self* can be beneficial. Individuals who are devoted to a life of purpose beyond the *self*, which almost always involves serving others in some way, tend to report and exhibit positive effects. They usually describe an overall sense of well-being, elevated energy and motivation, feelings of true accomplishment, and the experience of a lot of love in their lives, even without family or special loved ones. Service to others can cut through the all-consuming pattern of empty self-absorption, directing an individual's energy towards a truly rewarding and productive goal. For the person of faith, it goes even further. There is the sense of serving the spiritual family and God, which leads to an experience of personal integrity.

For sure, an individual does not have to have faith in order to have compassion or a purpose beyond the *self* and the related experiential rewards. But committed faith does provide a guiding framework that encourages endeavor towards higher spiritual values. It also immerses the individual in a greater understanding of a Divine system of love and Higher Truth and Power and our place within it. Compassionate behavior is *not* just a choice but a responsibility intrinsic to faith. It is the expression of our love of God and our spiritual brothers and sisters and one way that we can manifest the higher *spiritual* level on the *physical* plane.

From a perspective of faith, there is tremendous strength in this. Compassion is powerful. It doesn't only *feel* good and *do* good, but the spiritually committed person often has the perception that acts of kindness and generosity result in blessings or positive occurrences down-the-line. To *give* is to *receive*. This doesn't mean that it's all about "good works" or that some great cosmic balance sheet is documenting good and bad acts, and doing good with the primary intent of receiving reward is not spiritual at all. The idea is more that, through compassion, a *higher* energy of love is being nourished and exchanged. Again, we have the image of a web of *spirit*, and it's all connected. One act of love gives rise to another. *(Pass it on.)* At some point, the love reverberates back *(now possibly greater and maybe in a different form)* to the individual.

The person of faith begins to understand that everything counts. An act, even as seemingly minor as a genuine smile, is a connection among *souls* and an expression of the unity of all humankind. The spiritually committed person learns that, when we honor the dignity of others, we strengthen ourselves and our connection to God. Every interaction with another human being is an opportunity. One of the most spiritually powerful tools that we have as we go through the day is a compassionate attitude, to respect the humanity and *spiritual beingness* of each person that we meet.

The degree that we do so generates a reserve of spiritual Power. Whatever we do, whenever we do it, everything we do is important. When we act in accordance with the good of our spiritual brothers and sisters, we are contributing, giving back to God, who sustains us. We also increase the flow of God's Power into our experience and lives. At the same time, when we act in a way discordant with the unity, ultimately resulting in suffering or separation, we detract from that Power. We also diminish its effect in our lives and experience.

Just as the person of faith perceives gifts and opportunities coming from God, there may be the sense of being given potential *moments of redemption*. These tend to be experienced as a moral dilemma or fork in the road when God seems to have provided the individual with a choice and opportunity to take some *higher* spiritual action. Maybe it is to reach out to or carry someone in need… a true act of forgiveness… or stepping up to the plate in some selfless way to help others. Sometimes such *moments of redemption* seem relatively minor, or they may be pivotal points in a person's life. Sometimes there is the sense that the redemption offered does not have to do with the current situation or choice but some other significant issue from the past, such as a negative act or long held resentment. When the individual does make the *higher* choice, there is a feeling of transcendent connection and healing, a clearing out and release. It's as though something burdensome has been washed away, and there is now the ability to move on, *psychologically* as well as *spiritually*.

The person of faith comes to understand that, through compassion, there is great power in bringing love into the world. It is this higher *spiritual* love… that transcends both the pain and pleasure of the *physical* plane. This is why, even as a child, I instinctively knew that having a *soft heart* is such a precious thing. The other side of the pain that a *soft heart* can bring is the opening up of the awareness of God's great love and an intensity of feeling that connects us all. The *softer* the heart becomes, the more we are brought back to the position of a child, in touch with our own vulnerability and fallibility and that of others. This only strengthens the caretaking bond with God... in our hearts and in our lives.

Epilogue   **RUSH OF BLESSINGS**

It was one of those bitterly cold, wet and wintry days in New York city. Amidst the blackened remnants of the previous week's snow, bundles of *souls*, wrapped in scarves and mittens, moved slowly against the wind... in the manner of soggy clouds of indistinguishable forms. Unclear as to age or gender, their eyes and faces scrunched up against the biting cold, like fetuses in hooded parkas.

In line, the bundled couple before me inched gingerly around the icy puddles but were having trouble getting up the steps of the bus. I wanted shelter as did the growing throng behind me. The human breath, in combination with the bus fumes, was creating a freezing gray mist. With every slap of wind, the grumbling din grew louder. If the line didn't move shortly, there was going to be one of those ugly New York moments. The bobbing bundles ahead seemed to be obliviously struggling but resisted help. Then quickly one of the duo lifted the other up, shoving it through the door.

Progress. As I raced up the steps, the warmth of the bus exploded in the dank sweat and wet of everyone packed together, but what a relief after the cold... Just then, right in front of me, the bundle who had so much trouble getting up the steps started to slowly sit down in the lap of another New Yorker, lowering her bulky body in the manner of a circling, descending helicopter. The scream and biting retort from the seated passenger *(complete with New York accent)* were sharper than the wind outside.

The bundle startled, the fur-lined hood falling down to her shoulders, revealing an elderly woman, the exuberant joy of her countenance suddenly bared for all to see. Shuffling as quickly as he could from behind, her aged and rickety husband, his hood also falling, grabbed her arm while steering her gently towards one of the poles to steady her. As his coat flew open, his frame looked like a pair of twigs. "You tried to sit down on top of someone," he whispered lovingly.

"Oh my," she smiled at him with immense delight and playfulness, the twinkling romantic vibe between them more electric than any feral, out of control sexual encounter between tanned and toned 20-year-olds, the typical movie fare of today. There was a bit of breathlessness as she recovered from her blunder. "I almost sat on someone. Really?" Chuckling, shaking her head in self-awareness, "I would do that… these days." She erupted in throaty laughter and winked gleefully as he affectionately pinched her nose. "That's exactly the type of thing I would do… *these* days."

This scene still warms and inspires me over twenty years later. The enjoyment that people can have, no matter where they find themselves in life. Their utter joy of being… and being together. The love that binds. The light that seemed to glow around them. To be so old and faltering but so much in love. I imagine they are both gone now from the world but what an incomparable moment in time.

One of the things that a spiritual mindset teaches is that it's not perfection but the *wholeness* of experience that's important. Maybe it's the Hollywood influence, but we so easily get caught up in the set design fantasy. Love and happiness are supposed to mean romantic dinners or getaways… good-looking people, youthful *(if not actually young)*… spectacular sunsets with orchestral crescendos in the background… the beautiful family… the country club lifestyle… an endless vacation on coral sand beaches… the white picket fence… the A-list life. Most of us hold some idea, if not a comprehensive fantasy, of what perfection should be. Some strive to achieve it; others give in or give up, relegating their station in life to the B-list but still feed the dream vicariously through others or imagination. Yet, by holding such standards, even if we decide they are unattainable or silly, we can't help but compare and judge.

Perfection can be a cruel and misleading idol. People are always stunned *(and appear morbidly fascinated)* when someone who would seem to have it all commits suicide, struggles with addiction, or publicly does something so blatantly self-destructive. As a culture, we cherish our celebrity pantheon of gods and goddesses, anointed through the media, only to relish with even greater gusto when they tumble back down to ordinary climes. We delight in pitying the high school football captain and homecoming queen as past their prime *(and undoubtedly pining for their former glory)* once he starts to go bald and she gains weight after giving birth to four children.

But how do we know? We can never fully experience the heart of another, what is going on inside. Maybe the former cheerleader thinks being Mom is so much better... that every inch of expanding waistline is more than worth it as she chauffeurs around her screaming, loving little rug rats in the SUV? So often I have heard older, even quite elderly, people announce in such a definitive and heartfelt tone, "This is the happiest time in my life." It's not supposed to be, at least not within our superficial cultural stereotypes. It can't be perfect when you're eighty. Still, things are never what they seem.

Clearly, there is a human tendency to idealize perfection, assuming this is the key to a happy life. The perfect state implies the highest quality and absolute excellence but also a lack of flaws... the absence of fault or defect. Rather sterile overall, and this is where it gets tricky. We may set and reach goals, achieve success, and attain the highest of personal standards, but life is messy and so are we. Who doesn't struggle with perceived blemishes and failings, careless blunders, weakness, and deficiencies? In some way, at some point, however we define our ideal, all of us have to come to terms with the lesser parts of our journey and ourselves.

The spiritual perspective fosters a focus on wholeness, not perfection, which can only belong to God. The person of faith has to learn to accept the lack of perfection in one's *self* and others and *(at least from the human perspective)* in the finite, physical world. In every aspect of our existence, there will be mistakes and disillusionments… differences in opinion… peaks and valleys… and a lot of tedium in-between. That's all part of it. Life is what it is. People are who they are. We may be guided on a course towards a higher light and vision, but the course, itself, is never easy or even or entirely clean.

Wholeness embraces the totality of experience and, by doing so, seems to integrate, smooth out the rough edges, balance, and heal. There is usually a feeling of richness, depth, or fundamental meaning in how it all comes together, even if we never reach the sought-after pinnacle or find the answer, fix the problem, see the world, or heal the planet. Wholeness goes beyond and transcends our personal holy grail and whether or not we obtain it.

Sometimes a sense of wholeness is found in the moment, irrespective of time, when the individual is totally immersed in the immediate activity or bonds with other people. This can be in the most hideous surroundings or aversive circumstances, but there is felt a harmony and completeness within and outside the *self*. For the person of faith, there is always the wholeness of the love of God, connecting it all at any point in time.

For spiritual and nonspiritual people alike, there is also that sense of wholeness as to who we are... and over the course of our lives. When people look back, there may be a feeling of coming together and wholeness across time. A woven tapestry, in which each part, each design, each thread plays an integral part. This tends to become more apparent as the person grows older, and the interwoven themes and patterns become more evident. Especially those who have triumphed over tragedy or a difficult challenge may see the *negative* parts of their life as necessary in order to reach the *positive* place at which they eventually arrived.

Over and over, when people tell their stories of survival and transcendence, they describe extremely abusive and painful or out of control situations. They've gotten past it, often admirably, and there's kind of that feeling of "If I only knew then what I know now..." Then they add that they wouldn't change anything about their life although on the surface this seems contradictory. It's not that they are condoning what occurred or pleased that they had to go through what they did to get to where they are now. In fact, by telling their story, they seem to be seeking to help others get past or escape and avoid similar situations. But it is their story, a tale of metamorphosis and growth, which arose from pain. The growth and the pain can't be separated out. They wouldn't be where they are today if they hadn't been where they were before.

I had all these feelings when I moved back to the town where I had gone to college twenty-five years earlier. College hadn't been a good time. There was the major depression following the deaths of my father and sister, which was frightening, although within six months the most painful symptoms had resolved. I was still unmoored but did get on with the business of living, at least as a young person adrift in a university town. It was a turbulent, chaotic period, so it didn't seem unusual then, being adrift. There seemed to be a lot of us "adrifters" although that didn't make it any less painful or me feel any less lost. In some ways, everyone seemed to be searching or aimless until they weren't and then moved on. Maybe it was the age, being in my early 20s, not the times. It took about six or seven unhappy years before I had a sense of being back on a viable course.

So now it was over twenty-five years later. As I traveled near and through campus, in some places, there were no signs that even a day had passed. Here… the path that I walked to school… the ivy-clad buildings where I struggled not to bolt from class… the quad where drug-imbued sit-ins were held against the Vietnam War… the department where I worked before returning to graduate school… the bars… the games… the spring days under the trees… the get-togethers… breakups… transient joys… excruciating tears. A slideshow of memories but from a different perspective now through the adjustable lens of time.

Oddly, I wasn't sad at all. I remembered how painful it had been, how lost I had felt. Now it was like looking at a younger version of myself from a place of curiosity and dispassion. I didn't feel the pain, even as a visceral memory. Instead, I was simply overwhelmed with thankfulness, not for any external accomplishments or even pride at having pursued dreams and transcended earlier difficulties. My life just seemed like such a blessing. All of it. I felt so loved and grateful… for the joys, the truths, the lessons, the privilege of being… for my relationship with God.

There are times when I feel a rush of blessings, just how fortunate I am that I was led to faith and what faith has brought to my life. It catches me, takes my breath away, infuses and flows through every cell of my body… a flush of the warmth of life, an overwhelming gratitude.

In looking back, there was a turning point. Was it when I returned to God and silently spoke my first adult prayer? The misery of my college years had happened long before.

As I meandered around the tree-lined campus, I thought how stoic and impassive the old colonial buildings seemed to be. If only bricks could speak, how many dreams and disappointments, anticipation and trauma had gone before me and followed in the school's centuries of history. More will follow still. For me, something raw and painful did seem to have washed away, but it felt unconnected. I had gotten past it long ago.

What I did feel was a strong urge, to shout, to share... to say, "This is how beautiful it can be." How many lost and depressed young women sit in dorm rooms behind the ivy-covered walls, I wondered. Like a surreal dream sequence in a black-and-white film, it was as though I wanted to reach out beyond the distant fortress of wisdom and years gone by... to my younger *self*, all the younger selves... and *souls*... now wandering throughout campus. To do what? To give of my heart and my truth? Each of us finds our own path. I wouldn't have listened when I was young.

I began to dip into "If I only knew then what I know now..." All the years, the wrong and painful choices. How different my college years would have been... if I just had felt as directed, purposeful, and comfortable in my own skin as I do now. All that time wasted... the things I could've done but didn't do. Then it doubles back. Sure, I might have been happier and perhaps made more positive choices... for the time. Yet would these have been the right choices? How different my life might have been. Would I have stagnated or hit a wall of complacency? Would I have gone in a different direction entirely? If I had not been trying so hard to escape myself, would I have found myself? Would I not have traveled the trajectory that, in hindsight, does seem the only road to where I am now and where I want to be?

It is what it is. Like so many, faith is where I found a perspective of wholeness and arrived at my own destiny. Within a spiritual context, life intuitively makes sense. There is always God, loving, directing and unfolding.

God makes us whole because God sees us whole.

And, with God's love, we feel whole, maybe for the first time in our lives.

Not the end… but the beginning. A circle without end. Circles within circles.

psychmaster.com

PSYCHMASTER presents:

a unique DVD experience

Based on the book, SELF TO SOUL: A Vision of Psychology and Spirituality

approx, 61 min.

SELF TO SOUL
A VISION OF PSYCHOLOGY & SPIRITUALITY

LIVING PHILOSOPHY

ALSO INCLUDES
A SPIRITUAL QUEST
SOUNDTRACK CD

AN INSPIRATIONAL MEDITATIVE DVD
WRITTEN & NARRATED BY DR. JUDY MARSHALL

A new way of looking at eternal truths

Is there a God or spiritual unity beyond ourselves? How does this affect and transform us?

Photographed and edited in a cinematic style with an original musical score, **SELF TO SOUL: Living Philosophy** interweaves lectures by Judy Marshall, Ph.D. with exterior footage and surreal images to create a haunting, dreamlike panorama. Both experiential and narrative in presentation, while nondenominational in approach, **SELF TO SOUL: Living Philosophy** illustrates how spirituality is primarily experiential and can lead to transformation and emotional healing.

Includes alternate video "Visualization" track
DVD-ROM: PDF exercises

A Vision of Psychology & Spirituality

A book that presents an entirely spiritually-based view of psychological experience

by
Judy Marshall, Ph.D.

WORKBOOK *also available*
SELF TO SOUL:
Exercises of Reflection, Contemplation & Interaction

SELF TO SOUL: A Vision of Psychology and Spirituality is written in a poetic, evocative style that pulls for innate, underlying feelings and mystical reflection. At the same time, it is an intelligent discussion of universal spiritual wisdom and takes an honest look at what traditional spiritual principles suggest about psychology. Building on the work of Aldous Huxley and Joseph Campbell, it compares psychological and philosophical universals and describes a system of Divine "reality," our psychological place within it, and the importance of closeness to God in human existence.

p s y c h m a s t e r . c o m

PSYCHMASTER
MEDIA THAT EDUCATES & INSPIRES

*EXERCISES OF REFLECTION,
CONTEMPLATION & INTERACTION*

from the book
SELF TO SOUL
A VISION OF PSYCHOLOGY & SPIRITUALITY
WORKBOOK

psychmaster.com

PSYCHMASTER CDs on Psychology & Spirituality

available at psychmaster.com

WRITTEN & NARRATED BY JUDY MARSHALL, PH.D.

SURVIVING AS A SENSITIVE PERSON

Sensitivity can be a gift and a curse...

approx. 60 min.

On the negative side:
Emotional reactivity
Mood swings
Guilt and self-doubt
Lack of assertiveness
Problems with anger expression
Loss of boundaries
Suspicious perceptions
The potential for victimization

On the positive side:
Deep and finely-tuned emotions
Compassion for others
Genuineness and empathy in relationships
Artistic sensibilities and appreciation of beauty
Fertile imagination
Keen intuition
Spiritual inclinations

In our dog-eat-dog world, it is difficult to appreciate the positive aspects of sensitivity. How sensitivity plays out in various life areas and strategies for coping, as well as maximizing the great potential (i.e., the "silver lining" of sensitivity), are discussed.

HOLIDAY BLUES
The holidays can be a time of personal journey and affirmation (we move from one period of our lives to the next and are confronted with spiritual truths). What are specific coping strategies? When should professional help be sought?
approx. 60 min.

SPIRITUAL VS. MEDICAL MODELS OF HEALING
How do we heal? The "medical" model views our minds as similar to machines. The "inner light" model assumes a unique essence within, that can be a guiding force to transform our lives. In the "transcendence" model, we "get beyond" by turning a negative into a positive.
approx. 43 min.

WHAT IS SCHIZOPHRENIA?
What happens in schizophrenia? What causes it? Is there a typical course? Who becomes schizophrenic? Treatments and stereotypes are discussed, along with a plea for compassion. *approx. 72 min.*

A SPIRITUAL APPROACH TO DEPRESSION
How can a spiritual approach help us navigate one of life's most painful passages? Depression is something we encounter on our human journey, but is never our essence or purpose. "Coping strategies" based on spiritual principles are discussed.
approx. 64 min.

PSYCHMASTER CDs on Psychology & Spirituality
psychmaster.com

THE STIGMA OF MENTAL ILLNESS
In today's world, we are ill-informed about mental health and illness, but well-informed about physical health and illness. Ignorance breeds fear, denial, and more ignorance, which negatively impacts all of us. Some thoughts towards an attitude shift are discussed. *approx. 52 min.*

COPING WITH TRAUMA
When a human being is the victim of or exposed to violent events, there is always a psychological reaction. Often called "posttraumatic stress," reaction to trauma is presented as an expectable, self-protective emotional response. The possible complications and approaches to treatment are discussed. *approx. 57 min.*

PSYCHMASTER CDs on Psychology & Spirituality
AVAILABLE AT PSYCHMASTER.COM

WHY DO WE GET DEPRESSED?
There are many factors that contribute to the development of depression. In fact, you can have the same symptoms in two individuals, but the causes are different in each case. Depression can be biologically-based, due to toxic learned cognitions, or "reactive"/situational". Various typical causes are presented *approx. 41 min.*

WHAT IS SPIRITUALITY?
There are core principles, a "spiritual DNA," found in most belief systems. What is the relationship between spirituality, religion, metaphysics, and science? Spirituality is also primarily experiential. How do we recognize and access spiritual feelings? *approx. 72 min.*

PSYCHMASTER
PRODUCTIONS/PRESS

A different approach to psychology & mental health

PSYCHMASTER books, DVDs, and CDs seek to answer fundamental questions about spirituality and psychology, the reality of mental health and illness, coping with the challenges inherent in human existence, and achieving actualization and fulfillment. Based on the work of Judy Marshall, Ph.D., clinical psychologist, PSYCHMASTER CDs offer basic information about spirituality, sensitivity, and mental illness *(including depression, schizophrenia, and post-traumatic stress)* and explore experientially what it is like for the person struggling with mental suffering.

The idea is that education leads to recognition, understanding, and compassion, all of which must occur in order to deal effectively with real mental health issues – on both the personal and societal levels. In various CDs, and the *SELF TO SOUL* book, as well as workbook and DVD, Dr. Marshall's **nondenominational spiritual approach to psychology** is presented. This is based on the belief that a "living" spiritual commitment is the best psychological resource that we have for healing, relationships and in living our day-to-day lives.

p s y c h m a s t e r . c o m

MEDIA THAT EDUCATES & INSPIRES

Made in the USA
San Bernardino, CA
19 December 2013